100 THINGS
RAPTORS FANS
SHOULD KNOW & DO
BEFORE THEY DIE

100 THINGS
RAPTORS FANS
SHOULD KNOW & DO
BEFORE THEY DIE

Dave Mendonca

TRIUMPH
BOOKS

Copyright © 2015 by Dave Mendonca

No part of this publication may be reproduced, stored in a retrieval system, or transmitted in any form by any means, electronic, mechanical, photocopying, or otherwise, without the prior written permission of the publisher, Triumph Books LLC, 814 North Franklin Street, Chicago, Illinois 60610.

Library of Congress Cataloging-in-Publication Data

Mendonca, Dave, 1977–
    100 things Raptors fans should know & do before they die / Dave Mendonca.
        pages cm. — (100 things...fans should know)
    ISBN 978-1-62937-147-4
1. Toronto Raptors (Basketball team)—Miscellanea. 2. Toronto Raptors (Basketball team)—Anecdotes. 3. Basketball—Canada—Miscellanea.
4. Basketball—Canada--Anecdotes. I. Title. II. Title: One hundred things Raptors fans should know and do before they die.
    GV885.52.T67M46 2015
    796.323'6409713—dc23
                                    2015011350

This book is available in quantity at special discounts for your group or organization. For further information, contact:
    Triumph Books LLC
    814 North Franklin Street
    Chicago, Illinois 60610
    (312) 337-0747
    www.triumphbooks.com

Printed in U.S.A.
ISBN: 978-1-62937-147-4
Design by Patricia Frey
Photos courtesy of Getty Images unless otherwise indicated

To my amazing, beautiful, and supportive wife, Linda, thank you for your incredible patience; and to my basketball brother, Audley Stephenson, without you, this book wouldn't be as fun.

Contents

Foreword

I'm often asked where my love affair with the city of Toronto started. Well, it all began one afternoon on the campus of Georgetown University in 1994. Before the Raptors ever graced the floor of the SkyDome, the basketball fans of Toronto were treated to some great college basketball. The game—Georgetown versus Memphis—featured a star-packed lineup on each side. This was must-see basketball. George Butler, Lorenzen Wright, Allen Iverson, and Othella Harrington were all seen as future lottery picks in the NBA, and we were all headed to the famous Maple Leaf Gardens.

I had never really heard of Toronto. So I asked Hall of Fame coach John Thompson, "Where is Toronto?" He chuckled and said it's in Canada. My reply, of course, was: "Canada? Why so far for a game?" My teammates were just as shocked. We knew nothing about Canada other than it's cold and far from home. The first astounding feature of Toronto was the fact that it was actually a quick one-hour flight from the Washington, D.C., campus. Second was the look of the city, which also reminded me of my D.C. hometown because of its city lights and one-way streets. And the third feature that began my love affair was the friendliness of the people. It was all around the city from the airports to the bus stops to the coffee shops, hotels, and restaurants—you name it. The people's friendliness got my attention.

The game itself lived up to its billing as we edged Memphis in an overtime thriller that had the fans of Toronto on the edge of their seats. I can honestly say the DoggPound was born that night because the fans were firmly behind the Hoyas, and we felt the love. Toronto had made a lasting impression on me. I fell for it, and soon it would fall for me!

Fast forward a few years to the birth of the Raptors organization. I'm playing for the Detroit Pistons and loving it. When we would fly to Toronto for games, I was so excited to tell teammates about my old college story involving the city. But my love was under the surface because for many NBA players Toronto had a kind of negative connotation. We've all heard stories of bad taxes, bad schools, bad food, etc. You never heard of the many good things like good communities, good health care, low crime, and great sports fans.

So in February 2001, I received a call from the Pistons that I had been traded to the Toronto Raptors as the key player Toronto wanted. Initially, I experienced heartache because I was leaving my original DoggPound and the people and organization that had supported me for years. Second, I had the fear of acceptance in a new city and organization that didn't know anything about me. Third, I was a newlywed and had to inform my wife and stepdaughter we were about to move to Canada. I had a lot to be concerned about, and my mind was racing.

After speaking with Raptors general manager Glen Grunwald on the phone and hearing his excitement, he still seemed a bit hesitant about when I should join the team as he wanted me to have all the time I needed to adjust and make plans. My next move was not a calculated decision; it was on the spot and all natural. I decided to drive through a snowstorm that night to be on time for practice the next day to greet my new teammates. (This decision became legendary.)

When I put on the Raptors jersey that night, my heart pounded with anticipation. I was so excited to be a Raptor and to be playing alongside Vince Carter, Alvin Williams, and Mo Pete. But nothing had prepared me for what was about to happen when they announced my name to the sell-out crowd of 21,000. I received a standing ovation and the loudest DoggPound salute I had ever heard. And thus the DoggPound was reborn, and yes, I will always love my city.

DoggPound for life.

—Jerome "Junkyard Dog" Williams

Introduction

I'll always remember my first Toronto Raptors game. It was on my birthday, April 19th, in 1996. I was at the SkyDome, where the good guys, wearing the ferocious red dinosaurs on their chests, were facing the then-Washington Bullets in Toronto's penultimate home game of its inaugural season. I had been a huge basketball fan ever since I was a kid following the likes of Magic Johnson, whose on-court wizardry was always a treat to behold, and his Showtime Los Angeles Lakers and then later supported the early 1990s New York Knicks and their smash-mouth style of basketball led by ex-Lakers head coach Pat Riley.

When the Raptors arrived, I finally had my own NBA hometown team to root for.

Here was the spot where I'd take in my special game:

Section 524A, Row 22, Seat 110.

Ah yes, the 500 level.

It was the stadium's highest seating area that practically kissed the sky once the retractable lid was peeled back. I didn't care. As long as I was in the building watching hoops, everything was great. To me it didn't matter that the players looked like tiny ants from my seat. It was still an awesome experience. A crowd of 24,454 showed up, which looked funny in a massive 50,000-plus-seat stadium, but you could still feel the fans' energy every time the Raptors gave them a reason to cheer.

Despite Juwan Howard's game-high 42 points, Toronto sent me home happy with a 107–103 win, thanks to five players scoring in double figures, including Doug Christie's team-high 30. It was a terrific way to end a birthday.

Years later, while working as a national sports reporter for The Score Television Network (now Sportsnet 360), I covered the Raptors from 2001–2006. During that time I witnessed the downfall of Vince Carter, the rise of Chris Bosh, and some of the lowest moments in franchise history. I saw it all from my courtside media section seat. As a basketball junkie, I was in heaven. I couldn't believe I was being paid to watch live NBA games and interview players afterward.

After my TV reporting days, I was able to create a new way to stay in touch with the Raptors through a basketball podcast called *The Breakdown with Dave & Audley*. From 2008–2013, my co-host, Audley Stephenson, and I were able to speak with many current and former team personnel including Tracy McGrady, Damon Stoudamire, and Sam Mitchell.

Sam was always fun especially when you got him fired up. For example, we asked about one of his pet peeves. He replied, "I hate to hear people use the term *brutally honest*. I tell people this all the time—what is brutal to me is when you *lie* to me. How can the truth be *brutally honest*? I hate that term. I hate that phrase when people use that. To me, it should be *brutally lying*. That's when you're being brutal, when you lie to someone. When you tell someone the truth, man, you're not being brutal to them, you're being honest with them. We need to change that term. When has *honesty* ever been wrong?"

Sam, please never change.

He was just one of the various characters who were a part of the Raptors family over the years.

Through all of my fan and media experiences, I've been following the club from its infancy to the team you see today. It's been one heck of a ride, so I'm honoured to have the chance to write *100 Things Raptors Fans Should Know & Do Before They Die*. Within the following pages, die-hard team supporters will revisit some of the most entertaining, heartbreaking, and funny moments in franchise history. For those who just jumped on the bandwagon, it'll be a great education about Canada's only existing NBA squad. This club has come a long way since my first game in 1996 and even though the Raptors had a tough end to the 2015 playoffs, I'm still optimistic that their best days are yet to come. Hopefully you'll enjoy the trip back in time and will get pumped up for an exciting future ahead.

1 Vinsanity

On June 24th, 1998, the Raptors franchise changed forever. During NBA draft night, Toronto dealt its fourth overall selection, University of North Carolina forward Antawn Jamison to Golden State for its fifth overall pick, Jamison's UNC teammate, Vincent Lamar Carter, and cash considerations. In what would be one of the NBA's most intense love-hate relationships between a team's fan base and its superstar, Vinsanity was born.

The marriage began beautifully. In the early years, Vince "Air Canada" Carter thrilled Raptors fans with his electrifying and thunderous aerial assault on NBA rims across North America. As a result the accolades were piling up—a Rookie of the Year award, two All-Star selections, an eye-popping 2000 NBA Slam Dunk Contest win, and two trips to the playoffs—in his first three seasons. "He was a premier talent," Carter's former Raptors teammate, Jerome Williams said. "He was definitely one of those players who got not only the fans excited, but he got his teammates excited. Whenever you have a guy with that type of athleticism and talent level, there's a buzz in the air."

Toronto was in love. Raptors fans' memories of the franchise's losing ways before Vince arrived had now been replaced with his crowd-pleasing, high-flying acrobatics at the Air Canada Centre, which dominated nightly sports television highlight reels.

Alas, like many marriages, this one had its bumps. One of the biggest was before Game 7 of a 2001 second-round playoff series against the Philadelphia 76ers. Carter decided to attend his North Carolina graduation earlier that day. His controversial move confused and angered many Raptors fans and some teammates who felt

1

Canada Connection

Cleveland Cavaliers forward Tristan Thompson has a special connection with Carter. Growing up, the Brampton, Ontario, native went to Carter's basketball camp where he saw his hero up close. Years later, during the 2013 NBA All-Star weekend, Thompson spoke with his idol. "[Vince] remembered me from when I was in ninth grade," said the 2011 first-round draft pick. "He and I chit-chatted and had a couple of jokes. But Vince was one of the great players for [Toronto] and one of the great players of this league." Thompson then offered the ultimate compliment: "Vinsanity was my Michael Jordan. I looked up to him."

he should have stayed with the club. It reached a boiling point later when Carter—in the waning seconds of Game 7—missed what would have been a series-winning shot which ended the Raptors once promising season. All of a sudden Carter's golden image, in Raptors fans' eyes, lost some of its lustre.

In the next few seasons, he would experience various injuries, increased fan and media scrutiny suggesting he was quitting on the team, and issues with management, which ultimately forced a December 2004 trade to New Jersey.

Just like that, the love affair was over. Carter had become Raptors' fans most hated villain. With every future Toronto return, a reign of boos would always greet No. 15—until November 2014, when during an in-game video tribute to the Raptors former superstar, some cheered bringing Vince to tears.

Whether you despise or love him, you can't deny Vinsanity put Toronto on the NBA map and brought excitement and joy to global basketball fans, including the future Canadian NBA players he inspired. Carter, who averaged 23.4 points per game as a Raptor, is the most dominating, explosive, and polarizing player in franchise history. Despite his flaws you might see his on-court brilliance recognized with an induction into the Basketball Hall of Fame.

Vince Carter, an electrifying dunker, is likely the best—and certainly most exciting—player in Raptors history.

2 Wince Carter and the Breakup

On August 1st, 2001, fresh off their best playoff run in team history, the Raptors signed their franchise player to a six-year, $94 million extension on what then-Toronto mayor Mel Lastman declared as Vince Carter day. "It would have been tough to go elsewhere when he made it my day," said Carter, who averaged a career-high 27.6 points per game during the 2000–01 campaign. "I'm extending my contract and I'm going to continue to be a Raptor here and I'm really looking forward to it."

Locking up Carter was one of many moves Raptors general manager Glen Grunwald made during that offseason, including re-signing free agents Antonio Davis, Jerome Williams, and Alvin Williams and trading for 12-time All-Star Hakeem Olajuwon. Toronto was loading up to prepare for the next step in its championship journey. Some Raptors fans cautiously started to get excited again, slowly forgetting Carter's graduation day fiasco and missed last-second shot, which snuffed out a promising season.

But once the 2001–02 campaign was underway, Flight 15 wasn't taking off as explosively anymore. Carter was having chronic knee issues. Before you knew it, he missed 22 games before going under the knife in late March 2002. Then, during the 2002–03 season, he missed a career-high 39 games with more knee problems and an ankle sprain. To frustrated Raptors fans, it seemed like Carter fell to the floor every game grabbing his knee or ankle while wincing in pain. He was labeled as "a whiner," "soft," "Half-man, Half-a-season," "a quitter." Wince Carter had arrived.

The Raptors had to make do without their fallen superstar. In 2001–02 they made a furious late season run to sneak into the playoffs but would lose to the Detroit Pistons in the first round. Then in 2002–03 with the team battling multiple injuries, they missed the postseason thanks to an ugly 24–58 record, which allowed them to select future All-Star Chris Bosh in the 2003 NBA Draft. It was so bad that after a loss in the Raptors' final home game, Grunwald took a microphone and told the remaining fans, "We will not stand for this any longer." Hall of Fame head coach Lenny Wilkens was fired after the season.

Grunwald would replace the laid-back Wilkens with hard-nosed, first-time NBA head coach Kevin O'Neill. In 2003–04, even though Carter played 73 games, the O'Neill experiment didn't work. His demanding ways did little to inspire VC and a Raptors club, which finished a disappointing 33–49. Another lost season meant the end for O'Neill and Grunwald, a man Carter liked and who had been with the Raptors organization since 1994. Jack McCloskey took over as interim general manager until Raptors president Richard Peddie hired rookie NBA GM Rob Babcock.

This took Carter by surprise. During an April 2004 meeting with Peddie, VC was assured he'd be kept updated during the GM hiring process. In a Sportsnet interview with longtime Raptors season-ticketholder and Carter's close friend, Nav Bhatia, he said, "As for the hiring of the GM, Peddie didn't have to say he would keep Vince informed. He just said he would. And Vince believed him—until he found out after the fact that Babcock was hired. Vince suggested that Julius Erving be interviewed for the job. Well, Dr. J. arrived at the airport in Toronto, was in town briefly, and was never brought to the Air Canada Centre or anything like that. That's what my information is. Vince doesn't think Dr. J. received a proper interview. It didn't show respect to either Vince or Dr. J., two guys most people consider basketball superstars."

Bhatia, who attended Carter's 2004 wedding, added, "Vince loves Toronto and he loves the fans of Toronto. He has two condominiums in Toronto and he wants to live here for many, many more years. But he has serious problems playing for an organization that is run by Richard Peddie. He has problems with Jack McCloskey and [player personnel director] Jim Kelly, too."

Carter, according to Bhatia, not only wanted Peddie, McCloskey, and Kelly gone, but he also had issues with Toronto's inability to improve the roster. "Vince really thought there was going to be a good chance to get [Jamaal] Magloire and [Steve] Nash," Bhatia said. "He wanted them in Toronto because, as he told Peddie in the meeting, there was an obvious need to improve two positions—the No. 1 position and the No. 5 position. He wanted Magloire and Nash because they were perfect for the positions. They're both All-Stars and they're friends of Vince's. The fact they are also both Canadian would be good, he figured, because he recognized that would help the Raptors in terms of popularity in this country."

To add to VC's growing frustration, the team took away his mother's parking spot at the Air Canada Centre and the new GM fired longtime Raptors head athletic therapist Chuck Mooney, who worked closely with Vince. As the Carter and Raptors union continued to break down, the team hired its new head coach, Sam Mitchell, who entered a big mess. In a March 2013 *National Post* article, the former NBA Coach of the Year said after taking the job, he flew to Florida to visit the unhappy superstar. After Carter congratulated him, he confessed, "Mentally, I'm in a place where I've got some differences with the organization, and it's unfortunate that you have come into this…but my heart's not in it for the Toronto Raptors anymore."

With that bomb dropped, Mitchell had to forge ahead knowing his best player may not be around much longer. Since the Toronto media and Raptors fans knew Carter was possibly eyeing some sort of exit, they focused the spotlight on him more brightly. Once the 2004–05 season began, Carter received heavy criticism for his lack of effort on the court. His scoring numbers were down, and Mitchell was stapling him to the bench more often. Then, in

November 2004, likely out of frustration, Carter gave reporters this golden nugget: "I don't want to dunk anymore."

Of course, that sentence outraged Raptors fans who saw it as something a spoiled child would say. It just gave them more venom to spew at a man they once adored. Carter wanted out, and the rest of the NBA knew it. Thus, Babcock was backed into a corner. How could he possibly get fair value in a deal with Carter playing poorly and other GMs realizing he needs to make a move to end this toxic situation? Finally, on December 17th, 2004, Carter was dealt in one of the most lopsided trades in NBA history. No. 15 would take off to New Jersey for centre Alonzo Mourning (who did not report to Toronto), forward Eric Williams, forward/centre Aaron Williams, a 2005 first-round draft pick (Joey Graham), and a 2006 first-round draft pick (Renaldo Balkman), which was later traded to the New York Knicks.

According to *Sportsnet*, the day before the deal was done, Carter told Mitchell he didn't want to leave. When Mitchell mentioned that to Babcock, the GM said, "the deal had been agreed to." Translation—there was no going back. At the time, Raptors fans thought Vince quit on the team and the city, which fuelled their seething hatred for him even more.

Their suspicions were seemingly confirmed when after the trade, TNT's John Thompson asked Carter during an interview if he pushed himself as hard as he should have in the past, "In years past, no," Carter replied. "I was just fortunate enough to have the talent. You know, you get spoiled when you're able to do a lot of things and you *see* that and you really don't have to work at it. But now, I think with all the injuries and the things that have gone on, I have to work a little harder and I'm a little hungrier."

As you might expect, Raptors fans were blowing their tops after that. Carter's ex-teammate, Jerome Williams, reflected on his years playing alongside Vince, also criticized his effort. "As a player and as a teammate, I wish he would have actually taken those skills and developed them more," Williams said. "He would have been on the level of a Kobe Bryant and of some of the premier players like the Carmelo Anthonys and Dwyane Wades of today. He'd be right up there, but I think with injuries and not being able to really just get that eye of the tiger, his flame kind of dwindled there. Everybody is different. You can't make leaders out of people who weren't born to lead. I just don't think he was actually born to lead. He was born to be just a great, significant basketball talent. We expected more from him because that's the position he was put in by the Raptors and other organizations."

But Vince was also ticked off. In his first game back in Toronto on April 15, 2005, Carter dominated with 39 points in a 101–90 win to silence the hostile environment filled with loud boos and jeers every time he touched the ball. "I just kind of blocked it out," Carter said. "I'm happy with the way things turned out. Maybe they are not, but this was a fun game believe it or not."

The NBA Returns to Canada

Remember the Toronto Huskies? You probably weren't born yet, but they were the city's original NBA franchise. Actually, they were a charter member of the Basketball Association of America, which later became the star-studded league you see today.

On November 1, 1946, the Huskies hosted the New York Knickerbockers at Maple Leaf Gardens in the NBA's first ever game. The contest attracted 7,090 people, a good crowd considering Toronto was a hockey-loving city, and basketball wasn't a popular sport at the time.

Unfortunately, the Huskies would lose 68–66 and finished with a 22–38 record, which resulted in them folding after one season.

Over the years NBA basketball did visit Toronto from time to time. According to the *Toronto Sun*, the (now defunct) Buffalo Braves played 16 regular season games at Maple Leaf Gardens between 1971 and 1975. At one point, there was talk the Braves would eventually relocate to Toronto, but it never happened. During the 1970s three Toronto ownership groups pushed hard to attract an NBA team, but when the league offered one for the 1975–76 season, the $6.15 million franchise fee proved too rich for those pursuing the opportunity.

Toronto would be teased again in 1982 when Maple Leaf Gardens hosted a Cleveland Cavaliers and Philadelphia 76ers exhibition game, featuring NBA All-Stars Julius Erving and Moses Malone, which drew more than 15,000 people, sparking new hope an NBA team would return up north. Cavaliers owner Ted Stepien actually threatened to move his money-losing club to Toronto and rename them "the Toronto Towers" but ultimately decided to sell the team to Cleveland businessmen George and Gordon Gund before the 1983–84 campaign.

As a small consolation prize, Stepien brought the Continental Basketball Association (CBA) to Toronto. The Tornados, the first permanent Toronto professional basketball team since the Huskies left, didn't last long, only playing from December 1983 to December 1985 before moving to Pensacola, Florida.

In 1989 and 1992, Toronto would host more NBA exhibition games—this time at the retractable-roofed downtown stadium, SkyDome, which drew over 25,000 fans twice and continued to show the city could support a franchise. In 1993 the NBA took serious notice. Three bid groups were in the hunt, including Professional Basketball Franchise Inc. (PBF) led by Toronto businessman John Bitove Jr. In July then-Phoenix Suns owner Jerry

Colangelo headed an NBA expansion committee, which visited Toronto to meet the interested groups, examine their plans, and look at their suggested arena sites.

The PBF contingent impressed with its downtown arena idea involving a location on the subway line to help Torontonians travel to games without fighting winter conditions and the proximity to the city's financial core to attract major companies to purchase corporate boxes.

PBF's bid proved too good to ignore, so the expansion committee conditionally awarded the group a franchise for the 1995–96 season, and on November 4, 1993, the NBA's Board of Governors endorsed the decision.

The expansion fee price tag was a then-record $125 million, and it was agreed the club would play its first two seasons at SkyDome while its arena was being built. However, there was still a chance the deal could be revoked because the NBA possessed a longstanding opposition against gambling and didn't like the province of Ontario's sports betting game, Pro-Line, which allowed people to wager on NBA outcomes. After three months of

SkyDome—The Raptors' First Home

Known for its fully retractable roof, the downtown Toronto multi-purpose facility made its public debut on June 3, 1989. Since then, SkyDome (later called Rogers Centre in 2005 after Rogers Communications purchased it) has staged more than 2,000 events and welcomed more than 60 million visitors. Its seating capacity ranges from a few thousand to upwards of 50,000 for sporting events, concerts, family shows, trade shows, and conventions.

The iconic Canadian structure not only housed Raptors games between November 1995 to February 1999, but it also hosts Major League Baseball's Toronto Blue Jays, the Canadian Football League's Toronto Argonauts, and, from 2008–2013, the National Football League's Buffalo Bills.

negotiations involving the league, PBF, and the province, Pro-Line was forced to remove NBA games from its betting options, and the dispute was resolved.

The franchise now needed an identity. The club decided to stage a nationwide name-the-team contest for fans, which generated over 2,000 different entries. The final top 10 list included Beavers, Bobcats, Dragons, Grizzlies, Hogs (Toronto's nickname is Hogtown), Raptors, Scorpions, T-Rex, Tarantulas, and Terriers. On May 15, 1994, in front of a Canadian national television audience, the "Toronto Raptors" was unveiled. It was influenced by the popular 1993 dinosaur movie, *Jurassic Park*, and the logo would feature an aggressive-looking, sharp-toothed dinosaur dribbling a basketball.

The team colours were bright red, purple, black, and "Naismith silver" in a tip of the cap to Canadian James Naismith, who invented basketball in 1891. On May 24 the Raptors would introduce two-time NBA champion and former Detroit Pistons Bad Boy Isiah Thomas as their new executive vice president of basketball operations, general manager, and part owner. Thomas, a 1981 NCAA Champion with Indiana, had been admired by Bitove who also attended Indiana and followed his early Pistons days while studying at the University of Windsor across the river from Detroit. Thomas would assemble his management staff, including hiring Pistons assistant Brendan Malone as the franchise's first head coach and recruiting his former 1981 Indiana teammate and ex-Denver Nuggets vice president, Glen Grunwald, as his assistant.

The roster would then be filled via the NBA expansion and lottery drafts in anticipation of the Raptors' inaugural 1995–96 campaign. After all these years, NBA basketball was back in Toronto, this time permanently, where it finally belonged.

4 The Raptors Tip Off

On November 3, 1995, at the cavernous SkyDome, 33,306 fans watched the Toronto Raptors play their first regular season game in franchise history. Their opponent was the then-New Jersey Nets.

Once the game started, Ed Pinckney, a 1985 NCAA Champion, won the franchise-opening tip-off. Four-time All-Star Alvin Robertson would hit a three-pointer for the first Raptors points in team history. Robertson had quite the night, finishing with a game-high 30 points to help lead the baby Dinos to a 94–79 franchise-opening victory. Brendan Malone, who coached the Raptors that first season, had fond memories of that time. "What I

Opening Lineup

Here were the men who played on opening night:

Raptors

Starters
Guard, Damon Stoudamire
Guard, Alvin Robertson
Forward, Ed Pinckney
Forward/Centre, Carlos Rogers
Centre, Zan Tabak

Reserves
Forward/Centre, Acie Earl
Forward/Centre, John Salley
Guard/Forward, Willie Anderson
Forward, Tracy Murray
Guard, Jimmy King

Nets

Starters
Forward, Armon Gilliam
Guard, Kenny Anderson
Guard, Kevin Edwards
Centre/Forward, P.J. Brown
Centre, Yinka Dare

Reserves
Forward/Centre, Jayson Williams
Centre/Forward, Rick Mahorn
Guard, Vern Fleming
Forward, Ed O'Bannon
Guard, Chris Childs
Guard/Forward, Gerald Glass
Guard, Rex Walters

remember most about that first year were the crowds," said Malone who would be fired after only one season in Toronto. "There were usually over 30,000 people there. But there was such anticipation that first night, such an extravaganza."

Once the glow of that magical opening evening wore off, the Raptors would behave more like an expansion club by finishing the season in the Central Division basement with a 21–61 record. Regardless, after 49 years and two days since Toronto's original NBA (then the Basketball Association of America) franchise opened its first and only season, the long wait was over.

CB4

Chris Bosh's introduction to the NBA was a turbulent one. After being selected fourth overall in the 2003 draft (which also featured LeBron James, Carmelo Anthony, and Dwyane Wade), Bosh was coming to a Raptors squad that just endured a brutal 24–58 season, hired a new hard-nosed coach in Kevin O'Neill, and its franchise player, Vince Carter, was slowly getting unhappier by the day. If that wasn't enough, Bosh and his slim build had to play out of position in the centre spot once Antonio Davis was traded to Chicago in December 2003. That was a lot for a 19-year-old kid, who only had one year at Georgia Tech, to handle.

The Dallas native, however, would push forward and have a strong first year. In 75 games Bosh averaged 11.5 points, 7.4 rebounds, 1.4 blocks, recorded 13 double-doubles, and set a Raptors single-season rookie record with 557 rebounds. For his hard work, he landed on the 2003–04 All-Rookie first team. The second NBA season would present a new challenge for the burgeoning 6'11" star. With the December 2004 Vince Carter trade, Bosh was thrust into the role of franchise player sooner than expected. "If I want to be a great player, I have to step up one day and take on the responsibility," he said. "So whether it's me stepping up saying, 'I want to do it' or me being thrown into the fire, some way I'm going to have to take on that responsibility."

Under the guidance of new head coach Sam Mitchell, who replaced O'Neill in the summer of 2004, Bosh would thrive, recording 32 double-doubles, including a 24-point, 22-rebound effort against the Philadelphia 76ers on March 25, 2005. In 81 games that season, the NBA sophomore would have 16.8 points and 8.9 rebounds per night. His improvement continued in 2005–06 when he averaged 22.5 points and 9.2 rebounds a game in his first NBA All-Star season. Now out of Vince's shadow, Bosh was "the Man" in Toronto and living up to that status.

The Raptors re-signed him to a three-year deal plus an option for a fourth season, which would be worth $65 million. "The future is very positive for the franchise," said Bosh at a news conference at the Air Canada Centre.

With a new contract extension signed, it was time for CB4 (a nickname created by Raptors play-by-play man Chuck Swirsky,

The 2003 NBA Draft

Known for LeBron James, Carmelo Anthony, Bosh, and Dwyane Wade, the 2003 NBA Draft also featured eight future Raptors including Bosh (fourth overall pick), T.J. Ford (eighth), Mickael Pietrus (11th), Marcus Banks (13th), Carlos Delfino (25th), Leandro Barbosa (28th), Jason Kapono (31st), and two-time NBA champion Matt Bonner (45th). Other '03 draft notables include former All-Stars Chris Kaman, David West, Josh Howard, and Mo Williams. The draft also had one of the most lethal three-point shooters in NBA history in Kyle Korver, NBA champion Boris Diaw, NBA champion Kendrick Perkins, and the night's biggest bust, seven-footer Darko Milicic, who is now giving kickboxing a shot.

who combined Bosh's initials and jersey number) to help spring the Raptors back into the postseason for the first time since 2002. In 2006–07 Bosh would become an All-Star starter for the first time. He earned it with a solid first half of the season, which featured a 23-point, 22-rebound game against the Golden State Warriors in November 2006 and then a 41-point explosion against Dwight Howard's Orlando Magic on February 7, 2007. Bosh's leadership and growing production (22.6 points per game and 10.7 rebounds per game in 2006–07) would be one of the main reasons Toronto would win a franchise record-tying 47 games, clinch its first ever division title, and book a ticket to the playoffs.

In the postseason Bosh and the Raptors squared off against the old face of the franchise, Vince Carter and his New Jersey Nets, in the opening round. CB4 averaged 17.5 points, nine rebounds, and 1.8 blocks in his first playoff series, but Toronto would lose in six games.

After another All-Star campaign in 2007–08, Bosh would help guide the Raptors to a second straight playoff berth.

Facing the Orlando Magic, this first-round match-up featured a clash between two of the most talented young big men in the league, Bosh versus Dwight Howard. Bosh averaged 24 points, nine rebounds, and 3.6 assists while Magic star Howard put up 22.6 points, 18.2 rebounds, and 3.8 blocks per contest. The Raptors couldn't handle D-12's three 20-20 games and the rest of Orlando's attack, losing their playoff showdown in five games.

With Bryan Colangelo realizing Bosh might need some veteran frontcourt assistance, he acquired six-time All-Star Jermaine O'Neal in a 2008 offseason multi-player trade, which also sent point guard T.J. Ford to Indiana. While the Raptors roster was changing, Bosh was busy playing for Team USA at the Summer Olympics. It was there he strengthened his already developed friendships with LeBron and Wade. It would be a bond, which would come into play in the summer of 2010. But in 2008 their collaboration contributed to a gold medal for the Americans.

Coming off the high of his Team USA experience, Bosh's 2008–09 season began with the firing of Sam Mitchell only 17 games into the campaign. Canadian-born Raptors assistant Jay Triano would take over as head coach. Despite another All-Star season where Bosh averaged 22.7 points and 10 rebounds per game, the Raptors' Twin Towers experiment didn't work.

Since both Bosh and O'Neal needed room to operate in the low post, their styles never really meshed together. So after playing 41 games, the ex-Indiana Pacers big man was dealt in a multi-player swap to the Miami Heat with four-time All-Star forward Shawn Marion being one of the pieces heading to Toronto.

The move wouldn't do much for the Raptors playoff hopes. With a 33–49 record, they'd miss the postseason. Before the end of the 2008–09 campaign, the dreadlock-wearing Bosh got into some hot water. In response to a February 27, 2009, game, where Shaquille O'Neal scored 45 points against Toronto, the Raptors star said, "He was just camping down in the lane. I mean, if they're not calling three seconds…I thought it was a rule, but I guess not." Shaq implied that Bosh was soft by comparing him to a famous drag queen. "I heard what Chris Bosh said, and that's strong words coming from the RuPaul of big men. I'm going to do the same thing (in their next meeting) I did before—make him quit."

Yep, it was that kind of season for the Raptors and Bosh, who was now going into the final year of his contract before he could become an unrestricted free agent in 2010. The club offered him an extension, but Bosh turned it down. During that 2009 offseason, the Raptors made a slew of moves, including signing Bosh's former Georgia Tech teammate Jarrett Jack and trading for Orlando's multi-talented Hedo Turkoglu to entice their franchise star to stay.

In 2009–10 Bosh, who became a five-time All-Star in Toronto, would have his best season, averaging career-highs with 24 points

Though Chris Bosh eventually would leave the Raptors for the Miami Heat, Toronto selected a prized player in the star-studded 2003 NBA Draft.
(AP Images)

(including a Raptors career-best 44 points vs Milwaukee in January 2010) and 10.8 rebounds per game. The Raptors were in the playoff hunt late in the season, battling the Chicago Bulls for the final Eastern Conference postseason spot.

But on April 6, 2010, in Cleveland, Cavaliers forward Antawn Jamison flattened Bosh with an inadvertent elbow when both men jostled for position in the lane in the game's opening minutes. With blood dripping from his nose and mouth, Bosh had to leave the floor. Little did the Raptors and their fans know at the time, but it would be his final game in a Toronto uniform.

Bosh would have surgery to repair a facial fracture, and suddenly, the Raptors' playoff hopes were in jeopardy. In a pivotal game against the Bulls on April 11 in Toronto, the Bosh-less Raptors were blown out 104–88, and Chicago would win its final two games of the regular season to claim the eighth seed in the East. It was a tough way to end the year for Toronto, but it was only the start of the pain.

In the summer of LeBron, Bosh chose to head to South Beach in a sign-and-trade to join his Team USA friends James and Wade in a move that would eventually lead to two future NBA championship-winning seasons together. Reportedly, the trio had been plotting this for some time. Regardless, the end result gave the Raptors fan base another former star to hate. On his way out, Bosh did have a message for Raptors supporters on his website. "I just want to thank you guys for one of the best experiences of my life. As a die-hard sports fan, I know what it's like when a familiar face decides to leave and so I understand your disappointment. But know that this was my toughest decision, mostly because Toronto has been so great to me. I've loved every minute here and I just wanted to say thank you from the bottom of my heart. To a world-class city and its world-class fans, thank you."

After seven seasons, Bosh would finish as the Raptors' all-time leader in many categories including points, rebounds, and blocks.

On February 16, 2011, he'd make his Toronto return as a member of the Heat. Like Tracy McGrady and Carter before him, Bosh received some boos. They filled the Air Canada Centre the moment he stepped onto the court for pregame warm-ups and even when he was shown on the video screen during the U.S. national anthem.

Fans also directed some boos to LeBron when the camera panned to him.

It didn't matter. Bosh would have 25 points and six rebounds in Miami's 103–95 victory.

After the game the former Raptors star blew kisses to the crowd as he walked off the court.

Were they sarcastic or sincere kisses? "It's a sarcastic one to all the naysayers and it's real to all the good supporters," Bosh said. "People are going to take it the way they want to. The most important thing is the win tonight. We wanted to keep our momentum going."

VC's Slam Dunk Contest and Olympic Jam

Half-Man, Half-Amazing. The nickname certainly fit Vince Carter. Joining a Hall of Fame fraternity of high-flyers such as Michael Jordan, Dr. J, and Dominique Wilkins, "Air Canada" unleashed his own nightly aerial assault, which brought opponents to their knees and Raptors fans out of their seats.

Blessed with freakish athleticism, including jump-through-the-ceiling hops, Carter's ferocious dunks left many NBA big men, who attempted to block him, on the wrong end of ESPN *SportsCenter* highlights and/or on some kid's bedroom wall poster. Just ask future Hall of Famer Tim Duncan, four-time Defensive Player of

The Year Dikembe Mutombo, and four-time Defensive Player of The Year Ben Wallace. During an NBA All-Star Game, Duncan once told Carter, "Ain't no fair man, I got so little hops, and you got so much." Carter couldn't help but laugh.

VC had a full repertoire of dunks, including alley-oop, 360, reverse, windmill, tomahawk, etc. Not only did fans enjoy and respect Carter's dunking abilities, but his NBA peers did too. During a *Best Damn Sports Show Period* television interview, Los Angeles Lakers superstar Kobe Bryant gave Carter the ultimate praise when asked who'd win a dunk contest between himself, Carter, Jordan, Wilkins, and Dr. J in their prime. "I would say Vince. Vince is a special dunker," Bryant explained. "I think MJ did some stuff that was revolutionary for his time as did Dr. J. The way Vince dunks the ball, the way that he dunked the ball when he was in the dunk contest was just unbelievable."

Ah yes, *The 2000 NBA Slam Dunk Contest*.

One Iconic Dunker Helps Another

Leading up to the 2003 NBA All-Star Game, Vince Carter was criticized for not giving up his Eastern Conference starting spot to Michael Jordan who was appearing in his final NBA showcase. In a last-minute move, Carter allowed MJ to start, which gave basketball fans a thrill as Jordan would score 20 points including a clutch go-ahead jumper late in the first overtime. Afterward, Minnesota Timberwolves All-Star Kevin Garnett said, "It looked like old 23 crept back in the building and was trying to take the game." Ultimately, the West would win a 155–145 double-overtime thriller. Following the loss, Jordan stood up for Carter, a fellow former North Carolina Tar Heel. "I felt like he had taken a beating, and he shouldn't have," Jordan said. "I think he was being very respectful." As for Carter he understood what this opportunity meant to No. 23. "This is a storybook ending for Michael," Carter explained. "I'm sure I'll have another opportunity to be in the All-Star Game, and this is how it's supposed to be."

It would be Carter's official announcement to not only the NBA, but also the sports world that he had arrived. On that February night, the crowd in Oakland, California, was treated to an air show like no other. Carter dazzled the packed house, including a giddy Shaquille O'Neal, with a reverse 360 windmill, an elbow in-the-rim dunk (also known as "the honey dip") and a between-the-legs slam off a bounced alley-oop pass from his cousin, Tracy McGrady, which sparked VC afterward to mouth to a television camera, "It's over, it's over."

At that point, the contest wasn't even in the final yet. It didn't matter. All night basketball fans and current and former NBA players roared and stood on their feet, waving their "10" scoring cards in appreciation of the once-in-a-lifetime display they just witnessed. Carter's mind-blowing performance not only certified himself as one of the league's brightest young stars, but it also made Toronto relevant to the NBA universe.

Years later, when remembering that incredible night, Carter recalled being focused as soon as he stepped onto the floor. "This was my first opportunity, something I was looking forward to," Carter said. "I got in the zone once I got out there and could feel the energy. I was like, 'Oh yeah, this is it.'"

Carter's year of the dunk didn't end there. At the 2000 Summer Olympics in Sydney, Australia, the Raptors franchise player would deliver his greatest slam and arguably the best dunk ever. During a game between Team USA and France, the 6'6" All-Star would steal the ball, drive, and leapfrog over 7'2" centre Frederic Weis for a powerful one-handed jam. The French media called it *le dunk de la mort* (The Dunk of Death). "For me, that was probably the greatest play in basketball I've ever seen," said Jason Kidd, Carter's Team USA teammate. "Michael Jordan hasn't done that. Nobody has done that."

Team USA head coach Rudy Tomjanovich joked, "The only time I've seen a play like that is when I jumped over my four-year-old son on one of those Nerf ball sets." After the 106–94 Team USA win, Carter was modest about his jaw-dropping slam. "I don't rank mine. I just do them," he said. "I didn't think I was going to make it actually. I took off from a long way away."

Even Weis was surprised with Carter's springs. "I knew he could jump, but I didn't know he could jump over me," the 1999 New York Knicks first-round draft pick explained. "Everybody will know my face now or my number at least. It's going to be on a poster for sure."

Weis never signed with the Knicks and didn't play in the NBA. As for Carter, he would cap off that Olympic run with a gold medal during a year he'll never forget.

7 We Beat Michael Jordan

After the San Antonio Spurs destroyed the 1995–96 expansion Raptors 120–108 in front of Toronto's hometown crowd, it seemed the franchise's debut team would get drubbed even worse in the following game on March 24, 1996. After all they were playing the Michael Jordan-led Chicago Bulls, who went on to win a record 72 games and a title that year.

Surprisingly, the scrappy Raptors were giving the NBA goliath a handful in front of 36,131 delighted fans at the SkyDome. Toronto would actually lead 56–54 at halftime—not bad for a team with only 17 wins that was facing a 60–7 club at the time. But, of course, the Bulls would bounce back, outscoring the Raptors 30–23 in the third quarter to go up 83–79 heading into the final period.

Throughout the game Jordan was guarding Toronto's rookie sensation Damon Stoudamire, but the young star wasn't fazed, scoring a team-high 30 points and adding 11 assists. The Dinos also received great contributions from forwards Tracy Murray (23 points and 12 rebounds), Carlos Rogers (15 points), and big man Oliver Miller (14 points and 12 rebounds). With six Raptors scoring in double figures and Toronto surging in the fourth quarter, Jordan did his best down the stretch to get the Bulls the win, but his 36 points were not enough.

The Raptors shocked His Airness by squeaking out a 109–108 result in the biggest victory of Toronto's first season and one of the most memorable wins in franchise history. After the terrific performance, Toronto head coach Brendan Malone was loving life. "What a great win. Euphoric. It's a word. Look it up," he said. "Man, it's really a great feeling."

Even Jordan had praise for the first-year club. "This team has played us well all season long. The last time we were here, they had a chance to win it at the buzzer, so they played us well," said the future six-time NBA champion. "You have to give them credit."

When asked years later about that once-in-a-lifetime game, Stoudamire had nothing but warm memories. "Man, that was real special. That was a great game for us," said the point guard who averaged 19.6 points during his Raptors career. "We got a big victory against, ultimately, one of the greatest teams of all time who eventually went on to win 72 games that season. That was a defining moment, I think, for everybody. The city was ecstatic. All the players were ecstatic. That was just a great moment."

8 Mighty Mouse

The Toronto Raptors select Damon Stoudamire from the University of Arizona.

Booooooooooooo!

That was the scene on June 28th at the 1995 NBA Draft at SkyDome in Toronto. Damon Stoudamire, selected seventh overall as the franchise's first ever draft pick, was showered with boos after disappointed locals were hoping to receive UCLA star forward Ed O'Bannon, who was fresh off an NCAA championship and NCAA Tournament MVP. Instead Toronto chose a 5-foot-10 point guard, who as a senior at Arizona averaged 22.8 points and 7.3 assists per game.

In a 2010 podcast interview, Stoudamire said the frosty reception didn't bother him. "I didn't even care," said the guard who would play 200 career games as a Raptor. "I wasn't gonna let nobody steal my day. That was *my* day. It's like getting married, so that was *my* day."

Armed with plenty of motivation, "Mighty Mouse," a nickname earned due to his small, muscular stature and one that he took to heart as he got a Mighty Mouse tattoo on his arm, adjusted right away to NBA competition and turned those draft night boos into consistent cheers. The city began to embrace their first franchise star and watched as he would deliver a terrific 1995–96 rookie campaign, which included 37 double-doubles. Stoudamire would go on to capture the NBA Rookie of the Year award, averaging 19 points and 9.3 assists in 70 games.

After the young guard received his Rookie of the Year award at a press conference, Raptors general manager Isiah Thomas, who took a chance by drafting the former Wildcat, said in front of him

What Happened to Ed O'Bannon?

After an outstanding career at UCLA, O'Bannon wasn't able to find similar success when he was selected ninth overall by the New Jersey Nets in 1995. Due to knee problems, poor confidence, and being an undersized NBA power forward, he floundered, scoring only five points per game in two seasons with the New Jersey Nets and Dallas Mavericks. Former Nets teammate, the late Armon Gilliam, said, "He's a guy who didn't find his niche in the NBA. He wasn't in the right situation to grow and develop. He never got the opportunity to prove what he could do." After playing overseas then retiring in his early 30s, O'Bannon dabbled in car sales, high school coaching, and later challenged and won an antitrust lawsuit against the NCAA, which opened the door for college men's basketball and football players to earn money by selling their naming, image, and likeness rights.

and the media, "I shouldn't do this, but I'm going to kiss you." Then he planted one on a smiling Stoudamire's cheek.

The Raptors franchise player made quite the impression on fans and teammates. "Love Damon Stoudamire," said ex-Raptor Doug Christie who played with him from 1996 to 1998. "He was a friend at the same time as a teammate, had great times. We learned so much about ourselves as basketball players playing together up there in Toronto."

Mighty Mouse wouldn't lose steam in his sophomore season, averaging a career-high 20.2 points and 8.8 assists in 81 games, but in year three, he watched as the Raptors front office started to crumble. Because of issues with ownership, Thomas quit and accepted a broadcasting job with NBC. Stoudamire, who had developed a loyal bond with the 12-time All-Star, wasn't shocked by the news. "I'm not surprised at all. I'm more disappointed than upset," he said. "I think he meant a lot to this team. He brought these players here and got us started out on the right direction."

Stoudamire, who didn't appreciate how the Raptors treated Thomas, would later request a trade. In February 1998, during what would be the worst season in franchise history (16–66), Mighty Mouse was dealt in a multi-player deal to the Portland Trail Blazers. "The emotions were so high at the time, and I wanted to get to a winner so bad and have a chance to win," he admitted in 2010. "Going to Portland with all the young players they had, I just felt like that was a good fit for me."

It would mark the first of many disgruntled Raptors stars' exits. Years later, Grunwald said of Stoudamire, "He was the champagne that launched the franchise. He played with such heart. He was really affected when Isiah left as general manager. It would've been really interesting to see what would've happened to his career if that hadn't happened."

After the trade Toronto fans would boo him in his various returns as an opponent, but in 2013 he reflected and had remorse for the situation. "I was young," Stoudamire said. "Basketball is a business, and as you get older, it's more about building relationships, and that's more important than the selfishness in which I left here. For me, I wish I could have done that over again because it just wasn't done the right way."

Despite the messy ending, Raptors fans have forgiven their diminutive former star. In fact during a Raptors 15-year anniversary short video board presentation, which showcased some of Stoudamire's team accomplishments, the Air Canada Centre crowd gave him a standing ovation. In 878 career NBA games, Stoudamire averaged 13.4 points and 6.1 assists while suiting up for the Raptors, Trail Blazers, Memphis Grizzlies, and San Antonio Spurs.

Kyle Lowry, the Bulldog of Bay Street

Kyle Lowry had a reputation. In his past stints with the Memphis Grizzlies and Houston Rockets, the tough-minded young point guard had an attitude and was no stranger to challenging authority. The Philadelphia native showed promise on the court but was never fully given the keys to the Ferrari for a long period of time.

Memphis had 2007 first-round selection Mike Conley Jr., so the Grizzlies made him their guy while in Houston, Lowry did start more (71 of 75 games in 2010–11), but he clashed with head coach Kevin McHale, and then the Rockets wanted to shed salary and acquire draft picks, so they dealt the talented guard to Toronto in July 2012. "I didn't want to get traded," Lowry told Grantland. com. "I knew [Toronto was] trying to get Steve Nash. This is what they said: 'They wanted Steve Nash to be the point guard for two years and then me learn behind Nash and to get paid and be the starter after Steve called it a career.' I said, 'No, I don't want to be a backup. You're not trading for me to be a backup.' They did the trade anyway, but they didn't get Steve."

Once in Toronto, the Villanova University product would still have to wait for those Ferrari keys because longtime guard Jose Calderon was still around. Before the 2012–13 campaign, Lowry suffered an injury in training camp, which set him back, allowing Calderon to start the season. *"You all want me to be this guy?"* Lowry told Grantland. *"You guys traded a first-round pick for me to be this guy that sits on the bench, that plays 15, 20 minutes?"* I was not happy. It was part because I knew what I just came from being, which was almost an All-Star in Houston until I got sick and got hurt. I went from being almost an All-Star to back on the bench. I was not a bad teammate. I was just really in a world of my own. I was just like, *All*

Kyle Lowry, a tough-minded point guard and fan favourite, drives to the basket during the 2015 playoffs.

right, I'm going to go to work. That's all I'm going to do. I'm not going to fraternize. I'm going to go to work, come home, that's it. Because it wasn't my team. I was a role player."

At that point Lowry was so frustrated, if given the chance to re-sign in Toronto, he would have turned it down. "I'd tell you, 'You can kiss my ass,'" Lowry remembered. "I never thought I'd be back. Put it like this: I thought, *I'll do my two-year bid and I'm gone.*"

Things changed in January 2013 when Calderon was dealt to Detroit in a three-team trade which brought Rudy Gay to the Raptors. Lowry was not only re-united with his former Grizzlies teammate, but now he was *the* starting point guard.

Here are your keys to the Ferrari, sir.

In his first Raptors season, Lowry averaged 11.6 points and 6.4 assists in 68 games, including 52 starts. Lowry, though, still had some growing up to do. Once new general manager Masai Ujiri entered the scene, he challenged the young man. "Do you want to be a $3 million player, $2 million player for the rest of your career, and become a minimum player, or do you want to be a $10 million player or more?" Ujiri asked. "Talent says you are that type of player, but the attitude and the way you carry yourself says the other. You can be so much better."

After Lowry's friend, Rudy Gay, was dealt to Sacramento in December 2013, No. 7 thought he might also possibly be on the move. "I didn't think I was getting traded anywhere besides the Knicks," Lowry recalled. "I thought that was the trade, and Masai was truthfully telling me that I'm gonna trade you somewhere where you can be a starter. I honestly thought that was going to happen. I had two duffle bags ready to go."

It turned out Lowry wouldn't go anywhere, and Toronto would be a completely different club from there. The Raptors were a more balanced team, but Lowry was the heart and soul of the club. He was outstanding during the first half of the season, including in these games:

- December 28, 2013, vs the New York Knicks—32 points, 11 assists, and eight rebounds
- January 24, 2014, vs the Philadelphia 76ers—18 points, 13 assists, and 10 rebounds
- January 27, 2014, vs the New Jersey Nets—31 points, seven assists, five rebounds, and five steals
- January 29, 2014, vs the Orlando Magic—33 points, 11 assists, and seven rebounds

Coupled with Lowry's inspired play and the Raptors' overall improved performance, Toronto was leading the Atlantic Division. You'd think Lowry's efforts would be rewarded with a 2014 All-Star selection, but he would be unfairly snubbed. All-Star voters may not have loved Lowry, but Toronto became enamored with its bulldog. Despite being six feet tall, he takes charges in the lane, occasionally grabs rebounds amongst significantly bigger and taller players, and fights for everything he wants on the court. He's a hockey player disguised as an NBA guard.

No wonder Toronto loves him.

He'd guide the Raptors to a franchise single-season record in wins, Toronto's second division title in club history, and the team's first playoff appearance since 2008.

You can keep the Ferrari, sir.

In Lowry's Raptors playoff series debut, he was a handful for the Nets especially when he scored 36 points in Game 5. He even had a chance to extend Toronto's Cinderella season late in Game 7, but with the Raptors down one, Paul Pierce blocked his shot in the paint to seal Toronto's fate. Despite the tough ending, Lowry had a terrific season, putting up 17.9 points and 7.4 assists per game.

Then the big question became would the unrestricted free agent re-sign with Toronto?

In a 2014 summer dominated by LeBron James' return to Cleveland, Raptors fans were hoping their tenacious floor leader would come back. "I was very open to leaving," Lowry admitted. "I was like: *Look, I have a chance to go somewhere else, why not look at it?*...I did my pros and cons. I did my lists. I did my research. I did the—what the salary cap is two years from now, three years from now. I knew who was going to be a free agent. I wanted to make sure I was going to the best situation for me personally, but to also try to win as much as I possibly can."

After the Heat, Rockets, and others made overtures, Lowry decided to remain a Raptor by signing a 4-year, $48 million contract. "Toronto is just the right place for me," Lowry told Yahoo Sports.

Justin Bieber to the Rescue

In 2015 Kyle Lowry became just the third Raptors player to be voted an All-Star starter, joining Vince Carter and Chris Bosh. It's an exclusive club in franchise history, but one mega pop star tried to help Lowry get there.

That help came after Prime Minister Stephen Harper tweeted on January 6, 2015: "Canadian basketball fans should get behind @Klow7, who deserves to be an NBA All-Star. #NBABallot #wethenorth" Lowry was blown away, responding with a "wow thank you" tweet.

Canadian Justin Bieber decided to use his influence to do the same. On January 19, 2015, Bieber tweeted the following to his millions of followers, "Toronto has been killin it and @Klow7 deserves to be an nba all star. Make sure to voice for him. #WeTheNorth. Good luck buddy."

Oh wait, Bieber forgot something. In order for tweets to be counted as votes, the hashtag #nbaballot must be used. Despite the gaffe Bieber's tweet generated tons of attention, which helped Lowry get selected.

Ujiri applauded the move. "We made it known that our top priority heading into the offseason was to re-sign Kyle," the Raptors GM said. "He was a key to our success last season, and we are delighted that he wants to be here in Toronto to help us continue to build a championship program."

In the 2014–15 campaign, Lowry wouldn't rest just because he had a fat deal and some security. He helped lead the Raptors to the playoffs for the second straight year. One of his brightest moments in 2015 was being selected as an NBA All-Star starter for the first time.

Raptors fans, in full #WeTheNorth mode, played a huge role in Lowry's new accomplishment.

"Thank you to the wonderful Raptors fans across the NBA, especially in Canada!" Lowry said in a statement. "I am amazed by your passion for our team and the support you have given me. When I re-signed here this summer, I said one of the great things is being able to play for an entire country. This is further proof how really special that is."

Ujiri was pleased to see Lowry's evolution into an All-Star talent. "I am super [proud]," Ujiri said. "I texted him yesterday and I told him I'm so proud of him…He's not relaxing. He wants to win and he wants to try and win big. That's what he wants, and he's not just any player but your point guard, your lead player."

At the All-Star Game, Lowry would have 10 points, eight assists, and a game-high four steals, but what delighted Raptors supporters the most was his unexpected one-handed putback jam in the second quarter of the East's 163–158 loss. It was his first dunk in years. During the game Lowry yelled, "I got hops!" Referee Pat Fraher said, "I didn't know you had hops like that." Lowry answered, "I only do it 'cause it's the All-Star Game."

You can keep the Ferrari, sir.

10 Graduation Day and the Miss

After Vince Carter left the University of North Carolina following his junior season in 1998 to enter the NBA draft, he promised his mother, Michelle, he'd return to finish his African American Studies degree. Fast forward to 2001 when the Raptors made the playoffs for the second straight campaign and knocked off the New York Knicks in the first round for their first postseason series win in franchise history.

While facing the Philadelphia 76ers in round two, Carter and 2001 NBA MVP Allen Iverson staged an epic scoring duel, which helped to extend the back and forth series to a seventh game. Toronto was building something special that season, and the players and fans could sense it.

On May 20, 2001, the day of Toronto's biggest playoff game in franchise history, its most talented on-court weapon decided to attend his University of North Carolina morning graduation ceremony. During his graduation Carter sat beside future NBA centre Brendan Haywood but would leave about 20 minutes into the nearly two-hour ceremony before many of the speeches, including the commencement address from late ESPN sportscaster Stuart Scott. Actually, the All-Star didn't even get his diploma that day. At the time North Carolina undergraduates did not receive them during graduation ceremonies. Instead Carter was sent his in the mail. His graduation day decision irked Jerome Williams who said in a 2010 podcast interview, "I wanted to graduate when I was in school too, but I stayed in school to do it." After watching some of the festivities, Carter took a plane to Philadelphia in time for a pregame team meeting.

Fresh off a 39-point Game 6 performance, VC struggled early in Game 7 due to being a little winded and trying too hard. Despite his challenges, the game was tight down the stretch. In the fourth quarter's waning seconds and with the Raptors down 88–87, Carter missed a potential series-winning shot. Toronto's Eastern Conference Finals dreams were dashed. It was one of the most gut-wrenching moments in team history.

Intense scrutiny followed from Raptors fans, media, and some of Carter's teammates who, years later, still feel he made the wrong choice. "I really, truly believe we should have won the whole Eastern Conference championship that year," Williams said. "But I just think there were some wrong decisions made right at the end that really turned the tide—one being Vince's decision to go to his school and graduate with his class. That was a tough decision. I graduated, but I would have had them ship that in the mail as far as a once in a lifetime opportunity to defeat a team that was going to be tough to beat but definitely beatable. It came down to one last shot and wasn't able to knock it down."

Regardless of what his critics mentioned, Carter, who finished the game with 20 points, looks back on the whole experience and has no regrets. "That was a monumental moment in my career, personally and as a professional player," he said. "I was able to accomplish two of my goals: to make it deep into the playoffs was one and to graduate. So that day is something I will never forget and always cherish."

11 Raptors Make Their Playoff Debut

This team was different. While the rest of the world was worried about Y2K and how the onset of the new millennium could lead to an apocalypse, the 1999–00 Raptors were busy winning games in the hope of arriving at a destination the franchise had never been before—the postseason.

Toronto's general manager, Glen Grunwald, did his part. The roster already included experienced players like the intimidating yet lovable Charles Oakley and seven-footer Kevin Willis, and Grunwald added more veterans, including Antonio Davis, Dell Curry, and Muggsy Bogues, to complement the Raptors' young, talented duo of Vince Carter and Tracy McGrady.

These moves came on the heels of a 1998–99 lockout-shortened season, which saw the explosive arrival of Vinsanity and the club's dramatic improvement after a dismal 1997–98 campaign. Even though Toronto didn't make the 1999 playoffs, you could tell the team was building some momentum. As the 1999–00 year began, the Raptors started well with a 4–1 record including a 123–106 win in Detroit on November 11, 1999, where seven Toronto players scored in double figures.

The Raptors' collection of youth and experience seemed to be working well together. VC was more deadly on the court while McGrady was maturing, growing his skills, and becoming a great sidekick to his All-Star cousin. The veterans were doing their part too, as the team caught fire during an 11-victories-in-12-games-stretch from February 27 to March 19. Toronto's playoff dreams would soon be reality but not in a typical way.

On April 12 the Pacers beat the Raptors 77–73, snapping Toronto's three-game winning streak, but thanks to the Boston

Celtics' win over the Orlando Magic that same night, the Raptors clinched their first postseason berth in franchise history. It was an incredible turnaround for a club that only won 16 games in 1997–98 to make the playoffs two seasons later.

Toronto finished with a 45–37 record, which set up a first-round date with a New York Knicks squad that made a miraculous run to the 1999 NBA Finals. Before the series started, head coach Butch Carter surprised everyone. He filed a $5 million defamation lawsuit against Knicks centre Marcus Camby after the former Raptor told the New York media his ex-coach was a "liar" for having told him he'd be one of the Raptors' cornerstones prior to his trade to New York. The legal action was a distraction for Toronto, but Carter would drop his lawsuit before Game 2.

In addition to dealing with his head coach being in the head-lines, playoff rookie Vince Carter had to learn how to excel in the postseason where everything was a new experience—even the pregame preparation. "I remember the practices being so much different than the regular season, what [coach Butch Carter] was putting us through," Carter told the *Toronto Star*. "I remember Butch lining us up. He takes all the big men—and I'm talking about Oak, AD, Kevin Willis, Yogi Stewart, all of our bigs—lining us up and telling us to drive to the basket, try to finish, get ready for the hard fouls. It was something."

In Game 1 on April 23 at Madison Square Garden, the Mecca of basketball, Carter clearly struggled. He missed 17 of his 20 shot attempts but still scored 16 while Tracy McGrady had 25 points and 10 rebounds in his playoff debut. VC's poor outing was one of the reasons why Toronto lost 92–88. "I was overexcited. I wasn't my normal self," Carter said. "My mechanics were not what they'd be in a regular season game. That happens."

When asked about the series years later, VC had more insight regarding his first postseason appearance. "When we got in the game, it was a different *world*. I just remember being excited, you're in the playoffs, playing the world-renowned New York Knicks...I just remember missing a couple of shots and all of a sudden seeing a double-team here, a double-team there, start getting double-teamed bringing the ball up the court. It was just amazing."

In Game 2, Carter, who had a better performance with a game-high 27 points, would receive criticism for a decision he made late in this one. In the dying seconds with Toronto down one, VC opted to feed an open Dee Brown for a three-pointer instead of attempting his own shot to win the game. Brown missed, and the Knicks were victorious 84–83 to go up 2–0 in the series.

Many Raptors fans felt Carter, as the club's superstar, should have gone for the win himself instead of passing off the opportunity.

Regardless, the scene would now switch to Toronto for the Raptors' first ever home postseason game. On April 30 nearly 20,000 enthusiastic fans packed the Air Canada Centre to see if their squad could avoid elimination. Unfortunately, Toronto's young guys would falter. Carter scored 15 points on 5-of-17 shooting to cap a disappointing series while T-Mac only had 12 points on 5-of-14 attempts from the floor. The veteran Knicks would outscore the Raptors 26–17 in the final quarter to wrap up an 87–80 victory and a three-game sweep in the best-of-five series.

Just like that, Toronto's playoff ride was abruptly over. It was a tough defeat to absorb for the postseason rookies in the Raptors' dressing room. "It was everyone's first experience, all the young guys," recalled Alvin Williams who only played one minute in the series. "It wasn't a sense of being overwhelmed because our leadership was good, but everyone didn't step up the way we could have stepped up."

12 Raptors Revenge

The Raptors had a bad taste in their mouth. A 2000 first-round postseason sweep at the hands of the New York Knicks in your first ever playoff appearance will make you feel that way. But the 2000–01 campaign would be different.

Before that season Toronto hired Hall of Fame head coach Lenny Wilkens after kicking Butch Carter out the door. The Raptors marched on without future two-time NBA scoring champion Tracy McGrady, who left for Orlando, an unpopular move among the Raptors faithful, at the end of his three-year rookie contract.

Future Raptors fan favourite, Morris Peterson, would be selected 21st overall in the first round of the 2000 NBA Draft. During the season on February 22, 2001, Toronto traded point guards Mark Jackson and Muggsy Bogues to the Knicks for guard Chris Childs and a 2002 first-round draft pick (Kareem Rush). The move allowed Alvin Williams, who was involved in the 1998 Damon Stoudamire trade to Portland, to take over the starting point guard duties where he'd post eight regular season double-doubles, including a triple-double against the Atlanta Hawks on March 23.

Williams' teammate, Vince Carter, would have a career year. VC averaged 27.6 points in 75 games while scoring 30 or more 30 times. Add in power forward Antonio Davis' 13.7 points and 10.1 rebounds per game plus a cast of characters including the lovably crusty Charles Oakley and high-energy forward Jerome "Junkyard Dog" Williams, Toronto would win 11 of its final 14 regular season games to secure a then-franchise record 47 victories.

The Raptors were playoff bound again and would face the Knicks again. In Game 1 at Madison Square Garden, Carter was not his All-Star self, shooting only 5-of-22 from the floor for 13 points in Toronto's 92–85 loss. Just as fans may have been thinking, *Here we go again*, came Game 2, where Carter would have 22 points and get help from Alvin Williams (a team-leading 23 points), Davis (15 points and 12 rebounds), and Oakley (12 points and 10 rebounds) as Toronto's starters outscored New York's 77–55 in the Raptors' first postseason victory in franchise history.

The Raptors then headed to the Air Canada Centre in hopes of making more history in Game 3. Despite 20,217 fans hoping Toronto could earn its first home playoff win in franchise history, the Raptors struggled. Carter scored 20 points but only shot 5-of-21 from the floor while Alvin Williams, who averaged 21 points in the first two games, had just nine points. New York's attack, led by sharpshooter Allan Houston (24 points), four-time All-Star Latrell Sprewell (20 points), and Glen Rice (18 points off the bench) was too much for Toronto as the Knicks won 97–89 to take a 2–1 series edge. A few days after the loss, Oakley criticized Carter for failing to act like a superstar. "All I said was, 'Vince, this is your team,'" Oakley explained. "'Don't try to back down. You're a Dream Teamer.' All the things I said were true."

Carter's mother, Michelle, who had the reputation of being a very hands-on parent, wasn't pleased with Oakley's criticism. Of course, the grizzled veteran was happy to respond. "Hey, if she wants to be a coach, Lenny [Wilkens'] contract is going to be up in two or three years."

In Game 4 of the best-of-five series and with the Raptors on the brink of elimination for the second straight postseason, Carter took Oakley's advice and finally became Vinsanity. He exploded for a game-high 32 points, including a highlight-reel first-quarter dunk, which shook the ACC and set the tone for Toronto's first ever home playoff victory 100–93. "I went back so far I almost hurt myself," Carter said of his electric first-quarter slam, which sent the crowd of 20,282 at the ACC into a frenzy. "That was the first open drive I had the whole series. My eyes felt as big as my face." Knicks head coach Jeff Van Gundy realized nothing could stop Flight 15 from taking off. "It started from the first dunk," Van Gundy said. "We didn't guard him. We weren't as alert or aware. I thought he was excellent."

Under the bright lights at MSG, the Raptors were feeling good in Game 5. Early in the fourth quarter, they enjoyed a 12-point lead, but Van Gundy's undersized Knicks would fight back, pulling within 81–80 with less than four minutes to go. The Raptors stayed poised. Leading 85–83 with under 1:30 left, Carter grabbed an offensive rebound off his own miss and got the layup to put Toronto ahead 87–83.

Then with less than 50 seconds remaining, VC sent a bounce pass to Alvin Williams who sunk a jump shot dagger, which sealed the historic 93–89 Game 5 victory. At last the Raptors, who had all five starters score in double figures, got their sweet revenge by earning their first postseason series win in team history. "The monkey is off our back. We're moving on to bigger and better things," said Carter, who scored a team-high 27 points in Game 5. "We saw this as a good opportunity to make a name for this franchise."

Although VC received most of the attention, the underrated Alvin Williams had a productive series, averaging 17.4 points per game. But what Raptors fans and ex-teammates will always recall is his clutch shot that iced the series victory. "Oh yeah. I remember that play," said Morris Peterson who played seven seasons in Toronto. "I remember when he let it go, putting a lot of arc on it. He had been doing it for us all year. He had been knocking down big shots. I thought Alvin was a little undervalued so to speak, as far as what he brought to the table. All the time I was there, he was making big plays, and that's the play that stands out. I remember thinking to myself, *This is the NBA, it don't get any better than this.*"

When you ask Alvin about his important Game 5 dagger, he's modest about it. "The play was a lucky play," admits Williams who would average 12.5 points per game in his Raptors playoff career. "I just remember coming down, we were trying to find a good shot, but we were kind of trying to stall a little bit. I remember the shot clock going down, I had the ball in my hands, and I actually slipped and fell and lost the ball. Vince picked it up and kicked it to me real quick. There wasn't anything else to do but to shoot it. There wasn't any time left."

The Raptors would move on to face the Philadelphia 76ers in what would be a classic second-round playoff series involving an epic Vince Carter and Allen Iverson showdown, a Game 7 controversy, and a heart-wrenching disappointment for Canadian fans. But Toronto couldn't have experienced those moments without its crucial playoff breakthrough in Game 5 at MSG.

13 T-Mac Breaks Toronto's Heart

Then-general manager Isiah Thomas and other team officials were expecting to select the French-born San Jose State University guard/forward Olivier Saint-Jean (who later changed his name to Tariq Abdul-Wahad after converting to Islam) with the ninth overall pick in the 1997 NBA Draft. Thomas, though, was hoping a sleepy-eyed high school phenom from North Carolina's Mount Zion Christian Academy would still be on the board. To the GM's surprise, the 18-year-old kid was, so he made the pick.

The Tracy McGrady era had begun.

In his rookie season, the scrawny yet extremely talented high-schooler struggled to adjust to his new NBA life and the cold Canadian climate. *Sports Illustrated* revealed McGrady lived a lonely existence. He used to sit by himself in a lavish, pre-furnished three-bedroom, three-bathroom Toronto apartment, which overlooked Lake Ontario and once belonged to 1992 World Series Champion and Toronto Blue Jays pitcher Juan Guzman. The Raptors star-in-the-making was sleeping as much as 20 hours a day at times. The rookie's rough first year would get worse. On November 18th, 1997, Thomas informed his players he might leave if his plans to buy out the team's majority owner fell through. Once he finished his comments, he turned to his young draft pick and said, "Tracy McGrady, welcome to the NBA." Two days later, Thomas quit. The decision stung the teenager. "When I heard the news, it really hurt me because Isiah was like a father figure," McGrady said. "I felt lost, like everybody else was in a boat and I was drowning out in the water somewhere."

The roller coaster of emotions continued when four days later, Raptors forward Popeye Jones met McGrady in the locker room and said, "'Get your stuff, T-Mac. We're about to be traded to Philadelphia." At the time Toronto and Philadelphia newspapers were swirling rumours that Jones and McGrady would head to the 76ers for guard Jerry Stackhouse and forward Clarence Weatherspoon. The deal didn't happen, but the Florida native was even more stunned when he found out Thomas started up the trade talk. "You think you're playing for a solid organization and think you've put down roots. Then suddenly you feel like you're not needed."

On the court McGrady was also frustrated with head coach Darrell Walker who criticized his work ethic and consistently put him in the doghouse. But Butch Carter would replace Walker after he resigned on February 13, 1998, the same day disgruntled franchise star Damon Stoudamire was traded to Portland. Toronto

Tracy McGrady, who would leave the Raptors franchise before realizing his full potential, showcases his sweet stroke during the 2000 playoff series against the New York Knicks.

finished with a franchise worst 16–66 record. McGrady would describe his first NBA season as "hell."

The outlook, though, improved. In the 1998 NBA Draft, Vince Carter was picked and then dealt by the Golden State Warriors to the Raptors for Antawn Jamison. McGrady would not only have a great teammate, but also a family member. In July 1997, while at a family reunion, McGrady was approached by Vince Carter's grandmother and during their conversation, he found out VC was his distant cousin. "I started freakin' out," McGrady admitted. "I couldn't wait to tell Vince that we were related."

During the 1998–99 lockout season, VC and McGrady were inseparable. According to *Sports Illustrated*, they sometimes sat at opposite ends of the Raptors bus while speaking to each other on their cell phones. "They say they're cousins, but Siamese twins is more like it," joked guard Dee Brown.

That year Carter would explode on the scene with his array of gravity-defying and energizing slams on the way to a Rookie of the Year award while 19-year-old McGrady was continuing his progress. In the 1999–2000 campaign, Vinsanity and T-Mac were forming the ultimate Batman and Robin duo. Their athleticism and highlight-reel finishes were making the Raptors an entertaining club to watch and a playoff contender. In their ultimate bonding moment, T-Mac joined Carter, who made his first All-Star team, at the 2000 Slam Dunk Contest. McGrady bounced a pass to VC for his memorable between-the-legs jam, which helped secure his dunk title win.

In McGrady's final weeks with Toronto, fans begged him to stick around, displaying "Come Back T-Mac" signs and painting the slogan on their chests. T-Mac would finish his regular season campaign with 15.4 points per game while Carter averaged a team-leading 25.7 points as the Raptors earned their first playoff berth in franchise history.

In Game 1 of a first-round postseason game against the Knicks, McGrady was ready for the Madison Square Garden spotlight. He had 25 points and 10 rebounds in his playoff debut. As for Cousin Vince, he would disappoint with 16 points on 3-of-20 shooting. The veteran Knicks would sweep the Raptors, but the real action was yet to come.

As the free agent signing period crept closer, according to the *Chicago Tribune*, Grunwald decided to fire Butch Carter, who stirred up multiple controversies including asking for Grunwald's GM title, to prove to McGrady the franchise wasn't in chaos. That wasn't T-Mac's only concern. Did he want to stay in Toronto and be his cousin's second banana or was it better to blaze his own All-Star path elsewhere? Also, since he was a Florida guy and the Orlando Magic wanted him, being a 21-year-old playing in his home state sounded pretty good, especially after the soap opera he dealt with at times up north.

The Chicago Bulls also wined and dined the kid, including giving the former high school baseball player a chance to throw the ceremonial first pitch at a Cubs game. The Miami Heat also took a shot, but in the end, McGrady deeply hurt Raptors fans by signing

National Pastime

"Baseball is my first love," McGrady once confessed.

In a 2011 podcast, the two-time NBA scoring champion described when he fell in love with the game and why he didn't pursue it. "I started baseball at five years old and I played it all the way up to my junior year in high school, man. It was just something that I really enjoyed playing because I was really good at it. The reason why I didn't pursue baseball was because when I transferred in my senior year and moved to North Carolina, they didn't have a baseball team because I went to a private school."

In 2014 McGrady finally realized his dream. Now retired, he pitched for the Sugar Land Skeeters of the Independent Atlantic League. Despite having a 6.75 ERA over four appearances, he got the start in the Atlantic League All-Star Game where he recorded his first strikeout as a professional pitcher. "The ball is definitely going in the trophy case," he said.

a six-year, $67.5 million deal with the Magic. "Not too many superstars get a chance to play at home, and I just saw myself taking advantage of it," McGrady said at a news conference. He joined fellow free agent and Detroit Pistons All-Star Grant Hill, who also inked a contract, but his Magic career would be injury-plagued, leaving T-Mac to shoulder the load.

Regardless, Raptors fans were gutted. They had all these visions of T-Mac and Vince leading the team to great playoff success, but suddenly, those dreams were obliterated. On April 1, 2001, McGrady returned to Toronto with a chorus of boos greeting him. His cousin, Vince, would outscore him 28–24, but the Magic would win the game 104–101. McGrady told TSN, "I really embraced it. I felt like [Raptors fans] really cared about me and, you know, I still have a lot of friends up there. When I came back, I wanted to prove to them that I was going to put it in their face for booing me and I was going to try to silence them every chance that I got, but I still got a lot of love for Toronto. I mean, that's where it first started, and my heart is still there."

Raptors fans would continue to boo T-Mac for a decade or so. But, after the two-time NBA scoring champion retired in 2013, he tweeted this message to Raptors fans: "Thank you Toronto. Thank you for giving me the opportunity to begin my career in the NBA. You believed in me and there my journey began. This incredible city will always hold a very special place in my heart."

In December 2014 with McGrady on hand during a Raptors home game, his acrobatic Toronto dunks were displayed on the scoreboard, prompting fans to cheer, and then they gave him a standing ovation. All T-Mac could do was smile. "Time heals wounds, right?" McGrady said. "I didn't say anything toward the fan base or anything toward the organization. It was just a decision whether I wanted to leave or stay. That was it."

Did he have any regrets leaving Toronto? "Yeah, I wish I would've stayed because I didn't expect myself to pan out to be that type of player that I turned into," McGrady explains. "If you look back on what Kobe [Bryant] said a while back, he said if I'd stayed here, we probably would've been playing the Lakers in a couple of championships."

14 The Giant GM

Chicago native Glen Grunwald was used to picking up the pieces. Back in the 1970s, the high school All-American at East Leyden High in Franklin Park, Illinois, was a lanky 6'9" forward who led his Eagles to back-to-back undefeated regular seasons in 1975 and 1976. According to *Glory Days: Legends of Illinois High School Basketball*, Grunwald was so good, in 1976 that one national recruiting service ranked him as the top overall prospect in the United States. Legendary Indiana Hoosiers head coach Bobby Knight said he was "maybe the most highly rated player we've ever recruited."

The young man's future looked great until a 1978 summer basketball game when he suffered a left knee injury, which wiped out his entire freshman season at Indiana. His knee would be reconstructed, but the damage was done. As a senior Grunwald became a co-captain on the Isiah Thomas–led 1981 NCAA title-winning Indiana team, but wouldn't play in the championship game against North Carolina.

The Boston Celtics selected him in the fifth round of the 1981 draft, but he would never suit up in an NBA game. "Sure, I'll always wonder how good I could have been," Grunwald said in *Glory Days*. "It was tough not to succeed in basketball after high school. But I was part of a good college program and happy to be part of its success, however small. When you are injured, you feel you can get better, but the gradual realization is it won't be the same."

Grunwald, though, launched an impressive post-playing career. He went back to school, earning a law degree from Northwestern University in 1984 and a business administration master's degree from Indiana in 1986. After working as a corporate lawyer, he accepted a position with the Denver Nuggets in 1990 as their vice president and general counsel.

Once Toronto received an NBA franchise, Grunwald's old Hoosiers teammate and Raptors executive vice president Thomas decided to hire him in 1994 as the club's vice president of legal affairs and assistant GM.

Life was going well until the relationship between Thomas and majority owner Allan Slaight went sour, which led to Thomas resigning in November 1997. Suddenly, it was up to Grunwald to pick up the pieces. He took over the GM spot and had to put out some fires, including a trade request from former Rookie of the Year Damon Stoudamire. "The team obviously wasn't doing very well, and I was aware of a lot of turmoil in management because Isiah was trying to buy the team and then wasn't trying to buy the team," Grunwald told the *Toronto Star*. "There were some difficulties internally in the management, and Isiah had been such a big part of the franchise. He was sort of the foundation of the basketball part of it so when he left, the foundation sort of left with him. We had to sort of start over, and a lot of people who had been there and had been supportive and loyal to Isiah, their perspective on the franchise changed—namely Damon Stoudamire being No. 1 on that list. And there were others too, in the coaching ranks."

Ultimately, Grunwald dealt Mighty Mouse to the Portland Trail Blazers in a February 1998 trade, and then Raptors head coach Darrell Walker escaped as well. "With the Damon situation, injuries, and the change in management, [Walker] wasn't sure he was up to coaching the team," Grunwald explained. Walker's assistant, Butch Carter, would fill his vacant spot, and the 1998 NBA Draft, which was Grunwald's first as Toronto's GM, would welcome new talent. During that draft he acquired Vince Carter while trading the Raptors' fourth overall selection, Antawn Jamison, to the Golden State Warriors.

It was a franchise-altering move that eventually catapulted the Raptors to a new level of success, exposure, and high-flying fun. Grunwald was a fan of Carter's since his pre-draft workout, though VC had his doubters. "The criticisms were [that] he could be another Harold Miner, a great athlete who was never able to put his offensive game together in terms of shooting and ballhandling and things of that nature," Grunwald told the *National Post*. "In North Carolina with Dean Smith as the coach, they kept players on a pretty tight rein. He wasn't allowed to do all of the things that he could do. But he came in for his workout and he really just wowed us with his personality and his athleticism and his skills. He had great form on his jump shot. It was an unbelievable workout. I fell in love with him right then."

Carter would reward Grunwald's instincts by becoming a dominating and electric force on the court. "He was like a rock star," said former Raptors guard Dell Curry. "It was fun watching him. It was a little hectic on the other guys who had to fight through the crowds [of reporters] that were waiting for Vince. It was fun… Nobody wanted to sit beside Vince [in the locker room] because you knew you weren't going to have much space…We put all the young guys around Vince."

Another well-regarded Grunwald trade was the acquisition of Indiana's Antonio Davis for the draft rights to the highly touted but often-injured Jonathan Bender in the summer of 1999.

During the Raptors' playoff years in the early 2000s, the 6'9" Davis gave Toronto incredible value with his durability, defence, low-post scoring, rebounding, and leadership abilities.

Alas, Grunwald didn't always have the golden touch. In 2000 after the Raptors lost their first ever postseason series, Tracy McGrady would leave via unrestricted free agency. Despite no T-Mac, the Raptors would make the 2001 playoffs, but wouldn't get past the second round.

Regardless, you could sense the club was on the verge of something special, Grunwald likely felt that too, so he went on a spending spree. In the summer of 2001, he'd bust out his wallet and use loads of cash to re-sign Vince Carter (six years, $94 million), free agents Antonio Davis (five years, $64 million), Jerome Williams (seven years, $40.8 million), and Alvin Williams (seven years, $42 million). Plus, Grunwald would acquire Hall of Famer Hakeem Olajuwon in a sign-and-trade with Houston. Raptors fans had high hopes, but the 2001–02 team didn't deliver. Even though Carter and Olajuwon had injury issues, Toronto still made the playoffs. Unfortunately, the club wouldn't get past the first round.

From there, things would spiral downward for Grunwald and the Raptors. In an injury-riddled 2002–03 campaign, Toronto only had 24 victories, which frustrated the usually mild-mannered GM, who grabbed the microphone after the team lost to Miami in its final home game of the season to tell the remaining fans, "We will not stand for this any longer."

Grunwald would fire head coach Lenny Wilkens and then replace him with hard-nosed, first-time NBA head man Kevin O'Neill. "This season was a disappointment of the highest order for all of us associated with the Toronto Raptors," Grunwald said. "In discussions with Lenny about the future direction of the team, it became apparent to both of us that parting company would best serve his interests as well as those of the organization."

The terrible campaign allowed Grunwald to draft high in 2003, where he'd select Chris Bosh fourth overall. However, in 2003–04, the Raptors didn't respond well to the abrasive O'Neill who had a rift with Grunwald and would finish out of the postseason again.

Maple Leaf Sports & Entertainment President and CEO Richard Peddie had seen enough, firing Grunwald before the end of that campaign on April 1, 2004. "We didn't make the strides that we thought we would," said Peddie who appointed Jack McCloskey as the interim GM. "We're standing here with 30 wins. It's time for someone else to come up with a master plan. We feel it's time for a fresh new perspective to take us to the next level."

Despite Peddie wanting him to go, Grunwald had the respect of his players, and Vince Carter was one who was disappointed in the departure of one the Raptors' best GMs. "He was just easy to get along with. I still speak with him to this day. He's a guy you can talk to...I felt very comfortable with him and I appreciated the opportunity and, of course, the guy who first drafts you and gives you your opportunity, you won't forget him. It was tough to see him go."

15 Raptors Are First-Time Division Champs

In his first offseason as Toronto's president and general manager, Bryan Colangelo was a makeover artist. After the club's 27–55 season in 2005–06, the former longtime Phoenix Suns GM realized his team needed a big overhaul, so he went to work, bringing in a slew of new players including 2006 No. 1 overall draft pick Andrea Bargnani, Spanish forward Jorge Garbajosa, two-time Euroleague MVP Anthony Parker, speedy point guard T.J. Ford, and seven-foot Rasho Nesterovic.

The internationally flavoured 2006–07 Raptors did not mesh with all the fresh faces in the dressing room, losing eight of their first 10 games. But the revamped Dinos would start coming together in the first couple months of 2007. They'd have a 10–5 record in January with Chris Bosh being the leading scorer in nine of those 10 victories. He was just one of the reasons why Toronto's offence was averaging 102.1 points in its January wins.

Six Raptors scored in double figures to lock up a 103–91 victory against the Hawks on February 2 in Atlanta, meaning Toronto was over .500 (24–23) this late in a campaign for the first time since 2001–02 and *leading* the Atlantic Division as well. "It's getting unbelievable," said Bosh who had 24 points and 10 rebounds against Atlanta. "We trust each other, no matter what happens. We're moving the ball well, everybody's playing unselfish basketball, and that's what's helping us out a lot."

CB4's teammate, Morris Peterson, wasn't satisfied. "Now that we're in first place, we're not going to be the hunter, we're going to be the hunted," Peterson said. "We've got to play harder." Toronto wasn't slowing down, winning seven of its eight games before the NBA All-Star weekend, including victories featuring Bosh's season-high 41 points versus the Orlando Magic on February 7 and 25 points against Vince Carter's New Jersey Nets on Valentine's Day.

At the top of the Atlantic Division with a 29–24 record, the Raptors looked nothing like the Toronto squad that was 20–33 at the 2006 All-Star break. They were receiving contributions from many of their new additions including Garbajosa, but disaster struck on March 26 in Boston when he suffered an ugly, season-ending left ankle and broken fibula injury while trying to block a slam dunk. The Raptors would be fine thanks in part to the solid play of their strong one-two punch of guards T.J. Ford and Jose Calderon. Ford, who was the starter, had 20 double-doubles in 2006–07 while Calderon, in his second NBA season, chipped in with seven of his own. Toronto's top draft selection, Bargnani, also helped off the bench by scoring in double-digits 41 times. And

Parker provided steady offence with double-figure points in 49 of his 73 regular season games.

You add all this quality production, the intense guidance of head coach Sam Mitchell, and the terrific offseason moves by Colangelo, it would lead to a great moment on April 1, 2007. After a 107–94 win against the Charlotte Bobcats, the Raptors clinched their first playoff berth since 2002. "It means a lot to me," said Bosh, who signed a contract extension in July 2006. "It quiets the people who were like 'Why did you come here? Why didn't go you to the States?' It's just a good feeling that my beliefs have paid off and it's turned to reality." CB4 also was quick to praise Colangelo for the club's success. "He brought a winning attitude. He brought it out of everybody. It starts from management."

Mitchell was also a part of the team's revival. "When we were 2–8, everybody doubted us," he said, "but we didn't have any doubt in that locker room that we were a good basketball team."

Heading to the playoffs was extra special for Peterson, who suffered through some terrible years before returning to the post-season. "That probably was the toughest thing, some of the losses we had," Mo Pete said. "All the games we led and ended up losing. If I look at this day, I would go through all the other stuff just to be here today."

But the Raptors weren't done yet.

On April 6, armed with an offensive attack featuring six Toronto players scoring in double figures, the Dinos would win 94–85 in Philadelphia, and then Chicago beat New Jersey that same night to give the Raptors something no other team in its franchise history had accomplished—a division title. "Nobody believed we could be in this position, only the guys who've been in this locker room and...the organization," Ford said. "Everybody else was probably just looking for a good season. Now we're setting the standard for every year how Toronto basketball has to be played and what the expectations are."

The Raptors would go on to win a franchise record-tying 47 games, secure the third seed in the Eastern Conference, and have home-court advantage in the playoffs for the first time. Unfortunately, in the opening round, Vince Carter's Nets would beat them in six games, ending Toronto's stunning turnaround campaign, which would see Mitchell win the NBA Coach of the Year and Colangelo take home the Executive of the Year.

16 Masai or Messiah?

It must be awkward replacing your old boss while he's still working for your company.

What if you bump into him in the hallway? What exactly would you do? Do you wave? Do you cue up some small talk?

It's just weird.

After Masai Ujiri officially replaced Raptors general manager Bryan Colangelo on May 31, 2013, Colangelo possibly went through some of the above when he was asked to stay on as the president of team and business operations. Fortunately, for everyone involved, he stepped down in June.

Ujiri worked under Colangelo, who was a reigning NBA Executive of the Year when Toronto hired him in February 2006, as the Raptors' director of global scouting. He later became the club's assistant GM in 2008. Ujiri, a native of Nigeria, left Toronto in 2010 to return to the Denver Nuggets, where he was previously an international scout, to become their executive vice president of basketball operations, making him the first African-born man in charge of a major professional sports team in the United States.

While with the Nuggets, Ujiri was applauded for putting out fires in the Mile High City such as successfully trading the disgruntled Carmelo Anthony in a blockbuster three-team, multi-player deal, which gave Denver plenty of value in return and kept the club competitive in the tough Western Conference.

As for the Raptors, after the 2012–13 campaign, they were coming off their fifth straight non-playoff season. So the brash new Maple Leaf Sports & Entertainment (MLSE) president and CEO, Tim Leiweke, kicked down the door by jettisoning Colangelo and signing Ujiri to a five-year, $15 million contract. "We feel very lucky to have Masai in our organization," Leiweke said in a team statement. "He is a proven judge of talent, and we look for him to be a big part of creating a winning atmosphere, leading us to the playoffs, and, ultimately, delivering NBA championships for Toronto."

For Ujiri, the decision to return was a no-brainer. "To come back to the Raptors, to live in such a great city, and work in an organization that has committed all the resources necessary to win championships was a huge factor in the decision," Ujiri explained. "I have already developed a great relationship with Tim Leiweke and I can't wait to get back to Canada to build a team that is poised to take the next step in the NBA."

His new job wouldn't be easy. The Raptors franchise was at a crossroads as it prepared for the 2013–14 campaign. Fans were hoping they would tank for the chance to select highly regarded Thornhill, Ontario, product Andrew Wiggins first overall in the 2014 NBA Draft.

But, was the club ready to blow up the roster?

There was also the question of getting rid of some fat contracts. Could Ujiri move Toronto's favourite whipping boy, Andrea Bargnani, and his over $22 million remaining on his deal? Also, how long would Rudy Gay stay in a Raptors uniform? Gay arrived in Toronto via a January 2013 multi-player trade, but since DeMar

DeRozan already had the job of being the high-scoring wing player, it seemed a little redundant and expensive (Gay would make nearly $18 million in 2013–14) to have Rudy around.

Ujiri fixed one problem by getting the New York Knicks to take Bargnani for sharpshooter Steve Novak, former Raptor Marcus Camby, Quentin Richardson, a 2016 first-round pick, and second-round picks in 2014 and 2017. That trade alone won him fans for life in Toronto.

As for Gay, once the season tipped off, he was a magnet for criticism. Fans were blasting him on Twitter after his 11-of-37 shooting performance in a double-overtime defeat against the Houston Rockets on November 11. Despite scoring 29 points and hitting a game-tying three-pointer to force a second overtime, people didn't appreciate his inefficient, high-volume shooting.

Ultimately, Ujiri would ship Gay along with Quincy Acy and Aaron Gray to the Sacramento Kings for Chuck Hayes, Patrick Patterson, John Salmons, and Greivis Vasquez.

Little did anyone know at the time, the deal would transform the Raptors season in a completely positive and surprising way. All of a sudden, the trade gave Toronto an instant bench, including a solid backup guard, who was a former NBA starter, and without Gay, it allowed DeRozan and Kyle Lowry to touch the ball more. "He's a phenomenally talented player, but it just wasn't working," Ujiri said. "On the court you could tell [Gay and DeRozan] weren't in sync."

Colangelo had a differing opinions, offering a slight jab at his former employer. "I put a high premium on talent and character, and Rudy Gay has an abundance of both," said the former Raptors GM. "Obviously, [Kings GM] Pete [D'Alessandro] has a mandate to increase the talent level of his team as opposed to depleting it. This move is a pretty good indication of that."

As for Gay, he reflected on the deal a few months later. "Do I feel like I was treated fairly? I think I took the fall for a lot of things, but it's happened before and it'll happen again," said Gay who attempted more than 17 shots per game in Toronto. "We had a chance to be a really good team. Obviously they're a really good team now, but I still feel like we had a lot of time left to build and become a big threat in the East."

Ujiri felt otherwise.

17 Good-bye, Rudy and Hello, Record-Breaking Season

The post-Rudy Gay era began on December 10, 2013. The Raptors were back at the Air Canada Centre after a Western road swing, which saw the high-priced forward dealt to the Sacramento Kings in a multi-player trade. Of course, the NBA schedule was unforgiving, so that night Toronto, without its new reinforcements in the lineup, faced the veteran San Antonio Spurs. Tim Duncan and his boys beat up the Raptors 116–103. "I'm going to chalk this one up to travel," said Raptors head coach Dwane Casey, whose club landed in Toronto at 5:30 AM Monday after taking a Sunday overnight flight from Los Angeles. "We ran out of gas."

At that point, Toronto was 7–13 and had lost six of its last seven games. It was a tough skid, but soon the cavalry would come. The next game featured the Raptors debuts of Patrick Patterson, Greivis Vasquez, and John Salmons while Chuck Hayes didn't play because he needed to undergo baseline cardiac testing. Both Patterson and Salmons struggled, but Vasquez scored 12 points in 17 minutes to help the Raptors defeat the Philadelphia 76ers 108–100.

Fast forward to December 20 in Dallas, DeRozan hit a clutch go-ahead shot on a pump fake at the free throw line while being fouled in overtime to help sink Dirk Nowitzki's Mavericks 109–108. Two days later in Oklahoma City, the Raptors defeated the Thunder 104–98 to end OKC's nine-game winning streak. The Raptors were becoming road warriors, winning their fourth in a row away from the ACC for the first time since 2002." [It] just shows our mental toughness as a unit," Salmons said. "Sometimes it's fun to play on the road because it's just us against everybody else." During this stretch Toronto would win nine of 11 games. Suddenly, the Raptors were coming together as a more balanced unit and headed into 2014 with plenty of optimism.

On January 27 in Brooklyn, with Toronto down one late in the game, Patterson stole a Deron Williams inbounds pass and then later made the go-ahead jumper with six seconds left to sink the Nets 104–103. "We knew they didn't have any timeouts. We guessed right, and Patrick looked like Richard Sherman out there with that steal," Lowry said, referring to the Seattle Seahawks defensive back who watched the game with some of his NFL teammates.

Lowry poured in 31 points for the Atlantic Division-leading Raptors. Both he and DeRozan truly emerged once Gay left town. They were becoming one of the NBA's most underrated and productive backcourts. On February 5 in their first game against Gay since the trade, they combined for 39 points, but the Raptors would lose 109–101 in Sacramento.

Gay had a 24-point, 10-rebound, four-steal night against his former team. On March 7, though, Toronto got some payback against Gay, who only scored 15 points in his return to the ACC.

He did receive some boos but nothing major. Actually, the loudest jeers and cheers came when Gay hammered a one-handed slam but was called for travelling. "Honestly, I didn't even pay attention to it," Gay admitted. "Boo or cheer, either way I have to go out and do my job."

The Raptors' good times didn't stop there.

- On March 28 the club clinched its first playoff spot since 2008.
- On April 11 Toronto won the franchise's second Atlantic Division title.
- On April 13 the Raptors tied the franchise mark of 47 wins in a single season shared by Vince Carter's 2000–01 squad and Chris Bosh's 2006–07 club.

On April 14 against the lowly Milwaukee Bucks, the 2013–14 Raps had a chance to make team history. Before the game DeRozan, who suffered some lean years up north, briefly spoke with the ACC crowd before unveiling the Raptors' Atlantic Division championship banner. "It means a lot," DeRozan said. "With all the struggles that I've been through here, the losing. To see everything get turned around and be up there winning a division is definitely big. It's something that can never be taken away."

DeRozan would get the night off, but Vasquez would flourish as his replacement, scoring a game-high 25 points while dishing out seven assists in a 110–100 win, Toronto's franchise-record 48th victory of the season. "This is probably the best team I've ever been on," Vasquez said.

Trading Gay was the difference. Before the move, Toronto had a 6–12 record and after it went 42–22. Now, a nation full of Raptors fans were cheering on this resilient squad, taking great delight in a journey nobody wanted to end. Toronto was now on to the next step—a first-round playoff series match-up with Kevin Garnett, Paul Pierce, and Joe Johnson's veteran Brooklyn Nets. Heading into this showdown, both teams didn't like each other much especially after Raptors general manager Masai Ujiri dropped an F-bomb while describing his feelings about the Nets in an outside fan rally before Game 1. It was a circus atmosphere outside and inside the ACC with fans passionately roaring at every opportunity.

Unfortunately, the Raptors showed their playoff inexperience with a sloppy effort, including DeRozan's 3-of-13 shooting performance and Toronto's 17 turnovers during Brooklyn's 94–87 win. After Pierce hit a big three-pointer in the fourth quarter, he irritated the fans by raising his hands and gesturing to the crowd. "It was just emotions flying high, playoffs, close game, taking some shots, making some shots," Pierce said. "I really feed off the emotions of the crowd, especially on the road...I love those moments."

With Game 2 being a must-win, DeRozan brushed off his mediocre playoff debut and took charge, scoring a game-high 30 points as the Raptors would tie up the series with a 100–95 victory. "It's everything you dream about, especially when you become a professional athlete, to be at the highest level and have the trust of your coaching staff and your teammates to have the ball in your hands and win a game for them," DeRozan explained.

Fast forward to Game 5 with the series tied at two, Lowry bailed out his team by scoring a career playoff-high 36 points, including a go-ahead three-pointer in the fourth quarter after Toronto squandered a 26-point cushion in a 115–113 nail-biter to give the Raptors a 3–2 series lead. Toronto was one win away from earning a postseason series victory for the first time since 2001.

But in Game 6 back in Brooklyn, the Nets squashed that dream 97–83 with help from Deron Williams and his team-high 23 points. So, the scene returned to the Air Canada Centre for Game 7. The last time the Raptors were in a Game 7, Vince Carter clanked a potential series-winning jumper, which shattered the hearts of basketball fans across Canada.

Before this big showdown, Nets backup centre Andray Blatche expressed his confidence about his team's chances. "Guarantee it," he said. "We're going to go there and take care of business and go to Miami." How did the Raptors react? "I don't know who he thinks he is," Vasquez told reporters. "He's not KG or Paul Pierce or Jason Kidd. But we're not going to listen to this nonsense. He gotta earn that, and he hasn't yet."

After the pregame bluster had subsided, the Raptors were down 11 in the fourth quarter before Lowry and DeRozan combined for 14 straight Toronto points to get the Raptors within five. Then with Toronto trailing by one with 6.2 seconds to go, Lowry drove to the paint, lost the ball, regained it, and then tried to put up a shot, but Pierce blocked it to seal the Nets' 104–103, series-winning victory. "It sucked," Lowry said after the fact. "It was a disappointing moment because we were so close to going to the next round, and I felt like we could've done anything last year. It took me a little while to get over it, but it's something that you learn from. I don't think I dwell on it. Honestly, I never think about it until people bring it up…I'm not the first to get his shot blocked like that, and I won't be the last."

18 The 20th Anniversary

It seems like just yesterday guys like Damon Stoudamire, Tracy Murray, and Vincenzo Esposito were squeaking their sneakers up and down the SkyDome court. Wow, time flies.

To celebrate this anniversary, throughout the 2014–15 campaign, the Raptors honoured many former team personnel including Tracy McGrady, Antonio Davis, Alvin Williams, Charles Oakley, Stoudamire, Isiah Thomas, John Bitove, and even a teary-eyed Vince Carter, who had a video tribute when his Grizzlies visited the Air Canada Centre in November 2014.

It was the club's salute to all those who helped build the franchise to what you see today.

As well, in an added wrinkle, the club brought back more nostalgia by having its players wear the club's inaugural old purple dinosaur road uniforms from time to time. A lot has happened since those days. Now, the Raptors are a playoff-caliber squad with one of the NBA's most rabid fan bases. After a surprisingly good 2013–14 campaign, it would be a tough one to follow, but the 2014–15 team showed no signs of slowing down early on.

In fact, the Raptors enjoyed a fast start with an Eastern Conference-leading 13–2 record, including wins against Kevin Durant and Russell Westbrook's Oklahoma City Thunder, Marc Gasol and Zach Randolph's Memphis Grizzlies, LeBron James and the new-look Cavaliers in Cleveland, and two victories against Atlanta Hawks team that would go 60–22. On November 28, 2014, in Dallas, Toronto suffered some adversity when 2014 All-Star guard DeMar DeRozan went down with a torn tendon in his groin, which shut him down for 21 games.

His backcourt mate, Kyle Lowry, would shoulder a lot of the offensive load, including one night in Utah on December 3 when he scored a season-high 39 points in a 123–104 Raptors road victory. During DeRozan's absence, Lowry averaged 21.8 points per game while guiding Toronto to a 12–9 record. No. 10 would return on January 14 and score a team-high 20 against the Philadelphia 76ers in a 100–84 home win.

Now with Toronto's high octane backcourt intact, the Raptors would catch fire again.

This time they'd head into the All-Star break, winning nine of 11, including an 87–82 home victory against the defending NBA champion San Antonio Spurs. In Toronto's next game, a last-second DeRozan go-ahead jumper was the difference in a 95–93 February 11 win against the Washington Wizards.

At 36–17, the 2014–15 club was better than the previous year's record-breaking squad that had a 28–24 showing at the All-Star break. Another positive was that after a strong push by Raptors fans online, Lowry would be a starter in his first NBA All-Star Game. Everything was going great. Toronto had a comfortable first place Atlantic Division lead and was one of the top teams in the Eastern Conference.

But the second half was a different situation. From February 21 to March 10, the Raptors lost nine of 10 games while their defence gave up 106.4 points per contest. During that stretch on February 28 at Madison Square Garden, DeRozan added to the tough times when after getting a first-quarter steal, he tried to be fancy by attempting a breakaway 360 slam. He, though, missed the dunk in embarrassing fashion, which appeared on various TV sports highlight shows and in social media chatter across North America.

Even though their team was still in control of the Atlantic Division, Raptors fans couldn't help but feel uneasy. Things would begin to turn around on March 13 when Toronto snapped a 16-game losing streak against the Miami Heat with a 102–92 victory. Then on March 18 a special visitor made his way into the Air Canada Centre for the first time as an NBA player—the crown jewel of Canada's new wave of basketball talent and future 2014–15 NBA Rookie of the Year Andrew Wiggins. With Prime Minister Stephen Harper in attendance and ex-Raptors head coach Sam Mitchell guiding Minnesota as Flip Saunders' replacement, who was with his ailing father, the 2014 No. 1 overall pick would score 15 points in a losing cause as the Raptors won 105–100.

Regardless, for Wiggins, it was good to be home. "It felt welcoming," said Wiggins, who received a loud reception during pregame introductions. "I already love playing in Toronto…Even though we didn't win the game, I still feel appreciated and had fun."

Down the stretch, it still wasn't comfortable for Toronto. Lowry suffered some back issues, which sidelined him for a period of time, and the club's defence continued to be shaky at best. Fortunately, on March 25, despite the Chicago Bulls' 116–103 win at the ACC, the Charlotte Hornets and Boston Celtics also lost that night, too, which allowed Toronto to clinch its second consecutive postseason berth. Then on March 27, Dwane Casey's boys would lock up their second straight Atlantic Division title, beating the terrible Los Angeles Lakers 94–83. "Last year was so unexpected," DeRozan said. "We never looked at it as 'We can win our division.' All the odds were against us. This time around, the start that we had…we kind of were expected to win it. It's kind of different, but it still means a lot."

With the regular season winding down and the playoffs on the horizon, an old Raptors foe decided to stir things up. In an interview with ESPN's Jackie MacMullan, Washington Wizards veteran Paul Pierce said, "We haven't done particularly well against Toronto (0–3 in the 2014–15 regular season), but I don't feel they have the 'It' that makes you worried." Yes, this is the same Paul "The Truth" Pierce who blocked Lowry in the dying seconds of Game 7 to seal a Brooklyn Nets first-round series win against the Raptors in the 2014 postseason.

After Toronto beat the Hornets 92–87 to secure its single season franchise record 49th victory in the club's final 2015 regular season game, DeRozan reacted to Pierce's remarks.

"He said something last year," DeRozan said. "He just gotta say something. Just let him talk. I could care less what he said."

Toronto general manager Masai Ujiri, who was fined $25,000 for his F--- Brooklyn comment in April 2014, addressed Pierce's assessment. "I honestly don't have enough money to respond to him. But if I did have enough money, I think everybody knows how I would respond to it and how the whole of Toronto would respond."

Well, it turned out the No. 4-seed Toronto would end up facing the No. 5-seed Washington in the opening round of the 2015 playoffs. The Raptors were looking forward to shutting Pierce up. In fact before Game 1 on April 18, Ujiri, in what's becoming a yearly tradition, would fire up Toronto fans in Jurassic Park by vocalizing his feelings regarding Pierce's "It" comment: "We don't give a s--- about it!" Ujiri said this with NBA commissioner Adam Silver attending the game, so he was subsequently fined $35,000, and the Raptors had to pay $25,000. Pierce's trash talk was already hurting the team.

Once Game 1 began, the energetic sellout ACC crowd repeatedly chanted, "Paul Pierce Sucks!" It was quite clear the villain had returned.

The 2008 NBA Champion wasn't rattled. Instead, he'd take the pressure off his young teammates, John Wall and Bradley Beal, by scoring a game-high 20 points on 7-for-10 shooting, including a three-pointer that sparked a 7–0 run in overtime, which helped lead Washington to a 93–86 victory.

Afterward, Pierce savoured his evil persona. "You've just got to embrace it," he said. "It's not that I'm a bad guy. Everybody knows I'm a good guy, I mean off the court. That's just the role you portray to media on the court, on the road. Everybody is booing you. No one likes you. I embrace it. It fuels me, truthfully."

Pierce also responded to Ujiri's pregame message. "Typical Ujiri," the former NBA Finals MVP said. "You heard what he said last year when I was in Brooklyn. I could really care less. I think I can play the psychological war a little bit better than him."

As for the Raptors, Pierce's mind games were definitely a distraction. "Give him a lot of credit," said Greivis Vasquez, who would later be traded to the Milwaukee Bucks on the night of the 2015 NBA Draft. "He got everybody's attention, and if we keep talking about Paul Pierce, this is going to be the Paul Pierce series...Man, I'll tell you this, this is the last day I'm going to answer anything about Paul Pierce. What he's doing is motivating his team, talking trash, so why would we talk trash? I don't know if you're from Toronto, but we don't have any trash-talkers in our locker room."

In addition to Pierce's production, it didn't help Toronto that its starters were quiet offensively in the club's first ever postseason overtime game.

- Kyle Lowry was only 2-for-10 with seven points before fouling out in the fourth quarter, which prompted Beal to wave goodbye to him
- DeMar DeRozan scored 15 points but on 6-for-20 shooting
- Jonas Valanciunas was 3-for-7 with six points
- Terrence Ross scored six points on 3-for-11 shooting, including 0-for-6 from beyond the arc
- Even Toronto's top bench scorer, Lou Williams, struggled, scoring 10 points on 4-for-16 from the floor and 2-for-8 from three-point land

The Raptors also couldn't handle Washington's size, which featured the likes of 6'11" Nene Hilario, 6'11" Marcin Gortat, and 6'11" Drew Gooden. Toronto was outrebounded 61–48, including 19–10 on the offensive glass. And Casey made some head scratching moves by not playing James Johnson, a good defender with a big body who could have given Pierce problems, and starting Tyler Hansbrough.

This all added up to a nervous Raptors fan base hoping its team could somehow turn it around in Game 2. It wouldn't happen. On April 21 the Wizards' young backcourt made sure of that. Wall put up 26 points and 17 assists while Beal scored 28 in a 117–106 win to give Washington a 2–0 series lead. The Wizards were now heading home in full control, and Pierce was hoping not to visit the Great White North again. In fact, after the Game 2 victory, he was shouting on the way to the dressing room, "I don't want to go through customs no more!"

Also following the defeat, the Raptors' global ambassador, Drake was caught shaking hands with a smiling Pierce as he left the court, which soured many fans. If Drake's handshake with the enemy wasn't bad enough, for the second straight game, Lowry was a non-factor, scoring six points on 3-for-10 shooting before leaving with a bruised left shin in the fourth quarter.

On April 24 in Washington, DeRozan had an explosive start in Game 3, scoring a franchise playoff-record 20 points in the opening quarter on the way to a game-high 32.

His backcourt mate, Lowry, who was not only battling a shin bruise, but reportedly also had a cold and lingering back problems (after the series he'd admit he was fine), was still not his All-Star self, putting up 15 points on 5-for-22 shooting.

Regardless, the Raptors only trailed by two heading into the fourth quarter, but that was before The Truth let his game do the talking. Pierce scored 11 of his 18 points in the final period, including a three-point dagger with 16.3 seconds remaining, which provoked him to tell the crowd, "That's why I'm here!"

Thanks to the 37-year-old's knack for being clutch, Washington would win 106–99 to take a commanding 3–0 series advantage. "My adrenaline is through the roof right now...I'm just enjoying the moment. I love playoff basketball. I love everything about it," Pierce said. "At this point in my career, I'm savouring these moments because I don't know how many more of these moments I'm going to have."

No NBA team had ever overcome an 0–3 deficit to win a post-season series, and that wouldn't change. On April 26 the Wizards blew out Toronto 125–94 in Game 4 to earn a first-round sweep. "It was just embarrassing," Raptors forward Patrick Patterson said. "It was horrific. It was a letdown. It was just ugly."

It was a disappointing and humiliating way to end a 20th anniversary campaign that started so well. "We were just emotionally drained and we just kind of gave in to their onslaught as the game went on," Casey said. "That's kind of the way sweep games go. Either you're in it and, if you can handle the haymakers, you can survive. But we didn't survive."

19 Isiah Thomas

He'd cut your heart out to win. And he would put it right there on the floor in front of you and he'd step on it. That's Isiah.

—Pat Riley

The Baby-Faced Assassin was one of the greats. After growing up on Chicago's tough west side, Isiah Thomas, the youngest of nine kids, would star at Indiana University where he'd win an NCAA title in 1981. That same year the sophomore headed to the NBA draft where he was selected second overall by the Detroit Pistons. From there, the 6'1" leader of "The Bad Boys" would put together an incredible NBA career, which included two championships, one NBA Finals MVP, 12 All-Star appearances, selection to the NBA's 50th anniversary all-time team, and induction in the Basketball Hall of Fame.

In May of 1994, Thomas would officially retire after tearing his Achilles tendon but left the Pistons as the franchise's all-time leader in points (18,822), assists (9,061), and steals (1,861). He sought a new challenge. A short time after calling it quits, Thomas was recruited to build Toronto's new expansion team by Raptors owners John Bitove and Allan Slaight.

"Zeke" became the club's executive vice president, general manager, and part-owner.

During a May 24, 1994, press conference, Thomas would burst through a giant Raptors logo to officially announce his arrival, but it would also be the start of his other role—as a salesman. "We were coming into a country that the No. 1 sport is hockey, and the culture of sport is hockey, whereas in the U.S., basketball, baseball, football are culturally ingrained in the American system," Thomas said. "We have mechanisms in place to foster basketball at the grassroots, to get basketball inside the home, on the kitchen table, in the backyard, in the schoolyard…You had to really go door to door, knock on people's doors, talk to them about the sport, get on the radio as often as you could, get on television as often as you could, and really put your message out about the game and selling the sport. That was a 24/7/365 job."

In addition to his sales duties, Thomas would truly make his mark as a talent evaluator when it came to drafting players. Despite having zero GM experience, he was still able to pick some future gems, including 1995–96 Rookie of the Year Damon Stoudamire, 2006–07 NBA Defensive Player of the Year Marcus Camby, and seven-time NBA All-Star Tracy McGrady.

At first, Thomas' selection of Stoudamire wasn't embraced by the SkyDome crowd (fans wanted UCLA Bruins star Ed O'Bannon) on 1995 draft night, but the Raptors GM knew the University of Arizona alum would be a better fit. "In a lot of ways, it was a very controversial pick," Thomas said. "UCLA had won the championship, Ed O'Bannon was the darling of the tournament, everyone was saying he would be the ideal person to start a franchise with and what…After spending a good portion of time knocking on doors to get an understanding of the population and the culture, [I thought that] Toronto fans would love seeing Damon Stoudamire play. I thought he was relatable. He wasn't someone who was seven-feet tall that the average person couldn't

KG a Raptor?

KG is a lot of things—intense, competitive, a former NBA champion, league MVP, 15-time All-Star, and future Hall of Famer—but could you ever imagine him wearing a purple dinosaur on his chest?

According to the *Toronto Sun*'s Steve Simmons, Isiah Thomas wanted that badly.

In an April 2014 article, Simmons recalled a conversation with Thomas leading up to the 1995 NBA Draft regarding the 19-year-old from Farragut Academy. "I really want this high school kid. I love this kid," Thomas said. "I don't know if we can get him, but believe me, we're going to do everything possible. I mean, everything possible."

With the Raptors selecting seventh overall after losing a coin-toss to their expansion brothers, the Vancouver Grizzlies, Thomas watched as the Minnesota Timberwolves scooped up Garnett, their franchise cornerstone for the next 12 seasons, at the fifth spot while Toronto selected Damon Stoudamire. The Raptors missed out on the KG sweepstakes, but fortunately, Mighty Mouse helped save the day.

relate to. He was smaller in size so the average person watching him could relate to him, could buy into his story, and understand the values he possessed as a basketball player and as a person. You can build on those small, broad shoulders."

Besides his drafting prowess, Thomas' NBA resume enticed players to give the Great White North a chance. "Guys wanted to come and play just because of him because of what he had accomplished in the NBA," said forward Popeye Jones, who was traded to Toronto in 1996. "He was not only my idol, but he was an idol to a lot of current NBA players at the time. We had watched him growing up as youngsters."

Doug Christie, who was acquired by Thomas in a February 1996 trade with New York, credited the former Piston with his success. "It was the best thing that happened because Isiah was there," said Christie who played 314 games as a Raptor. "He sat me down and talked to me and said, 'You've been through a lot. I've followed you. I know what's happening with you, but I want you to do is, I want to go out there on the court and mess up.' And I looked at him like, *Mess up?* He's like, 'Just play your game. Don't try to fit in. Don't try to do anything. Mess up once. Mess up twice. Please don't mess up the third time. Just play your game.' That was the first time anyone kinda took the reins off me and said, 'Do your thing.' It just turned out fantastic. I love him for that. Isiah was great for that."

Unfortunately, Thomas' time in Toronto would soon go sour. After Slaight used a shotgun clause to buy out Bitove, he would become majority owner. "The biggest breakup for us came with Slaight and John because, as time has beared this out, John had the correct vision," Thomas reflected years later. "He had the correct plan, and had those two been able to stay partners, it would have been a beautiful thing. As we sit here 20 years from then, I think all of us ask this question: why did Slaight do it? Why did he want John out?"

In a November 1997 *Chicago Tribune* piece, it mentioned the Raptors GM was angry Slaight refused to allow him to make trades, including attempts to deal for SuperSonics All-Star Shawn Kemp, because the club didn't want to spend on big money players. Slaight denied the accusation. That was just a small piece of a rift between the two, which couldn't be repaired.

At one point Thomas attempted to buy out Slaight, but he didn't have enough money to do so.

He'd eventually resign in November 1997 and work for NBC television as an NBA analyst.

"If I had to do this situation all over again, I would investigate my partners a little bit more thoroughly before I decided to come to another country and do business," Thomas said. "Had I been able to work something out where you don't have to risk your fortune, then I would still be here."

20 Bryan Colangelo

Bryan Colangelo had the *GQ* style—always wearing high-collared, custom-made Italian shirts, slim-cut suits, and bold ties. Chris Bosh once called him "the coolest GM in the league by far." But would Colangelo have the substance to go with his fashion sense?

His pre-Raptors resume suggested he did. Colangelo was a successful, longtime Phoenix Suns general manager, including during the Steve Nash *7 Seconds Or Less* era where the club was an offensive juggernaut and when he won the 2004–05 NBA Executive of the Year award. He also had good pedigree as the son of Jerry Colangelo, the first GM of the Suns and a longtime sports executive who now serves as USA Basketball's managing director. "I've always given him advice," Jerry Colangelo said about his son in a 2009 podcast interview. "But, you know how sons are with fathers, they don't listen too often."

Word in 2006 was that Bryan Colangelo might head up north after the Raptors fired GM Rob Babcock in January. To fill in the GM gap in the interim, Hall of Famer and Raptors senior advisor to the president Wayne Embry took over on an interim basis and traded Jalen Rose and a 2006 first-round draft pick to New York for Antonio Davis, thereby, clearing a good amount of cap space for the next GM to play with. On February 28, 2006, that man would officially be Colangelo, who left the Suns to become the Raptors' team president and general manager.

The saviour had arrived. "The Toronto Raptors offer one of the best situations in the NBA, and I'm thrilled to be coming here after 15 years in Phoenix," said Colangelo, who drafted All-Stars Shawn Marion and Amare Stoudemire as Suns GM. "The Raptors have an ownership group committed to building a championship club, have some excellent young players around Chris Bosh, are positioned well against the salary cap, and reside in one of North America's premier cities. I couldn't be any more excited about the future of the Toronto Raptors and I'm eager to get started here."

Colangelo would get to work right away. He waived Antonio Davis in March 2006 and traded Babcock's disappointing 2004 pick, Rafael Araujo, to the Utah Jazz in June. A fan of European basketball talent, he dealt Matt Bonner (a very popular player), Eric Williams, and a second-round pick to the San Antonio Spurs for Slovenian centre Rasho Nesterovic.

The next big move was one that would stick with Colangelo for the rest of his Raptors tenure.

After finishing 2005–06 with a 27–55 mark, Toronto won the NBA draft lottery and had a top overall pick for the first time in franchise history. Heading into the 2006 NBA Draft, it wasn't considered a deep one. There were good college players like LaMarcus Aldridge from the University of Texas, Gonzaga's Adam Morrison, UConn's Rudy Gay, and Washington's Brandon Roy available, but there were no certified can't miss superstars in the bunch.

With that in mind, Colangelo decided to go in another direction. The Raptors selected a seven-foot, 20-year-old Italian talent with Dirk Nowitzki-like perimeter shooting skills as their first overall pick. *Welcome to the family, Andrea Bargnani.* The young man, who previously played for Benetton Treviso in Italy, became the first ever European to be chosen as the NBA draft's top overall selection. "At the end of the day, it came down to that we felt that Andrea Bargnani was really the best pick for the future of this organization going forward," Colangelo said. "It's not about today. It's about today and tomorrow, and we think that Andrea is a player that's not only going to help us in the short run, but we think he's going to grow into a terrific star in this league."

The new Raptors GM continued his roster overhaul by trading promising forward Charlie Villanueva to the Milwaukee Bucks for the speedy, talented, and oft-injured point guard T.J. Ford. Colangelo then added overseas help by signing free agents Anthony Parker (an American who suited up for Maccabi Tel Aviv in Israel) and Jorge Garbajosa (a rugged forward who played in Spain and Italy before heading to Toronto).

With all this activity, the sharp-dressed man was giving Raptors fans something they didn't have for a while—hope. The 2006–07 Raptors, featuring a mix of American and international players, would have an incredible turnaround, tying a franchise single-season record with 47 wins and securing their first division title in club history. Despite losing in the 2007 playoffs against Vince Carter's New Jersey Nets, it felt like the Raptors were moving in a good direction, and Colangelo was a big reason why. For his contributions he was named the 2006–07 NBA Executive of the Year.

In the 2007–08 campaign, the Raptors would make the postseason for the second straight year—this time with a 41–41 record—but would lose in the first round again. It was a slight setback, so the sharp-dressed man tried to improve the team. With Colangelo looking to upgrade the centre position, giving Bosh some defensive help in the frontcourt, he decided to pull off a major multi-player deal, which mainly featured Ford and the draft rights to future All-Star Roy Hibbert being shipped to Indiana for Jermaine O'Neal. For Colangelo, this trade was a risk. O'Neal was injury-prone, had big money left on his contract, and his numbers were in decline.

If that move wasn't surprising enough, once the 2008–09 season began, Colangelo fired head coach Sam Mitchell a day after a 39-point loss in Denver, which dropped the Raptors to 8–9. "Obviously, last night's game was just an absolute kick to the gut," Colangelo said. "When you look back, it's a culmination of things. Expectations are high. We want to win."

Mitchell's Canadian-born assistant, Jay Triano, would take over the head coaching duties the rest of the season, but the Raptors never really recovered. To make things worse, the O'Neal experiment flopped with the ex-All-Star missing games due to injuries before being dealt in a multi-player trade to the Miami Heat, which also brought Marion to Toronto.

The Raptors would miss the playoffs for the first of five consecutive seasons under Colangelo. During the tough years, Colangelo did have some good moves such as drafting youngsters DeMar DeRozan and Jonas Valanciunas and trading for players such as Amir Johnson and Kyle Lowry. Unfortunately, the Raptors fan base will remember him more for the transactions that didn't work such as the disastrous Hedo Turkoglu experience, letting Bosh go to Miami for essentially nothing in 2010 and acquiring the redundant Rudy Gay (the Raptors already had an offensive-minded wing player in DeRozan) in a January 2013 multi-player trade.

In May 2013 Colangelo's run as Raptors GM would be over, and the Masai Ujiri era would begin. New Maple Leaf Sports & Entertainment President and CEO Tim Leiweke relieved Colangelo of his GM duties, but the sharp-dressed man stayed on as team president in a non-basketball role. "Bryan's probably ticked off at me," Leiweke said. "There's no probably. He's ticked off at me. This isn't his perfect world either. But to his credit, he accepts it." Colangelo would eventually step down from that position in June.

In 2014, in a surprising bit of honesty, he confessed something you wouldn't normally hear from a current or former NBA executive in public. "I tried to tank a couple years ago," Colangelo said. "And I didn't come out and say, 'Coach [Dwane Casey], you've got to lose games.' I never said that. I wanted to have him establish a winning tradition and a culture and all of that, but I wanted to do it in the framework of playing and developing young players, and with that comes losing. There's just no way to avoid that, but I never once said, 'You've got to lose this game.'"

is flaws he still deserves some credit for the Raptors
/off relevancy since he assembled some of the team's
Colangelo did bring the style, sometimes brought the
_____, but always was willing to shake things up when needed.

21 Drake, the Raptors' Global Ambassador

On June 20, 2013, the Miami Heat defeated the San Antonio Spurs for their second straight NBA title. Afterward, LeBron James' friend and Toronto-born rap star Drake tried to enter the champagne-drenched Miami locker room, but security wouldn't allow him saying only media could enter. The Canadian replied, "I am media." That got him nowhere. Social media had a good laugh. "I think that'll be the last time I ever get shut out of a locker room," Drake said. "I don't know if that's ever going to happen in Toronto."

He's probably right because on September 30, 2013, the lifelong Raptors fan would become the club's official global ambassador, giving the struggling franchise a much needed hip element and marketing boost. "Today's probably one of the best days of my life," Drake expressed. "I want excitement for this team. I want them to be one of the biggest teams in this league. Everywhere I go, I preach the gospel that is the city of Toronto. I love this city with all my heart."

Aubrey "Drake" Graham's passion for the team runs deep. "I was a Vince Carter guy. I was a Damon Stoudamire guy. I was a [Tracy McGrady] guy," Drake said. "I've supported the franchise through our ups and downs. More than anything, I'm a Toronto guy. I'm a city guy. I care about the city more than anything in the world."

The Raptors' global ambassador, hip-hop star Drake, watches Raptors action from his courtside seat.

His new Raptors role started with him having a conversation with Maple Leaf Sports & Entertainment President and CEO Tim Leiweke and Raptors general manager Masai Ujiri. "I came into the venue one night and I guess was extremely outspoken about what I felt could change as far as the building goes," said the Grammy Award winner. "That sparked a discussion, and [we] sat down and decided we had the same visions. It just turned from a discussion to a reality."

On the same day his new role was announced, it was officially revealed that Toronto would host the 2016 NBA All-Star Game. "I'll be doing my best to curate the weekend and making it an exciting, safe, positive weekend for everybody who decides to come down to a different country, which is going to be very interesting for the All-Stars."

With Drake supporting the Raptors, there's a chance his hip-hop influence could attract big-time free agents to play up north. Well, in August 2014, he tested it out by directing a special message to an Oklahoma City Thunder star who attended his concert. "You know, my brother Kevin Durant was kind enough to come to the show tonight and watch us," Drake said at the performance. "I just want him to see what would happen if he came to play in Toronto. Let him know what would happen."

The crowd cheered and clapped for the four-time NBA scoring champion, but it turns out the NBA considers that tampering, so the league fined the Raptors $25,000. Reportedly, the league told Toronto it would drop the fine if the club stripped Drake of his ambassadorial title, but the Raptors declined. "I get texts: 'Do you know Drake? Have you met Drake?'" head coach Dwayne Casey said laughing. "He sits there every night, he hears me cuss out the referees every night…He knows all my cuss words."

Drake was also involved in some of the rebranding for the franchise, including the inspiring "We The North" campaign, which was a hit during the 2014 playoffs. That was the same postseason when Drake infamously used a lint-roller courtside on his pant leg.

When the Raptors revealed their new logo in December 2014, fans were lukewarm toward it, and even the Brooklyn Nets thought their design was copied. On December 19, 2014, the Nets tweeted "@Raptors Looks familiar." A day later, Drake denied the new Toronto logo was his creation, tweeting, "Actually this redesign was executed without me. My collaboration with Mitchell & Ness comes out next season."

Regardless of the logo hiccup, the franchise continues to rise, and its official ambassador is along for the ride. "It's just fallen into place," Drake said. "I don't think about what I add, I think it's more about the fans. If people are excited because they see me get excited—my goal is just to try and stay off the court and not get in trouble. What the franchise has given me as far as a purpose, confidence, an incredible hobby, I just try and give it back every night when I come to the games."

22 Kobe Drops 81 on Toronto

On January 22, 2006, the Raptors stepped onto the Staples Center floor for the second-to-last stop of what would be a 1–4 western road trip. Up until that point, it had been a tough season, which included a horrendous 4–20 start.

What would represent another Toronto lowlight would become a Kobe Bryant highlight show. The Raptors came out strong against the Lakers, leading Los Angeles by seven after the first quarter, by 14 at halftime, and by as many as 18 in the third quarter. Then the Mamba had enough. After scoring 26 in the first half, Bryant exploded for 27 in the third quarter.

He was carving up Toronto with a variety of pull up three-pointers, reverse layups, off-balance jumpers, dunks, and free throws. Throughout the game Morris Peterson, Jalen Rose, Matt Bonner, and Chris Bosh all took their defensive turns but were helpless against him. Because of Kobe's dominance, L.A. roared back to take a six-point lead after the end of the third quarter.

Heading into the fourth quarter, with 53 points and a date with history on the horizon, the future Hall of Famer continued his onslaught. Bryant was hitting from the baseline, driving through a sea of red shirts for more buckets, and sinking three-pointers in a one-man rampage that hadn't been seen since Wilt Chamberlain clubbed the Knicks with 100 points in Hershey, Pennsylvania, so many years ago.

Alas, Kobe's pursuit of Wilt would fall short, but late in the game, as Bryant sunk his 18th free throw, Lakers fans were on their feet, clapping and cheering for a man who accomplished something Michael Jordan never did—score 81 points in an NBA game.

Lakers television play-by-play man Bill Macdonald said it best: "Ladies and gentlemen, you have witnessed the second greatest scoring performance in NBA history." Kobe's numbers were staggering in LA's 122–104 comeback victory. He scored 55 of his 81 in the second half, including 28 points in the final quarter. "Not even in my dreams," Kobe said. "That was something that just happened. It's tough to explain. It's just one of those things. It really hasn't set in for me…I was just determined. I was just locked in, tuned into what was going on out there. These points tonight mattered. We needed them. The points I put in the basket were instrumental. It means a lot more." Bryant confessed to ESPN, "I still don't know how the hell it happened to be honest with you."

Lakers head coach Phil Jackson, who played against Chamberlain and coached Jordan, was impressed. "I've seen some remarkable

Reactions to Kobe's Performance

Hall of Famer Kareem Abdul-Jabbar

"It was a real treat. His ability to shoot from long range and also attack the hoop, split the defence, and get in close for opportunities near the basket is unique. He's made a niche for himself and he deserves it."

Late Lakers Owner Jerry Buss

"You're sitting and watching, and it's like a miracle unfolding in front of your eyes and you can't accept it. Somehow, the brain won't work. The easiest way to look at it is everybody remembers every 50-point game they ever saw. He had 55 in the second half."

Chris Bosh

"We were just watching him shoot. He takes the type of shots where you don't think they're going in, but suddenly he's rolling, so he's kind of hard to stop. We tried three or four guys on him, but it seemed like nobody guarded him tonight."

Morris Peterson

"I never seen anything like that. Take nothing away from that performance tonight. He showed why he's one of the premier players of this league. Once a guy like him gets going, gets into a rhythm, it's going to be a long night. It was a long night for us tonight. You really can't say much."

games, but I've never seen anything like that before. It's just a personal challenge for him to attack the whole team. It was not exactly the way you want to win a game, but when you have to win a game, it's great to have that weapon to be able to do it. We rode the hot hand."

In his career against the Raptors, Bryant has scored 40 points or more five times. In those games, the Lakers are a perfect 5–0.

Here's the list:

- 81 points—a 122–104 win in Los Angeles on January 22, 2006

- 48 points—a 117–99 win in Los Angeles on December 28, 2004
- 46 points—a 121–101 win in Toronto on February 1, 2008
- 41 points—a 118–116 overtime win in Toronto on March 8, 2013
- 40 points—a 104–101 overtime win in Toronto on December 17, 2000

Kobe's 81 set a Lakers single-game record and allowed him to join Elgin Baylor as the only men in franchise history to score 70 or more. Baylor had 71 points against the New York Knicks on November 15, 1960. And to think the Raptors could have selected Bryant in the 1996 NBA Draft. Oh well.

23 Raptors Pass on Kobe

The 1996 NBA Draft was one of the best in league history. Its only rivals would be 1984 (featuring Hakeem Olajuwon, Michael Jordan, Charles Barkley, and John Stockton) and possibly 2003 (highlighted by LeBron James, Carmelo Anthony, Dwyane Wade, and Chris Bosh). Fortunately for the Raptors, they were heading into the 1996 draft with the second overall pick.

After general manager Isiah Thomas hit a home run with his NBA Rookie of the Year Damon Stoudamire selection the year before, he had a decent chance of doing it again in '96 with the incredible crop of available talent. Once guard Allen Iverson was selected first overall, the best remaining players were: Kobe Bryant, Steve Nash, Ray Allen, Stephon Marbury, Shareef Abdur-Rahim,

Antoine Walker, Marcus Camby, Peja Stojakovic, Jermaine O'Neal, and Zydrunas Ilgauskas.

NBA Commissioner David Stern then took to the podium. "With the second pick in the 1996 NBA Draft, the Toronto Raptors select Marcus Camby from the University of Massachusetts."

The Raptors had just passed on three future Hall of Famers (Bryant, Allen, and Nash) and nine All-Stars in total. Of course, they didn't know it at the time. To be fair, Camby did have a good career, which included a 2006–07 Defensive Player of the Year Award and a 1999 trip to the NBA Finals, but he didn't last long in Toronto. In June of 1998, he was dealt to the Knicks for Charles Oakley, Sean Marks, and cash.

The Charlotte Hornets picked the 17-year-old Bryant 13th overall but would later trade him to the Los Angeles Lakers for Vlade Divac in July 1996. When asked why he skipped college, Kobe showed he was driven to succeed even then. "It's the ultimate challenge," Bryant admits. "If I was 40 years old and I'm sitting back, looking at my career, if I went to college and played in the NBA, maybe I'd have a great career, maybe not, but I'm still having that doubt in my mind, 'Could I have answered that challenge? Could I have responded to the challenge of the NBA?' That's something I didn't want to have on my shoulders, so I just really accepted it."

Five titles and 17 All-Star teams later, Kobe thanked the Hornets on Twitter, tweeting on July 1, 2014, "On this day 18 yrs ago, the hornets told me right after they drafted me that they had no use for me and were going to trade me. #thanku #lakers."

24 VC and the Nets Ruin the Playoff Party

The 2006–07 Raptors finally did it. They not only made the playoffs for the first time in the post-Vinsanity era, but they also clinched their first Atlantic Division title, too. Life couldn't be sweeter until they discovered their first-round postseason opponent: Toronto's Public Enemy No. 1, Vince Carter and his New Jersey Nets.

After years of suffering, it was time for the Raptors to show Vince they were just fine without him. Toronto had home-court advantage in the series, so in Game 1 on April 21, 2007, the electric sellout Air Canada Centre crowd of 20,330 was ready to spew venom VC's way.

During Game 1 the Raptors handed out red shirts to fans. Well, the Nets wore their road red uniforms while Toronto had their home whites, so it looked like Toronto fans were actually supporting New Jersey. "It was extremely weird," said Carter, who averaged 25.2 points per game in 2006–07. "I remember hearing about them going red and I was like, okay. And then we get to that day and we have on red uniforms…I'm assuming someone lost their job that day."

Once the game began, Carter heard boos all afternoon. He only made 5-of-19 shots for 16 points, but it was his playoff tested teammates, Richard Jefferson and Jason Kidd, who stepped up. Jefferson scored a game-high 28 while Kidd was two points shy of a triple-double (eight points, 15 assists, and 10 rebounds) in the 96–91 win.

As for the negative reaction VC received from fans, it didn't bother him. "I didn't come here to worry about the crowd and the response," Carter said. "I came here to win a basketball game."

For many of the Raptors, it was their first taste of the postseason. All-Star Chris Bosh, who had 22 points in his playoff debut, said the inexperience hurt them. "[The Nets] were definitely more poised than we were. They came out a lot more calm. The things we didn't do well, they took advantage of."

Before Game 2 on April 24, the night began with Sam Mitchell receiving his NBA Coach of the Year award as his players joined him at centre court while NBA Commissioner David Stern handed him the prize. Afterward, the Raptors would shake off their Game 1 jitters with help from Anthony Parker's 26 points and Bosh's 25-point and 13-rebound night to tie the series at 1–1 with an 89–83 victory. "None of this could have happened without those 15 guys in the locker room," Mitchell said. "The best part other than winning the basketball game was the presentation when those guys came out because we really care about each other. I work them hard, but they also know how much I care about them."

The Raptors benefited from another off-shooting game by Carter. He was only 8-for-24 from the floor, scoring 19 points but adding 11 rebounds. "I'm not worried about the shots going in," Carter admits. "If I remain aggressive, I'll play my way out of it."

In New Jersey for Game 3, the real VC showed up. Carter was a handful, driving to the hoop and hitting from the perimeter, shooting 15-of-23 overall from the floor in a dominating 37-point performance. But he wasn't alone. Kidd, a game-time decision due to a knee injury, suited up and was an all-around terror for Toronto's defence. He'd record 19 assists to go along with 16 points and 16 rebounds for his 10th postseason triple-double. Kidd and Carter proved too much for the Raptors as the Nets won 102–89 for a 2–1 series lead.

Game 4 would be an absolute demolition. The Nets only trailed for 15 seconds in this affair and led by as many as 33 at one point in a 102–81 victory to give them a commanding 3–1 series advantage. New Jersey's deadly duo of Carter (27 points, seven assists, seven rebounds) and Kidd (17 points, 13 assists, and eight rebounds) overwhelmed Toronto again. "We got it handed to us," Mitchell said. "It was tough for everybody in the organization. I told all the guys this is where you grow. You can't focus on how bad it was. You've got to focus on what you're going to learn. It's a waste to play this way and not learn anything from it."

The Raptors would stay alive in Game 5 at the ACC, thanks to the efforts of Jose Calderon, who chipped in with 25 points and eight assists off the bench, while four of Toronto's starters scored in double figures in the 98–96 victory. "Jose did a spectacular job tonight," Bosh said. "He made some big shots, especially when they were going under the screens. They paid a lot of attention to me so that freed him up."

Andrea Bargnani, the 2006 first overall pick, contributed 18 points. Carter put up 30 points in the loss as the scene switched back to New Jersey for Game 6.

This contest would be a close one late in the fourth quarter. Bosh, who had a team-high 23 points, banked in a jumper with 47 seconds remaining, giving Toronto a 97–96 edge. Jefferson would answer with a go-ahead layup with 8.3 seconds left to make it 98–97 New Jersey. Toronto wasn't out of it. The Raptors had possession and needed to convert one last shot to extend its season. Calderon tried to pass to Bosh, but Jefferson leaped for the steal, ending the Raptors year. "It was me trying to get the ball to Chris, and Jefferson cheated at the end," Calderon said. "It was right there. I was confident we were in the right direction. If we could get that one, I felt we could get Game 7."

Kidd averaged a triple-double in the series with 14 points, 13.2 assists, and 10 rebounds, and Carter, who'd score 21 in the Nets' Game 6 victory, averaged 25 points in the series.

25 Antonio Davis and the Metric System

The Davis brothers weren't actually related, but 6'9" power forward Antonio Davis, who was a 1990 second-round pick, and 6'11" forward/centre Dale Davis were an imposing part of the Indiana Pacers' frontcourt in the 1990s. A.D., who didn't suit up in an NBA regular season game until age 25 after playing overseas, was the bench guy during those successful Pacers clubs while Dale was the starter. In his six seasons with Indiana, Antonio participated in 67 postseason games and averaged 7.8 points and 6.5 rebounds.

But in the summer of 1999, A.D. would be on the move. The Raptors acquired him in a one-for-one swap for the draft rights to the much-hyped high school prospect Jonathan Bender.

Bender never lived up to the lofty expectations due to his knee issues, but Davis would prove to be quite the gem for Toronto.

Right away, the Raptors were adding a solid veteran who could strengthen the club's defence, provide some interior scoring, rebounding, and leadership to the club's young stars, Vince Carter and Tracy McGrady. "If I can lead by example and get my teammates fired up about playing defence, our offence becomes easier, and we become successful," said Davis who averaged nine points and 6.6 rebounds in 420 regular season games with Indiana. "That's what I'm trying to do."

Being in Toronto would be an opportunity for A.D. to start games, but there was a wrinkle. Since Charles Oakley was the club's main power forward, Davis would have to be an undersized centre. In the 1999–00 season, he'd do well in the role, putting up 11.5 points, 8.8 rebounds, and 1.3 blocks in 79 games, including 23 double-doubles while helping the Raptors reach their first postseason.

During Toronto's disappointing first-round loss against the New York Knicks, Davis averaged 13 points and 8.3 rebounds in the series. Davis and the Raptors would keep getting better. In the 2000–01 campaign, A.D. would put up 37 double-doubles in a year where he'd make his only NBA All-Star Game—albeit as an injury replacement. Amongst the league's brightest talents in Washington on February 11, 2001, Davis would start and have eight points and nine rebounds in the East's 111–110 comeback win against the West. That regular season Davis put up 13.7 points, career-highs with 10.1 rebounds and 1.9 blocks in 78 games as the Raptors soared into the playoffs for the second straight year. During that postseason run, A.D. was a handful, putting up 16.4 points, 11.1 rebounds, 1.8 blocks, and nine double-doubles in 12 games.

After Toronto's tough second-round series defeat against the Philadelphia 76ers, Davis, who was an impending free agent, would upset the club's fan base due to his remarks about Canada in an interview with American syndicated sports talk show host Jim Rome. "It's just that Canada teaches a lot of different things," Davis said. "You know, the metric system, when [my kids] go to school every day and they're singing the national anthem…As they grow older, there are some different things they need to learn… I'm a little worried about it now because they're really starting real school—first and second and third grades—and I think those grades are very important in their learning process."

General manager Glen Grunwald joked, "Tell Antonio that I will volunteer to tutor his kids in pounds and ounces and gallons and pints [if he re-signs]." Ultimately, Davis would return after signing a five-year deal.

In that 2001 offseason, Toronto's GM also traded Oakley and later acquired two-time NBA champion centre Hakeem Olajuwon, which meant Davis could now return to his natural power forward spot. Despite Olajuwon only starting 37 of his 61 games in 2001–02 due to injuries, Davis still played mostly at the 4-spot thanks to centre help from the likes of the athletic Keon Clark and seven-foot former NCAA champion Eric Montross.

That season, though, would be a roller coaster ride. On March 19, 2002, the Raptors suffered their 17th defeat in 18 games, which included a 13-game losing streak. The lows continued when Vince Carter, who endured an injury-riddled year, would need season-ending knee surgery. With no Carter and the team on a massive slide, Toronto, in its next game, walked into Cleveland and blew out the Cavaliers 94–80. It sparked a timely and surprising nine-game winning streak, which helped the Raptors go 12–2 down the stretch to sneak into the playoffs.

During the nine consecutive victories, Davis was a monster, averaging 19.8 points and 8.8 rebounds in that span.

Davis' strong results continued into the postseason, leading the Raptors with 17 points (a career playoff high) and 10.6 rebounds per contest in their five-game, first-round series loss against the Detroit Pistons. "He was our horse," ex-Raptors guard Alvin Williams recalled. "And there's nothing like having a big guy doing it because it was an inside presence that made everything easier for us guards—myself and Mo Pete. It just made it easier. We'd give it to him. They'd double him. He was a great passer, rebounder. Jumping on his back was something."

That would be Davis' final Raptors playoff series because after a terrible 24-win season in 2002-03, A.D. was not happy. In October 2003 Davis addressed the media after there were rumours he made a trade request. "I took time to look over what transpired over the summer," said Davis, who had three years and $37 million remaining on his deal. "I didn't go in there and tell them I think you should move me, but I also understand the nature of this business...When I look at our roster, I'm sure all of you have printed that I'm coming up on 35, and given my situation and my salary structure and all that, yeah, I have to wonder if this team is going to make moves and they haven't...If you're going to trade me, trade me. Whatever they are going to do, let them do it, so I can be situated."

In December of 2003, Davis would finally be traded, along with Jerome Williams and Chris Jefferies to Chicago for Donyell Marshall, Jalen Rose, and Lonny Baxter. It was a bittersweet moment since A.D. had been part of Toronto's first three post-season teams in club history. But on March 19th, 2004, when he returned to the Air Canada Centre as a Bulls player, Raptors fans quickly forgot his Toronto contributions, booing him every time he touched the ball. Davis would shake off the negativity, scoring 18 points and grabbing 14 rebounds in the 96–91 Chicago victory. "I came here for four years. I gave them everything that I had. I tried to be everything that they wanted me to be, and when you don't feel like people appreciate that, it does hurt," Davis explained. "For them not to understand my situation, that kind of hurts a little bit, too."

Raptors supporters would actually see A.D. in a Toronto uniform again when he was traded from New York to the Raptors for Rose once more and a draft pick in February 2006.

The deal happened a day after Davis' wife, Kendra, was charged with misdemeanor battery for allegedly throwing a cup of coffee at a woman during a traffic disagreement the previous fall.

Regardless, Antonio wouldn't stay with Toronto for long, only playing eight games before being waived in March. "After receiving a second opinion on Antonio's lingering back problems, it is very unlikely that he would return to competitive action this season with the Raptors," said the club's president and general manager Bryan Colangelo. "After lengthy discussions with Antonio regarding his physical condition and his general sense of disappointment over his personally difficult year, we have concluded that it's in the best interest of both the organization and Antonio Davis to simply release him at this late point of the season."

26 The DeRozan Era

Compton, California, is known for being a rough part of Los Angeles, but it's one that was also the birthplace of a future Raptors star who'd become a key member in the club's post-Chris Bosh success. After dominating at Compton High School, DeMar Darnell DeRozan attended the University of Southern California (USC) for a year and then joined a 2009 NBA Draft class, which included Oklahoma's Blake Griffin, Arizona State's James Harden, and Davidson's Stephen Curry.

The 6'7" shooting guard arrived at an interesting time in club history. In DeRozan's 2009–10 rookie season, he'd watch as Bosh, an impending unrestricted free agent, would play his final year in Toronto before jetting off to Miami to form a much-hyped super team with friends LeBron James and Dwyane Wade.

Prior to Bosh's exit, one of the highlights of DeRozan's first year was competing in the 2010 Slam Dunk Contest. The Raptors rookie wasn't afraid to attack the rack because he had been dunking basketballs ever since he accomplished the feat as a sixth grader. "It was at recess, just playing around, trying to show off that I could dunk, and I could pull it off," DeRozan said. "It was a little bet. When you're young everybody's trying to dunk, and I said I could dunk." In 2010 he'd use his aerial talent to make it into the Slam Dunk Contest final after entering the competition by winning the NBA's inaugural All-Star Dunk-In over Los Angeles Clippers guard Eric Gordon. Unfortunately, DeRozan would lose to defending champion Nate Robinson and then would come up empty again in the 2011 dunk showcase.

Regardless, in his second season, the 21-year-old, who started all 82 games, would put up solid numbers, including scoring 30 or more points six times. His best games were a season-high 37-point performance against the Houston Rockets on New Year's Eve 2010 and a 36-point, 10-rebound effort versus the New York Knicks at Madison Square Garden on April 5, 2011.

Without Bosh, DeRozan was becoming one of the main faces of the franchise.

Despite averaging 17.2 points per game in 2010–11, the young man endured a lot of losing thanks to the club's 22–60 record that season. In DeRozan's lockout-shortened third campaign, he took a step back, only having 16.7 points per contest in 63 games as Toronto would have another tough year with a 23–43 record. The Southern California kid averaged 18.1 points in 2012–13, including 37 against the Jazz in a triple-overtime defeat on November 12, 2012.

But losing was becoming all too familiar for DeRozan. Since he arrived in Toronto, from 2009–10 to 2012–13, the Raptors had a 119–193 record with no playoff appearances.

In 2013–14 things finally began to change.

After a December 2013 Rudy Gay trade, which opened up court space for DeRozan and provided the Raptors good role players in return, Toronto started winning consistently.

DeRozan and his hard-nosed teammate, Kyle Lowry, would power the club's offence on many nights. On December 20, 2013, in Dallas, No. 10 would be clutch. After the Raptors trailed by 19 at one point, they'd roar back to force overtime where, with under 1:15 to go and Toronto down one, DeRozan pump faked and then sank a tough 15-footer while being fouled, which gave the Raptors a one-point lead they'd never give up in the 109–108 comeback victory.

On January 22, 2014, in Toronto, he'd hurt the Mavericks again. With Lowry struggling, going 0-for-10 from the floor and 0-for-6 from three-point land against Dallas because of a stomach flu, DeRozan had to carry the club. He'd sink 15 of his 22 attempts from the floor in a season-high 40 point night in Toronto's 93–85 win. "Once I saw Kyle with his head hanging down and holding his stomach, I knew he wasn't feeling too well," DeRozan said. "I just told myself to try do as much as I can to win, try to pull this one off, and keep my team in it."

His performance even impressed a former Raptors superstar. "He's a very good player, very athletic," Vince Carter said. "I think he's really learning how to play under control now. When you have athleticism like that, sometimes you just go, you just play, and let

DeMar DeRozan, drafted by the Raptors in the first round of the 2009 NBA Draft, instructs his team during the 2015 playoffs.

your athleticism take over. He's now slowing down, and everything else is developing, and it's just making him a tough player."

DeRozan's talent would be recognized with his first ever NBA All-Star appearance, where he scored eight points in the East's 163–155 victory in New Orleans. DeRozan would keep up his scoring in the second half of the regular season, including a stretch where he had 32 or more points in three straight games (33 against the Cleveland Cavaliers on February 25, 34 against the Washington Wizards on February 27, and 32 against the Golden State Warriors on March 2). His club's magical year would eventually result in a division championship, a single-season franchise record in wins, and a trip to the playoffs for the first time since 2008.

In Toronto's first-round match-up against the Brooklyn Nets, DeRozan only had 14 points in his postseason debut in Game 1. But in Games 2 and 3, he'd score 30 in both of them to become the first Raptor since Carter to have 30 points in multiple playoff performances.

DeRozan's Raptors Make NBA History Overseas

On March 4, 2011, when Toronto stepped onto the court to face the then-New Jersey Nets, it wasn't your typical showdown. For the first time ever, an NBA regular season game was played in Europe.

The event drew an announced sellout of 18,689 at the O2 Arena in London, England.

Curious onlookers watched as DeMar DeRozan scored a game-high 30 points, but the woeful Raptors would lose 116–103. Despite the negative result, DeRozan's European-born teammate, Andrea Bargnani, enjoyed the atmosphere. "I loved the crowd," said the Italian who had 23 points. "I really felt the excitement."

On March 5, DeRozan would score 30 again, and Bargnani would have a game-high 35. But in the final seconds, the seven-footer would miss a potential winning shot to seal a heartbreaking 137–136 triple-overtime defeat and give Toronto an 0–2 record on its historic London trip.

"[DeRozan] is becoming a superstar in front of everyone's eyes," Lowry said. "He is doing it on the defensive end and the offensive end."

Even though the Raptors were eliminated by the Nets, it was still a great season in which DeRozan averaged 23.9 points per contest in the series and a career-high 22.7 points in 79 regular season games. In 2014–15 DeRozan was slowed by a 21-game absence due to a groin injury, but Lowry and the Raptors would keep winning until their star shooting guard could come back. He finally busted out with a game-high 35 points against the Philadelphia 76ers on March 2, 2015. Then on March 30 he torched James Harden and the Rockets for a career-high 42 points to go along with 11 rebounds in a 99–96 Raptors' win.

27 Tim Leiweke

Imagine starting a new job in a different city and country. Normally, most employees would play it low key to get used to the environment and people and then they'd be more comfortable speaking their minds after six months to a year in the new gig. *Um, not Tim Leiweke.* The former president and CEO of sports and entertainment conglomerate Anschutz Entertainment Group (AEG) came to Toronto with his guns firing like a wild west cowboy.

His ex-company, AEG owns Major League Soccer's L.A. Galaxy and is part-owner of the Los Angeles Kings and Lakers. So when Leiweke was in charge, the Lakers and Galaxy each won four titles while the Kings won a 2012 Stanley Cup. With that track record in mind in April 2013, Maple Leaf Sports and Entertainment (MLSE)—which owns the Raptors, Maple Leafs, and the MLS team Toronto FC—hired Leiweke to be its president and CEO, replacing the retired Richard Peddie. "I'm very excited because it's about a platform that's even larger than what we started with at AEG," Leiweke told the *Los Angeles Times*. "They have hockey where it's a religion, the NBA, MLS, the Marlies, AHL, and they own buildings and entertainment districts and have distribution channels, so it's really a unique platform. And again, it's far greater than what we started with at AEG and one that I'm enthused by because of the marketplace. It's a very dynamic, exciting, vibrant marketplace."

Leiweke's mission was clear. "We're not going to focus on growth outside of our core assets," he said regarding MLSE. "They want to win, and so that's priority No. 1: build a long-term contender in hockey, basketball, and soccer. And they have ambitions, and so we will grow, and that is a priority."

For the Raptors, Leiweke zeroed in on general manager Bryan Colangelo. In May 2013, with no playoff appearances in five straight seasons, Leiweke knew a change had to be made, so he relieved Colangelo of his GM duties but kept him on as team president until he stepped down in June. Later, Leiweke admitted the two couldn't co-exist. "I didn't get along with the GM," he said, "So we brought in somebody who sees the world the same way I do."

That person was then-NBA Executive of the Year Masai Ujiri from the Denver Nuggets.

Once Ujiri was on board, he started to reshape the club with big moves such as trading the disappointing Andrea Bargnani in the offseason then in December and shipping Rudy Gay to the Sacramento Kings in a blockbuster multi-player deal, which would transform the Raptors from tank mode to playoff contender.

Just before the 2013–14 season began, Leiweke, who was instrumental in convincing David Beckham to sign with the Galaxy, attracted more attention by recruiting Toronto-born rap star Drake to become the club's official Global Ambassador. If that wasn't big enough, the team also announced Toronto would host the 2016 NBA All-Star Game. "This is remarkable for our basketball team," Ujiri said. "We have a responsibility to grow our basketball team so it meets the momentum of the All-Star Game. This is awesome for the fans and awesome for the city."

Leiweke's moves were grabbing headlines and making the Raptors relevant again.

"What you're seeing is the remaking of a franchise, the remaking of what people think about us, the remaking of the demand in the marketplace for us," Leiweke said. "There's a reason that we led the NBA in new ticket sales the last few weeks. There's now a buzz about this organization."

It continued with the launch of the patriotic "We The North" campaign, which debuted before the 2014 playoffs to inspire national pride and support for the Raptors. This was a new age in team history. For Leiweke, his swift actions and demand for change were working.

In August 2014, though, he made the announcement he was leaving MLSE but would stay on until June 2015 (or until his replacement was found). It was a surprising decision since he hadn't been on the job long. "I have a dream, which is at some point or another I need to do my own company so I get up every morning scared to death that I'm going to fail and that it's my money, my equity, and it's all my responsibility," Leiweke said on Sportsnet 590 The Fan in Toronto. "And if I don't do that before I retire and call it a day, I will regret never making that decision."

As for his business idea, Leiweke wants to create a rival to StubHub on the resale of tickets in major markets and plans to work with sports clubs to make it happen. Because telecommunication giants and direct competitors, Rogers Communications and Bell, co-own MLSE, it also made his work challenging at times. "I live in a world today where, remember, 75 per cent of our company is owned by two companies that get up every day and try to figure out how to kill each other," Leiweke said. "So I'm like 'huh, I wonder what that does for my odds?' And then, I'm strong-willed and I've created a lot of change. Occasionally they get exhausted by my change and they don't agree with it, and I get that there's a different way of doing it that would be calmer, easier, more gentle."

28 Butch Carter's Strange Exit

Before the Raptors and New York Knicks started their 2000 first-round postseason series, Butch Carter co-wrote a book, *Born To Believe*, with his NFL brother, Cris, which criticized Butch's former Indiana University head coach Bobby Knight, calling him a "bully," "self-serving coward" and alleging he used "the n-word" at times. Butch would be the centre for more controversy when Knicks big man Marcus Camby, a former Raptors first-round pick, was asked about his ex-head coach in the New York media. He said Butch was a "liar" because—before he was dealt from Toronto to the Knicks—Camby claimed Carter told him and teammate John Wallace they would be cornerstones of the franchise. "No one likes him and no one wants to play for him," Camby said. "That is the kind of guy that he is." Upon hearing the news, Carter fired back by filing a $5 million defamation lawsuit against Camby. "I'm not going to allow my three sons to wake up and see in the national media that I'm a liar," Carter explained.

It should have been an incredible time to savour the Raptors' first postseason, but it instead became a puzzling debut. After losing Game 1 of the series, the Raptors head coach claimed his legal action helped shift the playoff pressure off his players' shoulders. "I

The Lenny Wilkens Era

After dismissing Butch Carter, Glen Grunwald turned to the winningest head coach in NBA history at the time—Lenny Wilkens. The Basketball Hall of Famer was hired in June and looked forward to the challenge. "I'm excited about it and can't wait to get started," Wilkens said. "I like the team. I like the city. I've watched the Raptors. I've coached against them. I thought last year they made a tremendous stride getting to the playoffs and I think their future is all upward."

Wilkens not only had been a successful coach, but also a successful player. Growing up on the Brooklyn, New York playgrounds, Wilkens developed his game, which ultimately led to playing at Providence College and then being selected sixth overall in the 1960 NBA draft. The point guard enjoyed a terrific career, which included nine All-Star appearances, a 1971 NBA All-Star Game MVP award, and a place on the NBA's 50th anniversary all-time team. While playing for the St. Louis Hawks, Seattle SuperSonics, Cleveland Cavaliers, and Portland Trail Blazers, Wilkens scored 17,772 points and dished out 7,211 assists. In 1989 he was inducted into the Basketball Hall of Fame.

During his coaching tenure, he'd guide the Raptors to a then franchise single-season record of 47 wins and a trip to the second round in the 2001 postseason and one more playoff appearance in 2002. Under his watch there were some exciting times in Toronto, but in 2002–03, the Raptors were hit hard by injuries and missed the postseason. After a 124–98 home defeat to the San Antonio Spurs in April of 2003, Wilkens set an NBA all-time record for most career coaching losses with 1,107.

The Raptors finished 24–58, sealing the end of their head coach in Toronto. Vince Carter, who missed a good chunk of 2002-03 with injuries, admitted the club didn't work well with Wilkens' laid-back approach. "We didn't really know our roles and what we were supposed to do," Carter said. "We should look for a coach that understands the game today. To heck with the past."

kept the media off them," Carter said, "but I couldn't keep [Latrell] Sprewell and [Allan] Houston off of them." Years later, though, Vince Carter questioned his head coach's lawsuit. "It was bad timing," VC said. "Every time we had an interview or media scrum, that was talked about. It was kind of a big distraction."

After facing increased criticism, Butch Carter would drop the lawsuit on April 26, saying in a statement, "bringing the courthouse into the locker room was not the best way to address this particular matter." Young Tracy McGrady was relieved for his head coach. "He's gone through a lot, and it's probably frustrating him. It's out of the way. We don't have to worry about that. The only thing we have to worry about is the New York Knicks."

The Knicks would sweep the Raptors, capping off a bittersweet end to Toronto's campaign. But the most bizarre incident was yet to come.

During Carter's end of season job evaluation with Raptors president Richard Peddie and general manager Glen Grunwald in attendance, he did something no one expected. "Butch Carter tried to talk me into making him the GM and Glen the team president—if he could get McGrady [an unrestricted free agent] to re-sign with the club," Peddie wrote in his book, *Dream Job*. "This struck both Grunwald and me as an end-around, one that would seriously undermine Glen's effectiveness."

When Raptors veterans like Antonio Davis heard the news, they were stunned. "I'm shocked by what Butch has done," Davis expressed. "It seems every time we get in a position to move forward, to get past all this stuff, something else happens, and we take another step back."

Years later, Carter mentioned his GM request wasn't about Grunwald. "What I was trying to do was get rid of Richard," he told the *Toronto Star*. Peddie wasn't convinced. "It was still a coup. I didn't feel he was trying to push me out," Peddie said. "He was trying to push Glen out. Who was really going to be making the decisions then? Knowing Butch the way I did, he would have wanted to make the decisions."

With all the turmoil, in June 2000 it was time to pull the plug. "I wish it had all gone differently," Grunwald admitted. "I wish Butch had done some things differently. His accomplishments in Toronto should not be discounted. However, in the end, that success was clouded by off-court distractions that were disconcerting to our fans and organization."

Since Carter's firing, he has yet to secure another NBA head coaching job, fuelling his speculation Peddie tainted his reputation around the league. "[Peddie] blackballed me," Carter mentioned. "They knew I was such a good coach that if I went somewhere else I was going to win. If there's one thing I can do, I can coach."

Peddie denied Carter's accusation. "Absolutely not. No one phoned me about coaches," he said. "Think about who their reference would be? If a general manager is going to phone about a coach, they're not phoning Richard Peddie. I don't believe Glen [blackballed Carter] either. Butch went a little off the rails, but he still did a nice job for us. There was no animosity with us and Butch."

29 F--- Brooklyn!

As the 2013–14 regular season winded down, some suggested the Brooklyn Nets were tanking—losing four out of their last five regular season games—so they could face the Raptors, instead of the Chicago Bulls, in a first-round playoff match-up.

The Raptors general manager wasn't concerned. "Good for them," Masai Ujiri said. "You know what? We haven't lost one—I know I haven't and I can sense from the players—second of sleep worrying about the Brooklyn Nets. At the end of the day, if we want to be a good team, we have to play good teams. We're not hoping for anybody. We're in the playoffs. You have to play. They can do whatever they want. We'll be right here."

Ujiri wasn't done talking. On April 19, 2014, at an outdoor Raptors fan rally just before Game 1 of Toronto's first-round playoff series against the Nets, the former NBA Executive of the Year drove the crowd wild by saying two simple words, which sent a clear message to anyone watching: *"F--- Brooklyn!"*

It was a statement to the Nets and the league that the Raptors weren't pushovers or laughingstocks anymore. But when speaking with reporters at halftime, Ujiri shared his regret.

"Wrong choice of words out there," he said. "It is really not about me. It is about the players and the playoffs. Just trying to get the crowd out there rattled—wrong choice of words. I apologize to kids out there and to the Brooklyn guys. Nothing against them. Just trying to get our fans going. That's it." Despite his remorse, Ujiri didn't hide his opinion about the Nets. "You know how I feel," he said with a chuckle. "Thanks guys. I apologize for not taking any questions, but you know how I feel. I don't like 'em. I apologize."

His words did little to inspire the Raptors, who lost Game 1. But after the 94–87 loss, Amir Johnson was quick to defend his GM's comment. "He's a very passionate man," he said. "We definitely have his back. I'm with him 100 percent. If he said f--- 'em, we all say f--- 'em."

Raptors guard Kyle Lowry was also in Ujiri's corner. "He believes in what we have and what we're doing, and that's what he is. He's a passionate and very emotional guy."

The Nets had a different take. "You gotta tell me who the GM is," Nets head coach Jason Kidd said. "I don't even know who that is. I could care less what they think about Brooklyn. We have a job to do, and that's to play the game of basketball." Kevin Garnett added: "It's all good. It's motivation."

Ujiri would be fined $25,000 by the NBA, and the Raptors would eventually lose in seven games. But the GM definitely provided a moment we won't soon forget.

30 Visit Jurassic Park

Maple Leaf Square is more than a public square along with a residential, office, and hotel complex in Toronto. The downtown gathering spot (later rebranded the Ford Fan Zone at Maple Leaf Square) received its name because the National Hockey League's Toronto Maple Leafs played at the nearby Air Canada Centre (ACC).

But during the 2014 NBA playoffs with Raptors supporters taking over the space and cheering ferociously in the thousands as they watched the games on giant outdoor monitors, Maple Leaf Square affectionately became known as "Jurassic Park." "The support for the Raptors this season in Toronto and across Canada has highlighted the fact that this is one of the most passionate markets in the NBA, and in my mind, this is just the first step in what we can accomplish," said Maple Leaf Sports & Entertainment President and CEO Tim Leiweke.

An estimated 10,000 people showed up at Jurassic Park, located in the open area outside Gate 5 at the ACC, to root for the Raptors in Game 7 of their first-round series. Before the final game against the Brooklyn Nets, even general manager Masai Ujiri addressed the crowd on stage, doing so for the first time since uttering the immortal curse words toward Brooklyn.

This time Ujiri kept it clean and said, "I just wanted to come out here and thank the best fans in the world. You guys know exactly how I feel."

Raptors fever was catching on pretty quickly and not just with Torontonians and the rest of Canada. During one of the club's home postseason games, rapper 50 Cent was spotted courtside wearing a "WeTheNorth" hat. And during Toronto's playoff series, former NBA champions Magic Johnson and Steve Kerr had nothing but love for the team's energetic followers. On April 30, 2014, Johnson tweeted, "The Raptors fans have been loud and enthusiastic inside and outside of the arena!" On April 19, 2014, Kerr tweeted, "Toronto is the East's version of Golden State. Unreal fan support regardless of team success. This scene outside the arena is amazing."

On the other side, with the Nets witnessing the Raptors' passionate fan base, team writer Lenn Robbins, who was running the club's official Twitter page during Game 5, actually criticized Brooklyn's followers for not being as enthusiastic. He tweeted, "#Nets fans take note—this is what a playoff crowd sounds like... set your DVR and take notes #RAPTORSvNETS—LR."

31 #WeTheNorth

In 2013–14 Tim Leiweke, the new Maple Leaf Sports & Entertainment president and CEO, not only fired general manager Bryan Colangelo, hired Masai Ujiri, and brought in Drake as the club's official Global Ambassador, he also rebranded the team with the "We The North" campaign. "This is the statement we want to make to Canada, and I think this is the chip we have, which is we're the north, and there's no one else," Leiweke explained. "It's just us, and everyone looks past us. But we're okay with that now. This is a crusade now. This is not just a rally cry; this is our identity. I think that's what we like about this is for the next two to three years. This is who we are and this is who we represent and this is who we fight for."

The Raptors were hoping to launch the first major phase of the brand overhaul in the fall of 2015 as a lead-in to the 2016 NBA All-Star Game in Toronto. That initial phase would be the "We The North" campaign. But something magical was happening—the team was winning, and a playoff appearance was inevitable. With Toronto's sudden surprising success, the club's rebrand launch had to start sooner than expected. "Without even looking at the campaign, the team became 'We the North,'" Leiweke said. "This is too great an opportunity. The team has taken on the personality of the campaign without even knowing the campaign. We've gotta go."

To create the campaign, the Raptors teamed up with Toronto ad agency Sid Lee. "We wanted to do something that was true to Toronto as a city, true to the people…and true to the vision that Masai Ujiri and Tim have for the team," said Dustin Rideout, Sid Lee's vice president of strategy. "Any sports team is not just selling tickets. They're selling memberships, and that's what we wanted to champion."

Just before Toronto's first-round playoff series with Brooklyn, the "We The North" campaign kicked off with the release of a gritty, urban, and goose bump-inducing 60-second video embracing the uniqueness of Toronto and the Great White North. The spot featured clips of the city's skyline, snippets of basketball action from various Toronto neighbourhoods, and a quick series of Raptors slam dunks. Drake was heavily involved in the inspiration of the video and, according to Leiweke, he also had input regarding logo plans and the choice of keeping the Raptors name.

The rebrand will add another level with the team wearing new uniforms for the 2015–16 season. As for the fans' reaction to the "We The North" video, they instantly connected with it, logging more than half-a-million views in the first five days of its posting. Before you knew it, whenever supporters mentioned the Raptors on Twitter, you'd see #WeTheNorth at the end of their tweets. It became a movement and a source of Toronto and national pride.

The Trail Blazers, however, pointed out to Raptors fans Portland is actually geographically more north than Toronto. The club tweeted, "Hey @Raptors fans, let's be friends. Technically #WeTheNorthToo."

Regardless, the Raptors' unexpected success coupled with the "We The North" campaign had jump-started this franchise again. After seasons of disappointment and mediocrity, the club's fan base was excited and felt an incredible sense of unity. The Raptors were relevant once more.

32 The Purple Dinosaur Jerseys

Back in the 1990s, combining the colour purple with a dinosaur usually made you think of the popular children's TV character, Barney. He was tall, had a big gut, and was the friendliest singing T-Rex you were ever going to meet. Unfortunately, in the NBA, if his likeness was stitched on the front of your jersey, he wouldn't exactly instill fear in your opponents.

The Raptors had an iconic jersey, which some considered a joke and compared it to our happy-go-lucky prehistoric friend. It was one of those uniforms where you either thought it was cool or you wanted to set it on fire. Toronto's purple road jerseys, featuring a growling cartoon red dinosaur dribbling a basketball on the front with his sharp toenails bursting out of his white sneakers, were worn from the franchise's inception in 1995 to 1999.

The Raptors' home uniforms had the same look, but they featured a white background and purple pinstripes. There, though, was just something about that purple uniform, which touched a nerve. In fact Raptors superstar Vince Carter once said, "The biggest concern to most of the players was the Raptor. A lot of guys had a problem with it. You look down there, and he is smiling and everything."

When looking at those retro threads, as a Raptors fan, you can't help but think of the franchise's early days, including young stars—Damon Stoudamire, Marcus Camby, Tracy McGrady, Carter—and watching games in the cavernous SkyDome. But the uniforms also opened up old wounds, including the losing seasons, the Isiah Thomas ownership drama, the Stoudamire trade, and the puzzling team name, which was somewhat influenced by the hit dinosaur movie *Jurassic Park*.

After years in extinction, the polarizing purple jerseys were brought back to life in time for the Raptors' 20th anniversary 2014–15 season. They were worn in selected home games throughout the year. With the franchise in full #WeTheNorth mode and on the rise, it was time to embrace its roots. "We are excited to bring back a piece of team history as part of our 20th anniversary celebration," Raptors general manager Masai Ujiri said in a club statement. "Our fans have shown affection for the original purple uniform, and I think our players will enjoy the chance to wear them."

Despite having its critics, the old purple jerseys have a fan in Raptors guard DeMar DeRozan. "It meant a lot, especially for me since as a kid I was amazed with the purple jersey, and that's what you think of when you think of the Raptors."

Vince Carter sports the infamous "Barney" dinosaur jersey the Raptors wore from 1995 to 1999.

Looking back, the purple road uniforms may not have been a timeless piece of art, but they were an unforgettable reminder of how far this franchise has come. Now, the future is bright with new uniforms for the 2015–16 campaign. Some will like them, and some won't, but this much is for sure, they'll never confuse them with a purple, smiling, and singing T-Rex ever again.

33 Dwane Casey

In the 1960s Dwane Casey grew up poor during the segregation-era in the small farming town of Morganfield, Kentucky, where the Ku Klux Klan had a major presence. "Guys with white hoods riding in their cars," Casey told the *Toronto Star*. "I knew what it stood for. I knew someone didn't like me. Growing up, you hear all these stories about the…You think of the boogeyman."

Despite the overall racial tension at the time, it wouldn't stop Casey from working on his basketball game. He became a talented hoopster but one that needed to earn money through many odd jobs, including as a driver for former Kentucky governor Earle Clements. That connection, arranged by Casey's grandmother who once worked for Clements, would pay off when the ex-governor called the University of Kentucky's president to suggest the basketball coach take a look at Casey.

After his freshman season at Kentucky, Casey needed to make some money, so in the summer he worked in a Kentucky coal mine. "I met men down there who had never worked a day above ground, they spent a lifetime down in those coal mines, and many of them paid for it with their health. They were always saying, 'Son, you don't want to work your whole life down here, so work hard in college.' It was quite a lesson for me." He also worked for his coach but in a less than glorious fashion. "I would work on coach [Joe B.] Hall's tobacco farm, cutting tobacco, putting it on sticks and hanging it in the barn," Casey told *The Globe and Mail*. "I had to find work. I knew I wasn't getting money from home."

His strong work ethic would serve him well in the future. As a bench contributor for the University of Kentucky, the 6'2" point guard won an NCAA title on March 27, 1978, when Kentucky defeated Duke 94–88. At the end of his playing days, the ex-Kentucky captain began his coaching career in 1979 as a graduate assistant under Hall. Then he went to Western Kentucky for five years before landing back at Kentucky on Eddie Sutton's staff as an assistant coach and recruiter.

In 1988 Casey's coaching career was in serious jeopardy when he was implicated in a recruiting scandal involving money he allegedly mailed to Claud Mills, the father of Wildcats recruit Chris Mills. During the drama Casey and Sutton resigned. The NCAA barred the ex-Kentucky guard from coaching college ball for five years until Casey settled a lawsuit against the express mail company in charge of delivering the envelope, which resulted in the NCAA lifting its ban. "I felt like I was never going to coach again," Casey admitted.

During his time in Bluegrass country, he recruited and/or coached future NBA players including Sam Bowie, Rex Chapman, Shawn Kemp, and Melvin Turpin to name a few. Since his recruiting scandal, Casey bounced around from the Japanese Basketball League (including providing some coaching help to Japan's national team) to an NBA assistant role on George Karl's Seattle SuperSonics teams to his first full-time NBA head coaching job with the Minnesota Timberwolves, which ended with his 2007 firing. "It was like, 'What did I do wrong?' I felt like it was a knock that I didn't work hard enough, that I didn't do enough," Casey said of his Minnesota dismissal.

He'd get another crack as an NBA assistant with Rick Carlisle's Dallas Mavericks in the 2008–09 campaign. It would be a successful ride capped off by a 2011 postseason in which his defensive system neutralized superstars like Kobe Bryant, Kevin Durant, and LeBron James on the way to the Mavericks' first NBA title in franchise history. Casey was a champion again.

For his efforts, the Raptors hired him in June 2011. "After a lengthy and detailed search for our new head coach, it became very clear that Dwane Casey embodies every aspect of what we defined as an ideal candidate," said Raptors general manager Bryan Colangelo. "Dwane's 16-plus years in NBA coaching circles working with some tremendous basketball mentors coupled with his proven ability as a defensive architect will serve as a great backdrop for the future approach of this team."

Colangelo revealed that hours after the Mavericks won their NBA title he received a phone call from their victorious head coach. "They just literally must have just walked out of the building, a few beers and a few glasses of champagne later, I'm sure," Colangelo mentioned. The Mavericks head coach then made the case for Casey. "Bryan, I want to know what it's going to take to get Dwane that job in Toronto," said Colangelo quoting Carlisle. "It's right for him. It's right for you. It's right for the situation. You need to strongly consider it."

Casey became Toronto's eighth head coach in franchise history. "Defensively, I'm going to be a hands-on control freak so to speak. The players will know how important defence is," Casey said. "I don't know a lot about of hockey. I know I'll learn about it. But we spliced in those guys checking players up into the window, into the boards, and that type of thing, and that's the way we want to play. We want to make sure people feel us when they cut through the lane. And that's a mind-set, and that's having a disposition—a bad disposition—when people come through your paint."

With Casey's guidance, the Raptors would set a regular season franchise record in wins, secure back-to-back playoff trips, but they'd also suffer a disappointing finish to their 2015 postseason run. It was a knockout punch, which could have destroyed anybody, but not this man who has been through a lot in his life including witnessing the ugly side of humanity. Like a scrappy fighter, Casey is back on his feet and ready for another round.

34 Sam Mitchell

During his head coaching days in Toronto, the former Mercer University star was opinionated, quotable, and a media person's dream. Sam Mitchell was never shy about telling people what he thought. "It's not about being afraid to express yourself," Mitchell told *The Breakdown with Dave & Audley* podcast in 2010. "It's about being honest with yourself and the people around you. I don't have time for people to try to figure out what I'm thinking and what I'm talking about. The simplest thing to do is just to tell someone what you're thinking, where your mind is right now, and what you think you need to do to be successful. If you do that, you save a whole lot of time and, generally, people respect you more."

He even took that direct approach as a player. Before beginning his coaching career, Mitchell was a 13-year NBA veteran forward who played with the Minnesota Timberwolves and Indiana Pacers. During the 1990–91 season, he enjoyed his best year, averaging 14.6 points and 6.3 rebounds per game. Although Mitchell wasn't an All-Star talent, his NBA wisdom proved incredibly valuable to a teenage franchise player-in-the making back in the mid-1990s—Kevin Garnett. "[Mitchell] took me under his wing, taught me a lot about being a professional," Garnett said in a YES Network interview, "how you view the league and not being like everybody else because everybody does things differently, the importance of work ethic. When I see young guys, I try to give them that same outlook."

Mitchell's straight shooting philosophy didn't always endear himself to everybody, but that was okay. "Don't get into politics or don't get into coaching, if you can't take criticism," Mitchell said. "I chose to become a coach. So don't feel sorry for me when people criticize me. That's part of the job. I knew that going in."

Mitchell was known for his combative coaching style. He wasn't afraid to challenge players, especially Jose Calderon, but the Spaniard responded by turning into a solid NBA point guard. A 2004 confrontation between Mitchell and Vince Carter would become infamous.

Mitchell, though, downplayed it. "Morris Peterson was lying on the training table," Mitchell said. "He got hurt in practice, slightly pulled his hamstring. I went down to the training room, where all the players were after practice getting treatment. I was talking to Mo. Vince came up behind me and put me in a bear hug and I stumbled and fell on one of the training tables. He starts laughing and saying, 'Coach, I got you, I got you.' And I said, 'Yeah, Vince, you got me.' And the players started laughing, and that was it."

Asked what his relationship was like with Carter, Mitchell had nothing bad to say.

"My relationship with Vince Carter, in all seriousness, was great. Vince told me when I got the job that his fight and disappointment was with management and he hated that I was brought into the middle of it as the coach. And all I said to Vince was, 'I've got to do my job, and if you are not playing up to your potential, I am going to take you out of the game.' And he said, 'Coach, you've got to do what you've got to do.' And we never had a problem, never had an issue."

In a 2005 Sportsnet.ca article, Carter's mother, Michelle, reportedly expressed a different take on the situation. "Sam was talking about the incident at the team's Christmas party to a bunch of people, right in front of Vince, his wife and myself," Michelle said. "He just came out and said Vince whooped his ass and I could tell it wasn't just a figure of speech. So I asked Vince what happened. He told me he couldn't take Sam's challenges anymore, so he picked him up and threw him on the massage table. That definitely happened. No question about it. And if anyone says it didn't happen, they're lying…I could see the signs of some irrational behaviour from Sam before what happened with my son, but for me that was the last straw. That's when I really started praying. I said, 'God, please get my child out of here.' Thank God my prayer was answered. But still, I feel sorry for the other players who are still in Toronto."

The Columbus, Georgia, native also wasn't shy about calling out his players in the media.

After a 102–86 loss against the Washington Wizards in November 2004, Mitchell didn't hold back.

"We're looking like the Washington Generals, and I'm not saying that to be funny," said Mitchell, mentioning the name of the Harlem Globetrotters' regular opponents. "Somewhere we have to find some men who want to play basketball. For those who don't, do everyone a favour and quit because it's embarrassing…I can't explain [the rebounding disparity]. We didn't move, we didn't box out, we didn't even jump, and we have athletes. We had guys with stats lines that read zero, zero, zero, zero. And I don't have to tell you who they were. You can read it for yourself."

In that game Jerome Moiso had zeros across the board—except for one personal foul—and Pape Sow had all zeros in his eight minutes of playing time. It wouldn't be the last time Moiso, the

6'10" big man, would feel Mitchell's wrath. "It's not really fair to this team for him to sit there and take up air. The frustrating thing for me, I look at Jerome Moiso sitting out there and he can go out and help us. And I'm asking him when. But it's hard to put him in the game over guys who come to practice and work hard every day, and he sits around feeling sorry for himself."

Another favourite target of Mitchell's was the Toronto sports media. Steve Buffery of the *Toronto Sun* interrupted Mitchell's pregame planning for a road contest with a question. "I've had enough of your b------t. I'm giving you a choice. I'm going into that locker room right now and I'm going to tell the players that you're gay or you're in the Ku Klux Klan. Pick one or the other." Buffery responded with, "You better tell them I'm gay." Mitchell would head into the locker room and yell, "Listen up everybody. Stumpy here is gay." Morris Peterson, who took a break from tying his shoes, was the only player around. He shrugged his shoulders and said, "Okay, Coach," before paying attention to his footwear again.

On the outside looking in, you'd think Mitchell hated the Toronto sports media, but here's the truth. "I never really took the stuff in the media personally," Mitchell admitted, "even when the media people wrote that I screwed up or didn't do a great job or had a bad game or whatever. Everybody's got a job to do."

After a turbulent 2005–06 season, he'd guide a revamped roster in 2006–07 to a franchise single-season-record-tying 47 victories, the club's first division title, and its first playoff appearance since 2002. For his effort he was named the 2006–07 NBA Coach of the Year.

"It's a little embarrassing," Mitchell said. "It's very humbling, considering the things we've been through. Not just me, my staff, the players who've been here, all the people who've been involved. It's a great honour. It kind of floors you. You're thankful and words just can't express it."

In 2007–08 the 41–41 Raptors weren't as successful as the 2006–07 squad, but Toronto still made the playoffs before losing to Dwight Howard's Orlando Magic in five games.

As the 2008–09 campaign began, Raptors general manager Bryan Colangelo wasn't happy with the on-court results, so after a 132–93 blowout loss in Denver, he fired Mitchell, who had an 8–9 record at the time, just 17 games into the young season. Mitchell finished with a 156–189 record in four-plus seasons. "I have a lot to be thankful for. They really gave me the opportunity to have a career in coaching, something I always wanted to do after I played," Mitchell told TSN. "It's a disappointment that I really wasn't given the chance to finish what I started, but you know what, I feel like I accomplished a lot of good things. I think the players that played for me all got better."

35 Looooooooou!

Lou Williams knows obstacles. In January of 2013, while with the Atlanta Hawks, the guard suffered a right knee ACL tear in a game against the Brooklyn Nets, which sidelined him for the rest of the season. Despite only playing 39 games, he was having a decent year with 14.1 points per contest.

After returning from reconstructive surgery to play 60 games in 2013–14, he was still not the same, but Raptors general manager Masai Ujiri would take a chance after acquiring the Georgia native in a 2014 offseason trade. The move was a shrewd one.

With the Raptors, No. 23 was instant offence off the bench.

He set a career high by hitting 152 three-pointers. Every time he sunk a shot, you could hear fans chant "Loooooooooou!" throughout the Air Canada Centre.

He also scored a team-record 21 points in the fourth quarter against the Cleveland Cavaliers on March 4. Not bad for a guy whose career was once in doubt. Williams was such a hit that Drake mentioned him in the song "6 Man" from his 2015 album, *If You're Reading This It's Too Late.*

Here are the lyrics:

> *"Boomin' out in South Gwinnett like Lou Will.*
> *6 Man like Lou Will, 2 girls and they get along like I'm*
> *[Lou Will].*
> *Like I'm Lou Will, I just got the new deal.*
> *I am in the Matrix and I just took the blue pill."*

Soon Lou's efforts were recognized league-wide, as he became the first Raptor to win the NBA's Sixth Man of the Year award after scoring a career-best 15.5 points in 80 games. "This ranks pretty high up there," Williams told *USA TODAY Sports.* "Oh yeah, this is extremely gratifying. Just the adversity that I've been through over the past couple of years, with things not working out in my hometown in Atlanta. Coming here and having an opportunity to win it in my first year here is just extremely gratifying. I couldn't be more thankful for it to happen at this time in my career."

Alas, Lou's Toronto stay would be a short one. He signed with the Los Angeles Lakers in July of 2015. Regardless, with the Raptors focused on acquiring more defensive-minded talent, they signed DeMarre Carroll from the Hawks to a four-year contract worth $60 million.

36 Vinsanity vs. The Answer

In the early 2000s, both Vince Carter and Allen Iverson were dominant young superstars but with different styles. Vince was a gifted athlete whose eye-popping aerial attack left everyone breathless while Iverson was a small, extremely quick, and talented scorer whose warrior-like heart was bigger than most. In a 2001 Eastern Conference second-round playoff match-up, these gigantic forces collided in an epic duel. "This is special because they both have their teams on their backs," Philadelphia 76ers president and part-owner Pat Croce said. "They're great basketball players, but more than that, they're exciting. They add an element of surprise when they get the ball. You don't know what's going to happen. They bring that anticipation and enthusiasm and they smile at the fans and interact with them. That's what the NBA needs. That's what we want. I want the people going nuts when Carter does something. I just want him doing it less than Allen."

The All-Stars traded punches right away in Game 1 with Iverson pouring in 36 points and Vince scoring 35, but the Raptors would win on the road 96–93. In Game 2, A.I. was a one-man wrecking ball. He crushed Toronto with a 76ers' single-game playoff record 54 points in a 97–92 victory. "I always feel the only person who can stop me is myself," Iverson said. "The only thing I care about is getting a win. If I shoot terrible and we win, that's all that matters." Carter, who had 28 points in Game 2, respected Iverson's performance. "He did the job, that's for sure, but the series is not over."

As the scene for Game 3 switched to Toronto, "Air Canada" dominated the stage.

Carter was lethal from beyond the arc, hitting a Raptors playoff single-game record nine three-pointers, including his first eight in a row. V.C. would answer A.I.'s 54 points in Game 2 by exploding for a franchise postseason record 50 of his own in a 102–78 Toronto win. "If [Carter's] that type of player that can turn it off and on like that, I'm scared to see what he'll do the next game," said Iverson who scored 23 in Game 3. "We expect him to have great games. We watched it on TV all year long. When players get in a groove, there's nothing you can do about it. If there was, we would have done it."

As for Carter he felt his long-distance shooting needed improvement. "I don't know. Three-point shooter doesn't sound right yet. I'm still working on that one. I still want to be an all-around player, not just get to the hole and dunk the basketball, not just pass, not just shoot, not just penetrate, but do it all at one time."

In Game 4 Carter would cool off with 25 points on 8-of-27 shooting while Iverson delivered 30 points to help the Sixers even the series at 2–2 with an 84–79 victory. Before Game 5 at the First Union Center, the packed Philly crowd of nearly 21,000 cheered as Iverson received his 2001 NBA Most Valuable Player of The Year award. It was an electric atmosphere, and Iverson made sure fans went home happy. The 6'0", 165-pound guard was unstoppable, sinking eight three-pointers on the way to a 52-point onslaught in the 121–88 win.

After only having 16 points in Game 5, Carter felt pressure to keep the Raptors season alive. In Game 6 at the Air Canada Centre, Toronto's adopted son would take over, scoring a game-high 39 points while Iverson was relatively silent in a 20-point outing. VC had forced a Game 7 back in Philadelphia. The morning of that pivotal contest, Carter decided to attend his University of North Carolina graduation ceremony to the surprise of many.

Once he arrived in Philly, he was set for the biggest game in Raptors history. But both he and Iverson weren't their elite level selves. A.I. scored just 21 on 8-of-27 shooting, though he was a terrific facilitator with 16 assists. Vince had 20, but the team, Raptors fans, and the entire country of Canada were hoping for 22. Unfortunately, VC missed a last-second jumper, which would have won Toronto the series.

Instead, it was Iverson and the Sixers moving on after an 88–87 victory. They'd go on to lose to the Los Angeles Lakers in the NBA Finals while Carter would deal with the intense backlash over his graduation ceremony decision and questions of what could have been.

37 A Dream Come True?

After his team lost a heart-wrenching seven-game second-round playoff series against the Philadelphia 76ers, Glen Grunwald didn't sulk. Instead the Raptors general manager went on an off-season spending spree. He re-signed Vince Carter and signed free agents Antonio Davis, Jerome Williams, and Alvin Williams to fat long-term deals. Then, in a sign-and-trade, he brought in two-time NBA Finals MVP centre Hakeem "the Dream" Olajuwon to the Raptors.

Granted, this was a 38-year-old version of the player whose signature "Dream Shake" move wasn't as lethal as it once was, but at least in Toronto's mind, Olajuwon was an upgrade in the 5-spot.

For many he was expected to retire as a Houston Rocket since he played there his entire career up to that point and at the University of Houston prior to that. The 1993–94 NBA MVP was a Houston icon, but his relationship with the Rockets organization became strained. During his 17th campaign, Olajuwon thought it would be his final one until the regular season got underway. Realizing there was more left in his tank, he wanted to keep playing, which led to a tense midseason showdown with the Rockets that involved a request to be cut.

Olajuwon and Houston head coach Rudy Tomjanovich worked out the issue, so all was good until No. 34 had a career-threatening blood clot in his leg. Medication would remedy the problem, ensuring his return to the court. Once the season ended, though, the Rockets only wanted Olajuwon if he agreed to a salary cap-friendly deal. Houston's final offer was $13 million over three years. *Thanks, but no thanks.* Olajuwon told the club he didn't want to play there anymore, so Houston then bid farewell to its beloved franchise star. "Hakeem's decision is disappointing for the entire Rockets organization," said Houston owner Les Alexander. "Hakeem Olajuwon has meant more to this franchise and this city than any other athlete in Houston history. It is with a heavy heart that we have agreed to his request."

In August of 2001, it was a new beginning for the future Hall of Famer. "I feel like a rookie again," said Olajuwon, who was dealt for a first and second-round pick. "I'm excited. It's a new opportunity to establish myself." Olajuwon, who signed a three-year, $18 million contract, also took a slight swipe at his old team. "Toronto realized I have value to their organization," he said. "This is a team that has a chance of winning an NBA championship."

Of course, some worried Olajuwon's advanced age and his recent blood clot could pose a problem, but Grunwald felt otherwise. "Our doctors have talked extensively with the Houston doctors and were comfortable that there are no serious concerns that may pop up."

When Olajuwon arrived in Toronto for his news conference, he had a surprise guest midway through—Vince Carter. "Vince is a great recruiter," Olajuwon mentioned after embracing VC. "My role is to make the game much easier for him. I'd like to make it easier for him to dunk on people."

With Olajuwon aboard the Raptors were one of the favourites to capture the Eastern Conference title. On October 30, 2001, Olajuwon would make his Raptors debut on the road against the Orlando Magic, recording 11 points, four rebounds, one block, and one steal in 23 minutes in the 114–85 blowout loss. On November 2 the Dream would make his first regular season Air Canada Centre appearance as a Raptor in the team's home opener. Against Dallas he'd put up 11 points, eight rebounds, three steals, and two assists in 27 minutes in a 109–92 victory against Steve Nash, Dirk Nowitzki, and the rest of the Mavericks.

During the first 11 games of the season, you could tell Olajuwon wasn't the Dream we once remembered, only averaging 8.5 points and 7.6 rebounds in that span. But then comes November 20 against the Detroit Pistons, when the All-Star Olajuwon briefly winked at us.

In that game he had 14 points, a season-high 20 rebounds, five blocks, and one steal in front of the ACC crowd. For one night, the old man could still fill a stat sheet.

Defensively, he remained a presence, recording nine blocks against the San Antonio Spurs on December 12 and seven blocks two other times, but back, toe, and leg injuries would limit him to 61 games and only 37 starts. Olajuwon posted disappointing regular season numbers—career lows with 7.1 points and six rebounds per contest. After the Raptors, without an injured Vince Carter, made a furious late season push into the playoffs, Olajuwon would come off the bench in all five first-round games against the Pistons, averaging only 5.6 points, 3.8 rebounds, and 1.4 steals per game. It would be the last time he'd play in the NBA. "It was a gamble and I think we lost on it." Grunwald said. "It didn't turn out the way we had hoped."

38 Chris Childs, What Were You Thinking?

Chris Childs was quite familiar with NBA playoff basketball. During the 1999 postseason, he was part of a magical New York Knicks run, which saw the Eastern Conference No. 8 seed head all the way to the NBA Finals before bowing out to David Robinson, a young Tim Duncan, and the rest of the dynasty-in-the-making San Antonio Spurs.

In fact, before the guard arrived in Toronto via a multi-player trade, he saw action in 56 playoff games. In the 2001 postseason, Childs provided the Raptors with some quality performances, including a 25-point effort in a Game 4 win against his old Knicks team, which forced their first-round series to a fifth and deciding contest. In Game 3 of Toronto's second-round series with the Philadelphia 76ers, Childs would also have 16 points and 10 assists in the victory. The veteran was used to playoff intensity and understood every possession was magnified because it could be the difference between moving on to the next round or cleaning out your locker to end another year.

During the first round of the 2002 playoffs against the Detroit Pistons, Childs, who came off the bench in Game 1, started Games 2 and 3 and flourished. In Game 2 he had a team-high 22 points and 14 assists and five rebounds. In Game 3 he had 12 points, a team-high 10 assists, and seven rebounds. He would receive the start again in the win-or-go-home Game 5. Former Raptors forward Corliss Williamson would get a basket for two of his 23 points in the paint with 26.5 seconds left to put Detroit up 83–79. With Toronto now down 84–79 and less than 16 seconds remaining, Childs kicked out a pass to Dell Curry who hit a three-pointer to bring the Raptors within two. After a Jerry Stackhouse free throw made it 85–82 Pistons, Toronto had one last chance with 10.7 seconds to go.

Childs raced up court as Chucky Atkins guarded him and then inexplicably decided to hoist what appeared to be a desperation running three-point shot and an attempt at drawing a foul, but it missed terribly with more than five seconds to spare. All of a sudden, the Raptors season was over. Their fans and the team were stunned. *Childs, what were you thinking?*

Some members of the Toronto sports media speculated Childs thought the Raptors were down by four, not three, so that's why he went for a four-point play. Another puzzling thing was once he headed up court there was still time to set up a play for someone like Curry who could have potentially tied the game.

There wasn't a need to rush a shot. It was a surprisingly poor decision for a veteran player who had been a part of quite a few postseason battles. Years later, his former teammates reflected on his pivotal mistake. "Yeah, I remember that," said Morris Peterson who only scored three points in Game 5. "You don't want to say one play costs you a game. Obviously, if we could take that back, we would."

Former Raptors guard Alvin Williams added, "It's amazing that it happened, but it was one of those situations where you get caught up in the game. Chris was playing very well, Dell Curry was making some huge shots for us, and it was just one of those things where we came up short. From 1999 on, we had built such a culture of sticking behind one another—on the court and off the court. It was unbelievable. It truly was a genuine relationship on and off the court. Once that happened it was one of those things where it's 'damn,' but it happened, and I still support him."

That would be Childs' last game in a Raptors uniform. He'd sign a free agent deal with the New Jersey Nets in the 2002 offseason.

39 Rob Babcock

Before replacing Glen Grunwald as Raptors general manager in June of 2004, Rob Babcock, who joined the league in 1987 as the Denver Nuggets' director of scouting, had just finished a 12-year run with the Minnesota Timberwolves in various roles such as vice president of player personnel, director of player personnel, and scout. But the Phoenix native had *zero* NBA GM experience.

Maple Leaf Sports & Entertainment President and CEO Richard Peddie looked past that and hired him anyway. There was some drama around the decision with Vince Carter previously wanting Julius "Dr. J" Erving in the role. "Vince doesn't know me," Babcock said. "I wouldn't expect him to be overly excited about Rob Babcock. I'm not a household name."

The new Raptors GM—with Carter's support or not—had a plan in mind. "Within two years we're going to be a very good basketball team," Babcock said. "I'm not really worried about how many wins we get right away, or whether we make the playoffs within the first year or two. Our goal is to establish our philosophy."

Because of Babcock's rookie GM status, Basketball Hall of Famer and two-time NBA Executive of the Year Wayne Embry was hired to be his senior basketball advisor. Babcock's first assignment was the 2004 NBA Draft where the Raptors had the eighth overall pick. During draft night on June 24 after the Suns selected Luol Deng in the seventh spot, Babcock was now on the clock.

The following future NBA contributors were still available:

- University of Arizona's Andre Iguodala (2015 NBA Finals MVP)

- High schooler Al Jefferson (averaged at least 21 points and more than 10 rebounds in a season three times)
- High schooler Josh Smith (averaged more than 15 points per game for eight straight seasons)
- Saint Joseph's Jameer Nelson (2009 NBA All-Star)
- High schooler J.R. Smith (scored in double-digits in nine straight seasons, including 18.1 per game in the 2012–13 campaign)
- Western Carolina's Kevin Martin (scored 20 or more points per game in five straight years)

But Babcock decided to shock everybody by picking 6'11" Brazilian centre Rafael Araujo out of Brigham Young University. "He's not a project," Babcock said. "He's not a stiff."

Raptors fans and the Toronto media heavily criticized the move, especially since Iguodala was picked right after Araujo at No. 9 by the Philadelphia 76ers. Also, since Toronto's unhappy superstar, Vince Carter, would be traded in December that year, it would have been nice to have a young wing scorer like Iguodala to take VC's place.

Instead, under head coach Sam Mitchell, Araujo wouldn't play much. In 111 career Raptors games, the Brazilian would only average 12 minutes on the court while scoring 2.9 points and three rebounds. Araujo, who would be dealt to Utah in June 2006, was a bust. "The biggest mistake was the drafting of Araujo," Babcock told the *Toronto Star*. "The mistake was made, and it was my fault."

Of course, Babcock's rough year would get much uglier as Carter was traded to New Jersey as part of the worst deal in franchise history. "Looking back on it, I would not have changed the way we approached it," Babcock said. "Any time a player comes out and demands a trade, it puts you in a very difficult situation. You know that you are not going to get value for that player, and player for player, we certainly did not get value at all, but we knew we weren't going to be able to get value...[Carter] clearly did not want to be there. It was clear from the first time I met him, talked to him about the situation. It was clear the first time he stepped foot on the floor and it was clear from the start of training camp all the way through until the time we traded him that he did not want to be there. When you have a player—and especially your best player —and he clearly was a fantastic player, but when you have your best player and the leader of your team who does not want to be there, you've got to move the guy. And absolutely all of us were absolutely certain that had to happen, we tried to get him in the fold, and it just wasn't going to happen. That's his prerogative, but it made it very, very difficult to trade him because everyone knew he did not want to be there."

The Raptors finished the 2004–05 season out of the play-offs and would do the same in 2005–06, but Babcock wouldn't stick around to see the conclusion. He was fired in January 2006. "Certainly the way it ended was very disappointing, that can't change," Babcock said. "I honestly felt we were on the right track. A lot of people thought I was too college-ish, too much of a college guy trying to establish a college atmosphere, but you know what? I honestly believe that's what works. I think it's been proven. The Seattle Seahawks won the Super Bowl [in 2014] with that type of philosophy, the San Antonio Spurs have been winning for years with that type of philosophy. I think it's a philosophy that's proven and a philosophy that works."

Well, it didn't work in Toronto, and everyone was a witness to the destruction.

Here's a look back at some of Babcock's other notable moves. In July of 2004, he inked troublesome point guard Rafer Alston to a six-year deal but would then trade him to the Houston Rockets for Mike James in October 2005. In June of 2005, Babcock confused the basketball world by selecting UConn's 6'11" power forward Charlie Villanueva seventh overall, even though the Raptors already had a similar and far superior player in 6'11" Chris Bosh. Babcock had three picks to play with in that draft, using the other two on the underachieving Joey Graham (16th) and Roko Ukic (41st), who'd only last one season in Toronto.

In August of 2005, Babcock made his best move, signing point guard Jose Calderon as a free agent. Despite that, Babcock will go down as the worst GM in team history.

40 Oakley, the Enforcer

Charles Oakley was basically an NBA cop. The hard-nosed ex-All-Star forward always patrolled and then punished perpetrators who messed with his teammates. Once you stepped over the line with "Oak," you could expect a razor sharp elbow coming your way. Michael Jordan's former Chicago Bulls bodyguard and Patrick Ewing's longtime New York Knicks sidekick wasn't exactly a warm and fuzzy figure, but that's what was charming about him.

This grizzled warrior could be grouchy and tell you what was on his mind without any filter, but when it came time to play, the power forward always backed up his talk with a maximum effort and was the ultimate team guy. "Sure, people told me Oak wouldn't do this, didn't want to do that," said former Knicks head coach Pat Riley. "But Oak is a leader and a hard worker. And I think he knows the coaching staff, the organization, and his teammates appreciate that. His teammates should respect him. He's sacrificing a lot of his game for them."

Before being traded to the Raptors in June 1998, the 1985 first-round Cleveland Cavaliers draft pick played in 129 postseason

Oakley vs. McInnis

During his time with Toronto, Oakley was reportedly dating a woman in Charlotte, North Carolina. When he called her house, Los Angeles Clippers guard, Jeff McInnis answered.

Oakley went hunting for McInnis right away, but he was nowhere to be found.

Then on December 1st 2000, the Clippers were in Toronto. "I saw Oakley coming out of the tunnel. He passed by Jeff McInnis, who was sitting on the bench, and socked him," wrote a reporter from the *Orange County Register*. "Jeff tried two or three times to get back at him, but players and coaches held him back."

Clippers head coach Alvin Gentry wasn't sure why this incident occurred. "It was a single hit. I just saw the aftermath of it, so who knows. We're not talking about the most mature group of people in the world when you talk about pro athletes, so it could have been anything."

Clearly, Gentry didn't know his NBA gossip.

For his assault, Oakley was suspended three games and fined $15,000. But the interesting thing was, the Raptors fan favourite told the Toronto media that the 6'4", 178-pound McInnis threatened his life. "Why would I threaten a 6'9", 260-pound guy?" McInnis said.

games, including one trip to the NBA Finals with New York in 1994 where in Game 4, he had 16 points and 20 rebounds against the Houston Rockets.

When Oakley arrived in Toronto, he brought a considerable amount of postseason experience, leadership, and toughness at just the right time. Toronto was on the rise with a young Vince Carter and Tracy McGrady who were poised to take the Raptors on a ride no one had experienced before.

In the 1999–00 campaign, Oakley would help Toronto make its first ever postseason appearance against his old club, the Knicks. Unfortunately, the Raptors would be swept in three straight despite Oakley having 10 points and 7.7 rebounds per game during the series.

Shooting a free throw during November of 2000, Charles Oakley was an intimidating post player with whom you did not want to mess.

The summer of 2000 would be an interesting one for Oak. During that time he'd play a dice game with Philadelphia 76ers big man Tyrone Hill. Hill lost and owed Oakley $54,000.

Time would tick on, but Hill still didn't pay up. You don't do that to Charles Oakley. Before a 2000 preseason game, the Raptors intimidator slapped Hill in the mouth. That started a scuffle, and neither were allowed to play. "Charles Oakley was probably one of the best guys just from the seriousness he had in the locker room and the attention to detail he came with the game. But when he slapped Tyrone Hill from Philly for not paying his gambling debts, I think that's funny," Jerome Williams said. "He would slap you. He'd slap you good, slap the taste out your mouth."

But it didn't end there. In April 3, 2001 in Toronto, Hill was still delinquent on his debt repayment, so Oakley confronted him after the Sixers' morning shootaround and threw a basketball at his head. Oakley was suspended one game and fined $10,000, but Hill eventually gave Oak his money.

In Toronto's 2001 first-round playoff rematch with the Knicks, Oakley was consistently trying to motivate Carter, but VC's mother, Michelle, didn't approve of Oak's criticism. Vince's mom said, "Those who did the talking weren't doing too much on the court." She'd also recommend Oakley take more shots. The veteran replied, "I don't take a lot of shots, so if she's got something personal with me, I'm not hard to find. She knows my number. I've got nothing against his mom, but she can't criticize me about something in the game…I wasn't trying to get on Vince. I've been telling Vince all year, you can ask him, 'Take it to the hole and you can kill these guys—you're one of the best players in the league.'"

Unfortunately, their feud didn't overshadow the reality Carter would later miss a crucial last second Game 7 shot against Philadelphia in the second round, which ended Toronto's terrific 2000–01 campaign. Oakley would average 9.3 points and 6.3

rebounds during that postseason run before being dealt to the Bulls in July 2001.

When looking back at his Raptors days, Oakley's teammates remember him fondly, including the man he was tough on—VC. "I remember the second day of practice Oak put his arm around me and he said, 'you know what? I'm gonna show you the ropes and make you a better player,'" Carter told *Off The Record*. "I was fortunate enough to have my cousin [Tracy McGrady] on one side and a savvy veteran like Oak on the other, day in and day out preparing me and giving me the opportunity to really learn the ropes and make it easier for me."

T-Mac also served up some praise. "The one thing I really appreciated about Oak, and Vince can attest to this as well, is he always had our back, no matter how young we were, he always had our back and we don't have that in the game today...If we got fouled hard in a game, you best believe somebody on that other team is gonna get fouled hard, and he just took care of us."

41 Mo Pete

Before the start of the new millennium, if you were a Raptors fan, you probably thought *The Flintstones* was just an old cartoon starring a loud prehistoric fat guy who yelled "Yabba Dabba Doo!" all the time. In April 2000 at Michigan State University, "Flintstones" meant something entirely different. At that time it was a nickname referring to a collection of three young men—Morris Peterson, Mateen Cleaves, and Charlie Bell—all Flint, Michigan, natives who would lead the Spartans to a NCAA title win against the Florida Gators.

Peterson, a junior, then declared for the draft and was selected 21st overall by a franchise that was on its way up. Mo Pete arrived at the perfect time with Vinsanity at its peak and the Raptors fresh off their first ever playoff appearance earlier in the year. In his rookie season, the kid with the sweet lefty three-point stroke played in 80 games with 49 of them coming off the bench, averaging 9.3 points per contest.

Peterson was fearless from the perimeter. It didn't matter that he was a first-year guy in the NBA, he'd still knock down threes in your face. On February 27, 2001, the Cleveland Cavaliers witnessed the show firsthand when Peterson hit seven three-pointers on the way to a season-high 29 points in a 101–89 win. Even in the 2001 postseason, head coach Lenny Wilkens showed confidence in the rookie by allowing him to play at crucial times.

In Game 6 of Toronto's second-round series against the Philadelphia 76ers, many remember Vince Carter's 39 points, which forced a Game 7, but few recall Mo Pete getting the start and scoring 17 points and having seven assists to help the Raptors avoid elimination. Even though the 2000–01 season would end in heartbreak, Peterson became a fan favourite. For his efforts Peterson would find a spot on the 2001 All-Rookie first team.

In the 2001–02 campaign, Peterson's scoring numbers would rise (14 points per game), but the Raptors had some obstacles, mainly the loss of the injured Carter for the 2002 playoffs.

To Toronto's credit, it moved on without him and faced Detroit in the opening round. Peterson delivered in Game 4 with 20 points as the Raptors extended the series to five games, but ultimately, the Pistons prevailed.

In 2002–03 Peterson was enjoying his best season to date, scoring 14.1 points per game, but the club around him was falling apart. The Raptors were decimated by injuries, including Carter, who just couldn't stay healthy. Ironically, Mo Pete would play all 82 games, including 80 starts, beginning an ironman streak.

From 2004–2006 he would see some of the lowest points in franchise history but still kept on playing through it all. In fact, in the 2005–06 season, Peterson had a career-high 16.8 points per contest, including a career-best 38 points in a game against the Phoenix Suns that year, but his team was terrible, owning a 27–55 record.

As the 2006–07 campaign began, Peterson's ironman streak would end in November at a franchise record 371 straight games. The veteran would also be the Raptors all-time leader in games played at 542. Besides his durability and long range shooting touch, Peterson was also known for making improbable circus plays. For example, one time he was driving to the basket, a defender swatted his headband over his eyes, but he still converted on the no-look layup.

On March 30, 2007, against the Washington Wizards, Peterson added to his resume.

Toronto was trailing by three with 3.8 seconds left. Washington's, Michael Ruffin intercepted a long inbounds pass and then tossed the ball high to burn some time, but it wasn't high enough. The ball found Mo Pete, who heaved a desperation three-point, game-tying buzzer-beater to force overtime, in which Toronto would ultimately win 123–118. "When I saw [Ruffin] tip it, I looked and I saw I had a chance to get it, and it turned out the ball just came to me," Peterson said. "I looked at the clock real quick, and there was like one second, and I just threw it up. Thankfully it went in, gave us another chance." Bosh, who scored 37 points, enjoyed the last second frantic scene. "Wild stuff, I don't know, man, you've got to go to the libraries on that one. I took Mo's shot as a second chance for us. When stuff happens like that, you've got to win."

The Raptors had a solid season with a then-franchise record-tying 47 victories to go along with their first Atlantic Division title and first-round playoff match-up with Carter's New Jersey Nets. For Mo Pete, who only started 12 of his 71 regular season games in 2006–07, it was just great playing on a winning club again. He had a quiet postseason series until scoring 17 points in a Game 5 Toronto win, but the Nets would beat the Raptors in six games.

Unfortunately, with general manager Bryan Colangelo looking to rebuild, Peterson wasn't in his plans. So, once his contract ran out at the end of the year, the Raptors chose to move forward, ending a long run together. "It was really tough, especially being there for seven years," said the Raptors all-time leader in three-point field goals made (801). "I had known a lot of the guys on the team. It got to the point I knew almost everybody in the arena, too. I would be there in the summertime, at night. I used to give some of the security headaches because I would come in there at one or two in the morning wanting to shoot. It's just an experience that I won't forget how loyal guys were to Toronto.

"Toronto, by far, has some of the best and most loyal fans in the NBA. Still to this day, I get emails and I get letters. I get people writing all the time talking about their experiences in Toronto. That's something that I hold true to my heart, like my first girlfriend."

42 Watch Vince Carter's Top 100 Dunks

Whether you hate or kind of like Vince Carter, you can't deny "Air Canada" is arguably the greatest dunker of all time. No offence to Air Jordan, Dr. J, and Dominique, but Vinsanity's acrobatic, creative, stylish, and powerful slams had a way of electrifying a crowd few could match.

If you're really a Toronto Raptors fan, do yourself a favour and check out "Top 100 Vince Carter Dunks" on YouTube. This highly entertaining 10-minute video showcases Vince's insane springs as he stages an unstoppable aerial assault on opposing defences throughout his NBA and University of North Carolina career.

The best part is witnessing him posterize many notable players including Tim Duncan, Dikembe Mutombo, David Robinson, Dirk Nowitzki, Ben Wallace, Alonzo Mourning, and, of course, poor soul Frederic Weis in a slam for the ages.

43 Man, We Love These Guys!

Charles Oakley, Jose Calderon, Kyle Lowry, Matt Bonner, and Morris Peterson will always feel positive vibes from Toronto's basketball supporters because Raptors fans love underdogs who give maximum effort every game, overcome obstacles, are productive, and who respect the city of Toronto. Oh, it doesn't hurt if you're bald and grab a lot of rebounds, too.

Here are some of the underrated Raptors who have a special place in the hearts of Toronto's basketball fans.

Alvin Williams

The quiet combo guard and clutch postseason performer played on three Raptors playoff teams. "I came in at a time where there were a lot of questions about the Raptors and athletes about wanting to actually be in Toronto," said Williams who averaged a career postseason high 13.8 points per game during the 2001 playoffs. "Once I had the chance to be in Toronto and then I got the opportunity to leave Toronto [as a free agent], I decided to come back because I really wanted to be there. I think the fans respected that. I think the fans appreciated that. I think that's where the respect and the love that they showed me came from. I wasn't the best player, but I played hard and I wanted to be there."

Jerome "Junkyard Dog" Williams

An outgoing, enthusiastic, headband-wearing, super-energized, hard-working rebounding machine had an adoring group of supporters affectionately called, "The DoggPound." "Fans gravitate toward authenticity, hard work," said Williams, who played in 180 games as a Raptor. "They want to see a consistent product on the floor. Whatever players are giving them that consistent product, they pay for, they buy the jersey."

And he had a great and fitting nickname. Who dubbed him Junkyard Dog? "Rick Mahorn and Grant Long. Of course, those are former Bad Boys with the Detroit Pistons," Williams told the podcast, *The Breakdown with Dave & Audley.* "As a rookie, they were just appreciative of my hard work and tagged me with the Junkyard Dog because I was a Georgetown alumni graduate. They really wanted to put me down as one of the hardest working guys in the NBA, and that's the nickname they came up with—Junkyard Dog."

Amir Johnson

He was a big man who played hurt, never whined, and always embraced the city. Heck, at one point, he even got the Raptors logo shaved into the back of his head and once purchased a bunch of Drake CDs and gave them out for free to people in the streets. "What can I say? I love Toronto," Johnson admitted. "And I love the fans."

Anthony Parker

The solid shooting guard and fan-friendly citizen arrived in Toronto after playing in Israel and then became an important member of the Raptors' first division title squad and playoff teams in 2007 and 2008.

Jorge Garbajosa

"Garbo" did a little bit of everything. The Spaniard, who sometimes smoked cigarettes, provided toughness with an elbow or two. The forward also pulled down rebounds and hit some perimeter shots. Fans enjoyed his game but were saddened when his Raptors career abruptly ended due to a nasty broken leg and ankle injury in 2007.

Tracy Murray

T for Three!
Murray, who was an original Raptor, was money from beyond the arc, including hitting six triples in a 40-point game against the Denver Nuggets in March 1996. He always wore a bright smile and personable vibe, and fans couldn't help but like the smooth-shooting forward.

Reggie Evans

A bald, rebounding monster, who was an undersized power forward, he never lacked effort on the court. "You have so many people who go out there and work so hard from 9 to 5 to make an honest living and buy a Raptors ticket," Evans said. "They want to come here and see somebody work just as hard as they do in the real world. A lot of times, they appreciate it more to see a guy go out there and bust his butt. That way they get their money's worth when they see the Raptors play."

Despite his short stay in Toronto, which included a 47-game absence due to a broken foot, Evans and the club's fan base had a nice connection. "We love each other. We feed off each other. We've got a bond with each other, and it just feels good to have a good relationship with the fans."

Jamario Moon

Here's a guy you can root for. After going undrafted in 2001, Moon bounced around various basketball leagues, including a stint with the Harlem Globetrotters until the Raptors took a chance on him in 2007. The 6'8" forward, who was a January 2008 Eastern Conference Rookie of the Month winner, would become a fan favourite for his high-flying jams, blocked shots, and—of course—cool name.

44 Primo Pasta

During a legendary television commercial, you see Andrea Bargnani draining shots in the Raptors practice facility as the then-Maple Leaf Sports & Entertainment director of culinary and executive chef Robert Bartley describes how Primo Pasta is an important part of Bargnani's pregame preparation. Toward the end the kicker comes when you see Bargnani about to dig into his plate of pasta and say, "Primo Pasta and Sauce," and then his voice is abruptly cut off, which leads directly into this cheesy jingle—"Quick and nutritious, simply delicious, everyone knows...it's Primo!" The spot ends with Bargnani eating his pasta and nodding his head in enjoyment.

Many members of the Raptors fan base bashed the spot. YouTube it and you'll see the loads of negative comments. Yes, Bargnani's time in Toronto was always a magnet for criticism.

It started in 2006 when general manager Bryan Colangelo selected the seven-foot sharpshooter, who played for Benetton Treviso in the Italian League, as the NBA draft's first overall pick over the likes of LaMarcus Aldridge, Rudy Gay, Rajon Rondo,

Kyle Lowry, and Paul Millsap. At the time some Raptors fans questioned the move. They didn't know much about the 20-year-old since he was overseas, but by his frame and shooting touch, it was easy to compare him to Dallas Mavericks seven-foot All-Star Dirk Nowitzki.

In Bargnani's NBA regular season debut against Vince Carter's New Jersey Nets on November 1, 2006, the European wasn't impressive, playing under nine minutes, having more fouls (three) than points (two) on the night. In his home debut on November 3rd, Bargnani was a little better with four points, five rebounds, and one block in just more than 10 minutes against the Milwaukee Bucks.

It would be a slow adjustment process for the rookie, but he'd show signs of improvement, including a 23-point effort against the Orlando Magic on December 13 and an 18-point, 10-rebound, and six-block performance against the Warriors on December 17. Bargnani, who was mainly a contributor off the bench, would go on to win the Eastern Conference Rookie of the Month awards in January and February 2007 and would join fellow European Raptors freshman Jorge Garbajosa at the Rookie Challenge Game during the All-Star weekend in Las Vegas.

In March, Bargnani would have his appendix removed, but he returned in time for Toronto's first playoff series since 2002 during a season where the club won its first ever division crown. The Italian would be relatively quiet in his first three career NBA postseason appearances against the Nets, but Raptors head coach Sam Mitchell decided to start him in Games 4, 5, and 6, and the young man responded by averaging 17 points in those contests.

VC's Nets would bounce the Raptors in the first round, but Bargnani, who'd score 11.6 points a game in 65 regular season appearances, would go on to be named to the NBA All-Rookie Team.

In 2007–08 Bargnani took a step back in his development with his poor shooting (38.6 percent in 2007–08 compared to 42.7 percent in 2006–07), decreased rebounding results, and his consistent foul trouble issues. He was also ineffective against the Orlando Magic in five playoff starts, averaging only 6.4 points in Toronto's 2008 opening round loss. Clearly, more was expected of Bargnani. "It rests on his shoulders. It's always a big 'if' when you're talking about personal development," Chris Bosh said. "If he doesn't work, it's not going to happen."

In season three Bargnani would have a bounce-back year with increases in points (15.4 points per game), field goal percentage (45 percent), three-point field goal percentage (a career-high 40.9 percent), rebounds (5.3 per game), and blocks (1.2 per game). He became more aggressive driving to the basket instead of relying too much on his perimeter shooting.

Also, he was starting more, including some games with newly acquired big man, Jermaine O'Neal, and Bosh in the same lineup. In those contests Bargnani would play small forward in Toronto's tall frontcourt and produced some decent results, including a 29-point, 10-rebound effort. After O'Neal's trade in February, Bargnani would remain a consistent starter, but the Raptors would miss the playoffs for the first time in his NBA career.

In the offseason, since Toronto was encouraged with No. 7's resurgence, the club re-signed him to a five-year, $50 million extension. *Il Mago* (Italian for the Magician), a nickname given by his former Benetton teammate, Riccardo Pittis, would not let the new deal make him complacent in 2009–10. In a career-high 80 games, Bargnani averaged 17.2 points, a career-best 47 percent shooting, and pulled down 6.2 rebounds per game.

After Bosh left in the summer of 2010, the Raptors would lean on the seven-foot talent to be the team's go-to guy. Offensively, the sweet-shooting Italian enjoyed his best scoring season, including a career-high 41 points against the New York Knicks in Madison

Square Garden on December 8, 2010. In 66 games Bargnani, despite some injuries, averaged a career-best 21.4 points, including 30 or more points nine times that season, but he couldn't help a Toronto squad, which sorely missed Bosh and finished 22–60.

Over the next two seasons, including the 2011–12 NBA lockout-delayed campaign, more injuries would severely restrict the Italian from reaching new heights. During that time he'd only play 66 games combined and became a major source of frustration for Raptors followers and the team. In December 2012 it didn't help that Bargnani allegedly criticized his club in an interview with an Italian newspaper, saying the then-struggling Raptors were "pretty much the worst team in the NBA."

He denied making the remark, but it didn't matter. The fan base was already growing tired of him. In January of 2013, Mitchell revealed how he wasn't given the chance to guide the franchise's first ever No. 1 selection the way he wanted to. "I wasn't allowed to coach Andrea the same way I was allowed to coach Jose [Calderon]," Mitchell told Sportsnet 590 The Fan. "I was a hard ass on Jose. I was hard on him, but look at the type of player he turned out to be. I was not allowed to be that tough on Andrea because within the organization we felt he couldn't take it. And my whole thing was—if he can't take it, then we can't build around him. And no one thought Jose could take it, and Jose did. I think because he was the No. 1 pick, and a lot was invested in him, I just think people in the organization thought my coaching style would be too tough on Andrea."

Bearing the burden of being a No. 1 overall selection carrying a franchise, including getting pounded by the fans and media, wasn't easy for the usually quiet Bargnani. In July of 2013, new GM Masai Ujiri took care of it by trading him to the New York Knicks for Marcus Camby, Steve Novak, Quentin Richardson, a 2014 second-round pick, a 2016 first-round pick, and a 2017 second-round pick. "All I've got to say about Toronto is that it was a good seven years," Bargnani said. "I was lucky to play there, and that's really it. I don't want to really talk about fans, what happened and frustration."

The Knicks' No. 77 would make his regular season return to Toronto on December 28, 2013. Bargnani was booed during pregame introductions and jeered every time he touched the ball, finishing with 12 points in a 115–100 loss. It was an underwhelming performance and representative of a player who could have been so much more during his time in Toronto. "It didn't go well," Sportsnet columnist Michael Grange said. "Bargnani was a franchise talent who lacked the drive to be a franchise player."

45 Jose Calderon

Before coming to North America, Jose Calderon was one of Europe's top point guards, but he decided to put his name into the 2005 NBA Draft to see if there would be any takers.

He watched as numerous names were called except his. "I didn't expect to be in the NBA," Calderon told *Sportsnet* magazine. "I was just going year by year and I knew every year I was getting better, but I was never drafted. So I was kind of like, *Whatever*. I was playing well and I was happy [in Spain]."

Fortunately, he got a call from Raptors general manager Rob Babcock, who had seen him play overseas, and the talented Spaniard would sign with Toronto in August 2005. The 24-year-old was known as a quality playmaker but had a tough time shooting in his first NBA season in 2005–06, averaging 5.5 points in 64 games. That year Mike James was the starting point guard while Calderon was mainly coming off the bench during the Raptors' terrible 27–55 campaign.

During the 2006 offseason, Raptors president and GM Bryan Colangelo, who had replaced Babcock earlier in the year, closed the chapter on James, who later left as a free agent, in favour of trading for 23-year-old Milwaukee Bucks point guard T.J. Ford, who was talented but missed the 2004–05 season with a spinal cord injury, in exchange for Charlie Villanueva.

When healthy, the six-foot Ford was a fast and athletic threat who once delivered an impressive putback jam, using his pogo stick-like springs, over seven-foot Los Angeles Clippers centre Chris Kaman.

Calderon's style was completely different. He was a classic pass-first guard who used his smarts and instincts to make others around him better. With the younger and more exciting Ford on the scene, Calderon took a backseat. Ford played 75 games (starting in 71) and was quite effective with 14 points, 7.9 assists, and 1.3 steals per contest. The 2003 Naismith College Player of the Year formed a good 1–2 punch with Calderon, who saw action in 77 games (including 11 starts), averaging 8.7 points while shooting 55.1 percent from the floor and dishing out five assists a night. Toronto's productive guard play was one of the reasons why the Raptors claimed their first division title in 2006–07.

The point guard tag team would continue until December 11, 2007, against Atlanta. After stealing the ball, Ford went in for the layup, but Hawks big man Al Horford hit him on the head, knocking Ford down with the back of his head also bouncing off the floor. He was out indefinitely.

With Ford out, Calderon would seize the opportunity. In his 56 starts that season, he averaged 13 points, 9.1 assists, and 1.2 steals. Over 82 games, he put up 11.2 points, 8.3 assists, and 1.1 steals. Looking deeper, Calderon was extremely efficient, shooting 51.9 percent from the field, 42.9 percent from beyond the arc, and

Handling the ball during the 2007 playoffs, Jose Calderon was also a superlative free throw shooter.

90.8 from the free throw line. He also took care of the ball, finishing the regular campaign with a league-leading assist-to-turnover ratio of 5.38:1. "I started playing more comfortably. I felt confident, and my teammates were confident in me," Calderon said. "Chris Bosh helped a lot…and he was 'the Guy.' When you've got the Guy on your side, it makes it easier."

Not only was CB4 supportive, but Raptors fans were, too. They were falling in love with Jose's game. Once Ford fully returned, he was the backup, but rumours swirled he wasn't pleased about it. "Saying that I'm unhappy or that I don't like the situation, I never said that, and I don't think I ever showcased that," said Ford in response to media reports he allegedly sulked after losing his starting job. "Everyone in this league wants to play. I want to play. Just because I get mad for a split second does not mean that I'm unhappy about an entire situation. That's just the competitive nature when you are out there battling. But people don't see it that way…[Calderon has] played so well this season. It has been a big year for him, and he showed the whole NBA that he's capable of being a starter in this league. I really respect what he's been able to do this year. I think he earned everything he's received."

At one point, Calderon reportedly told head coach Sam Mitchell he wanted Ford to start because he felt it was best for the club. Ford started all five games in a 2008 first-round playoff match-up against the Orlando Magic, averaging 11.6 points and 6.6 assists while Calderon had 11.8 points and seven assists per night. Alas, the Raptors would lose in the first round for the second straight year.

During the summer of 2008, Ford was traded in a multi-player deal to Indiana for Pacers big man Jermaine O'Neal, and Calderon would sign a five-year, $45 million extension. "We couldn't be happier for Jose to be in a position to sign a long-term contract and lead this team as its starting point guard," Bryan Colangelo said. "Every step along the way of his young NBA career, Jose has elevated his performance and made others on the floor better. Jose is a tremendous asset for this organization."

The 2008–09 season would prove to be an up-and-down ride for Jose. Mitchell was fired, and Calderon had some injury woes, which kept him out of the lineup. Once he returned he'd set the second-longest consecutive streak for free throws made in NBA history with 87. On March 29, 2009, against the Chicago Bulls, he'd tie Damon Stoudamire's single-game franchise record with 19 assists. He'd also shoot an NBA single-season record 98.1 percent from the free throw line. These achievements were great, but the Raptors missed the playoffs with a 33–49 record.

Before the 2009–10 campaign began, Toronto brought in point guard Jarrett Jack. He came in handy when Calderon was injured and missed some time. The 2005 first-round pick played well and even held onto the starting spot once the Spaniard returned. Suddenly, it was like the Ford/Calderon platoon again. Jack started 43 of his 82 games while having 11.4 points and five assists per contest. Calderon made 39 starts in 68 games, recording 10.3 points and 5.9 assists a night. Calderon's lustre was starting to fade especially with increased criticism over his defensive deficiencies. Unfortunately, Jack and Calderon's offensive efforts wouldn't lead Toronto back to the playoffs.

The 2010 Raptors offseason proved to be traumatic with the continuation of the franchise tradition of watching cornerstone players leave town. This time, it was Chris Bosh heading to South Beach. Toronto was in contract-shedding mode, so Calderon was on the trade block.

In fact, a deal that would have sent the Spanish guard and Reggie Evans to Charlotte for Boris Diaw and Tyson Chandler was about to happen until Bobcats owner Michael Jordan shot it down. So, Calderon remained.

Well, that was awkward.

The Raptors tried dealing their other point guard, and on November 20, 2010, after only playing 13 games, Jack was involved in a multi-player trade to New Orleans, which brought Hornets guard Jerryd Bayless and forward Peja Stojakovic to Toronto. Despite nearly being dealt, Calderon continued to soldier on as Toronto's starting point guard, ending his 2010–11 season with 9.8 points, 8.9 assists, and 1.2 steals per game. Heading into the 2012–13 campaign, Calderon would have competition yet again for his starting point guard job. In July of 2012, Toronto acquired Kyle Lowry from the Houston Rockets in a trade. "Look, I just try to be professional," Calderon said. "This is my team, and until somebody tells me different, I'm going to give everything I can. I've never had a problem with anybody. I have a great relationship with Kyle right now. We both just happen to play the same position."

Calderon would start 30 of 45 games before being shipped to the Detroit Pistons in a three-team, multi-player trade in January 2013. But during his time in Toronto, he was a professional, a gentleman, and a class act.

46 We Love Toronto

Raptors fans have heard it for years. NBA players don't want to play in Toronto because of the higher taxes, cold weather, and even the metric system. Despite the negativity there have been quite a few former and current Raptors who've expressed their love for Canada's largest city, including a once-admired-then-viciously-despised superstar. "I did not hate Toronto. I love it to this day. I still have friends there. I grew up there. I became who I am today right there in Toronto," Vince Carter said in 2012. "Toronto gave me my opportunity to be a basketball player, to fulfill a dream. I won the Rookie of the Year there. I won the dunk contest there. I've done all the wonderful things. My career highs all came right in that uniform...I have no ill feelings. I am very appreciative of the organization."

The Raptors' first ever lottery pick had nothing but praise, though the area represented unfamiliar territory. "I had never been to Toronto. I had never been to Canada except, I think, I went to the [Jackson 5] tour in Vancouver in like 1985, but I was like 11 years old," said Damon Stoudamire who played 200 games for Toronto. "This is a first class and very underrated city. I tell people that all the time. I love coming and enjoying the city when I'm back...It reminded me of like a New York without all the crime. It wasn't as dirty and grimy. It was nice because the people were nice. I had never met so many nice people in my life."

Ex-Raptors head coach Sam Mitchell also gave credit to the club's supporters. "People underestimate the fans in Toronto. Toronto is a very passionate basketball city. Toronto fans are great. They're very knowledgeable. I enjoyed my four-and-a-half years there. I miss them."

In the early days of the franchise, a trip to the Canadian frigid north was definitely a foreign experience. At the time, many players, including Doug Christie, didn't know what to expect. After he was dealt from New York to the Raptors, Christie had this reaction: "Toronto? Is that in the NBA? What the heck?"

For those NBA players brave enough to work for the Dinos, some of them had interesting adventures. In *The Breakdown with Dave & Audley* podcast interview featuring ex-Raptors Sharone Wright and Tracy Murray, Wright jokingly recalled Murray's success with Toronto's lovely ladies. "[Murray] had all the girls, I mean, *all* the girls back then...When it came to the chicks, there was only one guy that I could say was the David Beckham of Toronto...Let's just say this right here, Tie Domi, Mats Sundin, and those guys, they didn't have a chance. They hated Tracy, put it that way. For real, Robbie Alomar and those guys, they hated Tracy."

There were…uh…other things to enjoy about the city, too. Reggie Slater, who played 134 games with the Raptors, enjoyed the city's multiculturalism and open-mindedness toward basketball. "Toronto is awesome as far as great people, great diversity. The crowd, even though especially when I was there, hockey was the mainstay, people still accepted basketball. In fact people welcomed us with open arms," Slater said. "I was fortunate enough to play with some really nice guys, really competitive guys. I can't say a damn thing about my experience in Toronto. I love it over there."

Another player who couldn't get enough of the city was Amir Johnson. After the forward from Southern California was traded to Toronto in 2009, he felt the good vibes as soon as he arrived. "I walked around downtown a little bit and I kind of got like a humble feeling," told the *Toronto Sun*. "Everybody was so polite and so cool, and that's when I started loving Toronto."

During his time in the "the 6"—a nickname coined by Drake which is reportedly inspired by the No. 6 in Toronto's 416 and 647 area codes—Johnson immersed himself in the community and checked out popular events such as Caribana, Nuit Blanche, the Zombie Walk, and the Much Music Awards. He even made time to venture out to Toronto's western and eastern suburbs. "I like going down [to Mississauga]," he said. "They have a couple of malls that are pretty cool and a couple restaurants. And I go down to Scarborough for bootleg DVDs. I don't want to give up the spot, but they have legit, great DVDs."

Johnson clearly embraced the city, but why don't high profile NBA free agents see it as a viable destination? "Most of the things they hear about is the tax, and it's just too cold and too far," Johnson admits. "But once you get out here and get a couple of years out here, I'm pretty sure they'll begin to like it…And the move [the Raptors] made with Drake, I think the younger class [of NBA players] will want to just see what Toronto's all about."

47 Meet The Raptor

Ever since 1995, this talented performer has delighted NBA fans with cheeky humour, acrobatic athleticism, non-stop energy, boyish charm, and the ability to transform into an inflatable version of himself that once ate a Brooklyn Nets fan.

What's not to love about that?

This giant of the industry is no other than The Raptor.

This crowd favourite has entertained fans even during the Dinos' worst seasons. In those years, you could argue he was probably the best part of the in-game experience. The great thing about The Raptor is he's always moving, dancing, jumping, dunking, high-fiving kids, pumping up the crowd, hugging people, and clowning around with opponents, fans, officials, and cheerleaders (some have been devoured whole) all in the name of good clean fun.

No matter if he's on centre court, in the stands or on the large scoreboard, The Raptor is always engaging and up to something. "The big scoreboard played a skit in which The Raptor, walking around Toronto, came across a Heat fan playing Queen's "We Are the Champions" on a boom box," wrote Grantland's Zach Lowe. "Cut to The Raptor finding an aluminum baseball bat and smashing the boom box. Next skit: The Raptor is in yoga class, hilarious on its own, since a large dinosaur performing downward dog next to a bunch of young women in yoga clothes, everyone acting as if this is perfectly normal, is a great joke by itself. But lo and behold, the same Heat fan, wearing a Dwyane Wade jersey, happened to be in The Raptor's yoga class, and he was one of those annoying grunters. Cut to The Raptor tossing a giant yoga ball, quite hard, flush in the guy's face. Brilliant."

Unfortunately, during a 2013 preseason event in Halifax, Nova Scotia, The Raptor suffered a torn Achilles tendon and was originally expected to miss the entire 2013–14 season.

"I called him. I talked to him," Raptors head coach **Dwane Casey** said. "I was disappointed. My daughter cried; she was upset. He's a good man. He'll bounce back. He's in good hands with the physicians. The Raptor will be back, he will be back. We need his spirit."

In The Raptor's absence, his dinosaur cousin, Stripes, filled in the best he could.

But on March 23, 2014, The Raptor returned after being sidelined five-and-a-half months, while undergoing rehab, and everyone couldn't be happier. "We're so excited to have him back," said Anton Wright, manager of Raptors game operations. "Our fans have missed him greatly, his special style of entertainment. We're glad our fans will be able to experience that once again."

48 Just Plain Ugly

16–66. It's a terrible win-loss record shared between the 1968–69 Phoenix Suns, 1979–80 Detroit Pistons, 2014–15 Minnesota Timberwolves, and your 1997–98 Toronto Raptors.

After having a 30–52 showing in 1996–97, a nine-win improvement over Toronto's first campaign, you figured the Raptors would continue to go forward. Things began well during the 1997 NBA Draft when general manager Isiah Thomas picked a talented high schooler from Mount Zion Christian Academy with the ninth overall selection—Tracy McGrady. The 18-year-old was a lanky and athletically gifted 6'8" kid who would prove to be an NBA scoring machine years later. But on draft night, he was just a young man with plenty of promise who could be a Raptors star for years to come.

Toronto seemed to be on the way up until July 1997, when the club found out its young 6'11" big man, Sharone Wright, was nearly killed in a car accident in Macon, Georgia. According to the Bibb County Sheriff's department, Wright was driving his car over the speed limit when he dodged an animal and lost control. After his vehicle flipped over several times, Wright suffered a broken left arm, shoulder, collarbone, and bruised ribs, but his two passengers were not seriously hurt. It was reported Wright was running late for an appearance, but after the accident, he said critics accused him of drinking and driving. "I mean, I almost died, and people are saying these things," he said. "You've got some real negative, nasty, evil people in this world." Unfortunately, Wright was never the same. "The crash killed me playing at a high level," he admitted. "You take away basically my whole left side and the ability to play with power the way I had played, and I was a shadow of the player I once was."

It was definitely an ominous way to lead into the 1997–98 season that would become a franchise lowlight. Early in the new campaign, Toronto had a 1–2 record going into its November 6 home game with the Seattle SuperSonics. The Sonics, who'd win 61 times that regular season, were led by Vin Baker's 35 points and Gary Payton's 19 points and 13 assists in the 109–92 victory.

Little did the Raptors and their fans realize that would be the beginning of an epic nosedive, which would set the tone for an incredibly turbulent year. The defeats started to mount for the Dinos, who battled some injury woes, and some were not even close.

- **November 12:** The New York Knicks, with help from Larry Johnson's 27 points, blew out the Raptors, 93–70.
- **November 15:** The Indiana Pacers, led by Chris Mullin's 20 points, served up a 105–77 thrashing at SkyDome.
- **November 20:** In Houston the Rockets, who had eight players score in double figures, pounded the Dinos 127–97.
- **December 3:** In Utah, Karl Malone's 23 points and 15 rebounds helped the Jazz win 115–98.
- **December 5:** In Phoenix, Jason Kidd had a 14-assist performance in the Suns' 110–91 victory.

Toronto did have some close games during that stretch too, but after suffering a December 9 defeat against the Charlotte Hornets, the Raptors became the new owners of a streak they wanted nothing to do with—a franchise-worst 17 straight losses. The ugliness wasn't only on the court, but in the boardroom as well.

During the losing skid in November, Isiah Thomas resigned due to his stormy relationship with majority owner Allan Slaight and his failed attempt to buy him out.

"It's a quitter who leaves now," Slaight said. "It doesn't sound like the real Isiah Thomas. A winner wouldn't walk away with the way things are going now. To leave now at whatever we are, he would have 'Quitter' branded on his forehead."

Once the popular Thomas announced his departure, it would hit the team hard.

"I know the guys have very, very strong love for Isiah Thomas," Raptors head coach Darrell Walker said. "I know when they find out, they're not gonna be very happy."

He was correct. Toronto's star guard, Damon Stoudamire, who was mentored by Thomas, wanted to escape the chaos. Other players also spoke out. "The reason why I came here was because of Isiah Thomas," Raptors forward Walt Williams said. "I can't envision what happens from here. We just have to go out and play. That's all we can do."

Imagine young T-Mac who had to soak this in. He was stunned. "It's just crazy," said McGrady said. "I guess this is my introduction to the NBA. I'm glad to get it over with in my rookie year." Even Marcus Camby's agent offered his take. "I can honestly say every player on the team wants to leave with Isiah," Alex Johnson said. "There's no reason for players to stay in Toronto. To lose a cornerstone like Isiah is a big blow. Isiah got these kids to buy into a concept. I don't think the current owners understand the sense of family and loyalty players have here."

Thomas' former Indiana Hoosiers teammate, Glen Grunwald, would assume the GM duties. On February 13, 1998, Stoudamire's wish was granted when he was dealt to his hometown Portland Trail Blazers in a multi-player trade. "I'm glad to be going to a situation where I can win," Stoudamire said. "The Blazers are an up-and-coming young team that will be going to the playoffs every year. I'm going to give them every opportunity to sign me."

If that wasn't tough enough, once the Stoudamire deal was done, Walker, who wasn't happy with the club's new direction, resigned as head coach, and his assistant, Butch Carter, took over. The Raptors finished the season losing 16 of their final 17 games, including 13 consecutive defeats at one point. "We didn't win a lot of games," said ex-Raptors forward John Wallace, who had a career-high 14 points per game in 1997–98. "But we always went down fighting."

49 The 1998–99 Lockout Season

Vince Carter was waiting to be unleashed. Because of the NBA's third lockout in league history, the soon-to-be rookie superstar had to be patient as the league and its players union worked on hammering out a deal. The lockout would last from July 1998 to January 1999.

As a result, the start of the season was delayed, which meant teams had a shortened 50-game schedule. With fewer contests played in less time, that meant VC and the Raptors had to deal with back-to-back-to-back games on a few occasions including:

- March 15 (vs. the Charlotte Hornets), March 16 (vs. the New Jersey Nets), and March 17 (vs. the Detroit Pistons)
- March 21 (vs. the New York Knicks), March 22 (vs. the Nets), and March 23 (vs. the Chicago Bulls)
- April 19 (vs. the Orlando Magic), April 20 (vs. the Atlanta Hawks), and April 21 (vs. the Washington Wizards)

In those back-to-back-to-backs, Toronto had a 7–2 record. One of the reasons why was Vinsanity. During that stretch his best performances were: 28 points vs. the Pistons, 23 points, 12 rebounds, and four blocks vs. the Knicks, 23 points and 11 rebounds vs. the Bulls, and 20 points and 15 rebounds vs. the Nets. Despite the insane schedule, Carter wasn't looking like a rookie.

"My first year with the Raptors was the 98–99 season," said former longtime play-by-play commentator Chuck Swirsky. "That season opened up in 1999 in February, and it was a blur. We had 50 games in like 100 days. It was just so quick and so fast, and Vince arrived on the scene and was dominant. I mean, he was throwing down, as we know, some wicked jams. His elevation was off the charts. People were just stunned. Their breath was taken away every time he showed at an arena and hit a big shot or more importantly took it strong to the rack."

One of those times was in a March 1999 game against the Hawks in Atlanta. Dikembe Mutombo, the Hawks' 7-foot-2 shot-blocking menace, was notorious for finger wagging his opponents after denying them above the rim. That didn't stop a 22-year-old rookie from driving baseline, jumping up, and slamming it down over Mount Mutombo and then staring at him afterward.

Something was different about this Carter kid. He arrived at a time when the franchise just moved from the SkyDome into the brand new Air Canada Centre in February 1999. It was a fresh beginning for a club, which knew nothing but high volume losing in its first three seasons.

Suddenly, with guys like Carter, his happier and improving cousin Tracy McGrady, the addition of grizzled veteran Charles Oakley, and a seemingly stable head coach, Butch Carter, on board, the team's fortunes were getting brighter.

In fact, during the lockout season, the Raptors enjoyed some signature wins, including an 88–87 victory against Reggie Miller's Indiana Pacers and a 93–91 triumph against David Robinson, a young Tim Duncan, and the rest of the future 1999 NBA champion Spurs in San Antonio. Yes, the Raptors would finish that quick campaign with a 23–27 record and no appearance in the playoffs, but the league was starting to realize this franchise wasn't going to be a doormat for much longer.

The NBA would have another work stoppage in 2011, but Raptors fans would always recall the 1998–99 lockout season being the one where their club finally showed signs of success. An exciting ride was on the horizon.

50 Done Deal

Raptors fans are very familiar with what trades didn't work and how destructive they were to the franchise, but what about the ones that did deliver? There were several that shaped this team into a playoff contender at different points in the Dinos' existence.

Here are the biggest ones:

Vince Carter for Antawn Jamison at the NBA Draft

The official 1998 deal was that Golden State's fifth overall pick (Carter) and cash were sent to the Raptors in exchange for their fourth overall selection (Jamison). Both players—and former college teammates—sealed the move by trading their team caps with each other while on stage with NBA commissioner David Stern standing between them.

General manager Glen Grunwald orchestrated this monumental swap, bringing the Raptors a superstar talent who would catapult the franchise into the sports mainstream.

Jamison, who played three years with Carter at the University of North Carolina, was a two-time NBA All-Star, but Toronto got the better end of this transaction.

Kyle Lowry for Gary Forbes and a First-Round Pick

That's all the Houston Rockets received for Lowry? GM Bryan Colangelo pulled off a steal in July 2012, which eventually led to Toronto's strong-willed point guard becoming an All-Star leader who'd help bring the Raptors back to respectability.

Antonio Davis for the Draft Rights to Jonathan Bender

Grunwald took a gamble by giving up a first-round pick, but it paid off when the Indiana Pacers bench player became a solid starter in Toronto and one of the club's reliable anchors on three Raptors playoff teams in the early 2000s. As for Bender, the athletic big man was drafted out of high school but never lived up to his hype because injuries derailed his NBA career.

The Rudy Gay Seven-Player Trade

GM Masai Ujiri delivered a masterstroke with a 2013 deal that transformed the Raptors from a club that heard the words "tank" and "Andrew Wiggins" a lot to a playoff contender. The trade gave Toronto an instant bench with Greivis Vasquez, Patrick Patterson, Chuck Hayes, and John Salmons coming from Sacramento in exchange for Gay, Quincy Acy, and Aaron Gray.

Charles Oakley, Sean Marks, and Cash for Marcus Camby

Grunwald, realizing his young squad needed toughness and leadership, acquired Oakley in this June 25, 1998, trade. The playoff warrior, with his intimidating presence and opinionated personality, wasn't afraid to motivate Vince Carter when the team needed him most. The deal also worked out for the New York Knicks who, with Camby's help, advanced to the 1999 NBA Finals.

Antonio Davis for Jalen Rose and a First-Round Pick

After the firing of Rob Babcock in January 2006, interim GM Wayne Embry made this move with the Knicks, which cleared a considerable amount of cap room for the next GM, Bryan Colangelo, to work with. During that offseason Colangelo would then re-tool the roster to create the 2006–07 Atlantic Division champion Raptors.

Amir Johnson and Sonny Weems for Carlos Delfino and Roko Ukic

For Colangelo the centrepiece of this August 18, 2009, trade was Johnson. Prior to this transaction, the Pistons' 2005 second-round pick, who wasn't playing much with Detroit, was already dealt to Milwaukee in June 2009. Colangelo was happy to scoop up the kid and a decent player in Weems for Delfino, who wasn't expected to return to Toronto, and the Rob Babcock second-round draft selection in 2005, Ukic. Johnson would prove to be a very useful forward for many years to come.

Other Notable Trades

June 2014—Lou Williams and Lucas Nogueira from the Atlanta Hawks for John Salmons

June 2006—T.J. Ford from the Milwaukee Bucks for Charlie Villanueva and cash

February 1996—Doug Christie, Herb Williams, and cash from the New York Knicks for Willie Anderson and Victor Alexander

December 2003—Jalen Rose, Donyell Marshall, and Lonny Baxter from the Chicago Bulls for Antonio Davis, Jerome Williams, and Chris Jefferies

January 2001—Keon Clark, Tracy Murray, and Mamadou N'Diaye from the Denver Nuggets for Kevin Willis, Garth Joseph, Aleksandar Radojevic, and a second-round pick

June 2006—Rasho Nesterovic from the San Antonio Spurs for Eric Williams, Matt Bonner, and a second-round pick

October 2005—Mike James from the Houston Rockets for Rafer Alston

July 2010—Leandro Barbosa and Dwayne Jones from the Phoenix Suns for Hedo Turkoglu

June 2006—Kris Humphries and Robert Whaley from the Utah Jazz for Rafael Araujo

Marcus Camby, Steve Novak, Quentin Richardson, and Draft Picks for Andrea Bargnani

In the summer of 2013, Ujiri became an instant fan favourite when he unloaded the often injured seven-foot Italian to the Knicks for Camby, Novak, Richardson, a first and two second-round selections. It didn't matter that only Novak would suit up for Toronto, Ujiri still came out on top by acquiring three draft picks and getting rid of Bargnani's hefty salary remaining on his contract.

Morris Peterson's Draft Rights in a Three-Team Deal

In January of 1999, the Raptors, Minnesota Timberwolves, and Denver Nuggets teamed up on this trade. Toronto received Micheal Williams (yes, that's how you spell his first name), Zeljko Rebraca, a 1999 first-round pick (Jonathan Bender), and a 2000 first-round selection (Morris Peterson) while Chauncey Billups and Tyson Wheeler were dealt to Denver.

Grunwald would obtain one of the franchise's most loved players in Mo Pete, who would be on three Toronto playoff teams in 2001, 2002, and 2007.

Alvin Williams, Kenny Anderson, Gary Trent, and Draft Picks for Damon Stoudamire, Walt Williams, and Carlos Rogers

The February 1998 trade looked like this: Stoudamire, Williams, and Rogers to the Portland Trail Blazers for Anderson, Williams, Trent, two first-rounds picks and one second-round pick. Grunwald was in a tough situation with Stoudamire wanting out of town, but in receiving Williams, the longtime Raptor would become a fan favourite and good playoff performer in the early 2000s.

51 What's Your Name?

Back in 2014, Charles Barkley famously butchered the pronunciation of Raptors centre Jonas Valanciunas on TNT's NBA coverage, but when Sir Charles does it, we find it funny and charming. Over the years, though, the following Raptors players frustrated many who bravely attempted to say their names out loud.

Be afraid no longer.

Here's how you say some of the toughest ones in Raptors history:

- 2004 First-Round Pick, Centre, Rafael Araujo—ha-fay-el ar-RU-joe
- Centre, Mengke Bateer—MONK BAH-teer
- Centre, Primoz Brezec—PREE-mohsh BREHZ-its
- Forward, Pops Mensah-Bonsu—PAHPS MEHN-sah BAHN-soo
- 2014 First-Round Pick, Forward, Bruno Caboclo—Bruno cuh-BO-clo
- Forward, Jorge Garbajosa—hohr-HAY gar-BAH-hoh-sah
- Centre, Mamadou N'Diaye—MAH-ma-due en-Jye
- Centre, Rasho Nesterovic—RAH-shoh neh-STEHR-uh-vich
- Centre, Lucas Nogueira—Lucas no-GARE-uh
- Centre, Aleksandar Radojevic—Alexander Ra-doy-a-vich
- Centre, Uros Slokar—OO-rosh SLOW-car
- Centre, Pape Sow—pop sew
- Forward, Peja Stojakovic—PAY-zhah stoy-AH-koh-vich
- Centre, Zan Tabak—zhon tah-BOCK

- Raptors General Manager, Masai Ujiri—mah-SIGH u-JEER-ee
- Guard, Roko Ukic—Ro-ko OO-keech
- Guard, Ben Uzoh—Ben ooh-zo
- Centre, Jonas Valanciunas—YO-ness vah-lan-CHEW-niss
- Guard, Greivis Vasquez—GRAY-viss VASS-kez
- Centre, Jake Voskuhl—Jake VAHS-kuhl
- Forward, Hedo Turkoglu—HEE-doh TURK-ah-lou

52 The NBA's United Nations

Zan Tabak and Vincenzo Esposito were Raptors pioneers. In 1995 the Croatian centre and Italian guard were the first foreigners to ever play a regular season game in franchise history.

At the time, little did they know, they'd blaze a path for many future international NBA hopefuls who would one day suit up for Toronto.

The Raptors foreign player invasion intensified in the 2000s when general manager Bryan Colangelo, who was a big fan of overseas talent, was in charge. In 2006 he drafted Andrea Bargnani first overall; signed Spanish forward Jorge Garbajosa and two-time Euroleague MVP Anthony Parker, who was an American playing for Maccabi Tel-Aviv; traded for Slovenian centre, Rasho Nesterovic; and hired former Benetton Treviso GM Maurizio Gherardini as Colangelo's assistant GM and vice president.

Over the years, Toronto was a United Nations of sorts featuring players from countries such as Argentina, Brazil, China, Italy, and Spain, to name a few. When evaluating the Raptors' best ever international talent, men such as Jose Calderon and Bargnani (stop booing!) are at the top of the list. Even though, they received all the press, there were some underrated foreign-born players who could hoop.

Here are three of them who provided Toronto some international flavour.

Jorge Garbajosa

The former Spanish League Finals MVP played 11 seasons in Europe before signing a three-year contract with the Raptors. "Jorge Garbajosa has contributed toward winning at every stop in his professional career," Colangelo said. "We anticipate he will bring experience, leadership, and toughness to this basketball team."

The 6'9" forward did exactly that. Wearing Vince Carter's old No. 15, he was a glue guy, who did the little things that contributed to winning basketball on the 2006–07 Atlantic Division champion Raptors squad. His efforts were recognized with a December 2006 Eastern Conference Rookie of the Month award, and he'd later be named to the 2006–07 NBA All-Rookie first team after averaging 8.5 points and 4.9 rebounds in 67 games.

But on March 26, 2007, in Boston, Garbajosa's Raptors career was changed forever. In the fourth quarter, he tried to block a jam by Celtics big man Al Jefferson and then landed awkwardly causing a gruesome dislocated left ankle, ligament tear, and fractured fibula, which all required surgery. After the fall happened on the television broadcast, you could hear Garbajosa yelling in pain while fellow Spaniard Calderon tried to comfort him.

Garbajosa was out for the 2007 postseason and was never the same. In the 2007–08 campaign, he played seven games before having another left ankle surgery in December 2007.

In June of 2008, the Raptors released him. "After a long, difficult, and sometimes emotional process stemming from a traumatic injury to a key player, it was concluded that parting ways was the

Drafted No. 1 overall in the 2006 NBA Draft, Andrea Bargnani, an Italian, was part of the Raptors' ethnically diverse roster.

best thing for both Jorge and the Raptors organization," Colangelo said. "We wish Jorge nothing but the best with his basketball future."

Leandro Barbosa

"The Brazilian Blur" was known for his speed on the court. After being a part of some high scoring Steve Nash teams with the Phoenix Suns, the guard was traded to Toronto in the Hedo Turkoglu July 2010 multi-player deal.

The 2015 NBA champion never started a game with the Raptors but was solid off the bench. In Barbosa's first year with Toronto, he would score 20 or more points 10 times and would hit 72 three-pointers while putting up 13.3 points per game. But his stay wouldn't last. During the 2011–12 season, he'd be dealt again—this time to the Indiana Pacers.

Carlos Delfino

The Argentinian arrived in Toronto via a trade from Detroit, which saw two second-round picks go to the Pistons. A slick shooter and decent defender, Delfino was an effective member of Toronto's second unit in the Raptors' 2007–08 campaign. In the 2008 playoffs, he scored 16 points in Game 2 and 14 points in Game 5 before Toronto lost to the Orlando Magic. In his lone Raptors season, Delfino averaged nine points and 4.4 rebounds in 82 games.

After playing 2008–09 in Russia, he didn't want to come back to Toronto, so in August of 2009, he and Roko Ukic were dealt to the Milwaukee Bucks for Amir Johnson and Sonny Weems. "After drafting DeMar DeRozan and trading for Marco Belinelli, Hedo Turkoglu, and Antoine Wright, Carlos made it clear he would prefer to play elsewhere if he were to return to the NBA," Colangelo said. "There were limited sign-and-trade scenarios available, but acquiring Amir Johnson in this deal gives us another long, talented, young big man whose best basketball is ahead of him."

53 Salami and Cheese

Chuck Swirsky's best on-air hits include:

- "You can get out the salami and cheese, mama. This ballgame is over!"
- "Onions, baby, onions!"
- "Oh my Bosh!"
- "That was sick, wicked, and nasty!"

From 1998 to 2008, the high energy Raptors play-by-play man entertained many Canadian basketball fans with his enthusiastic and creative broadcast style. "The Swirsk," who performed television and radio duties, became a fan favourite, best known for his colourful catchphrases, especially his "salami and cheese" call. "It started with receiving a letter from a viewer, and they couldn't break away from the television set because they were really into the Raptors, and they wanted to know, 'Can you please let me know when the Raps win a ballgame, so I can finally head to the refrigerator to make a sandwich?…By the way, I like salami and cheese.' This happened like four or five years ago," Swirsky recalled. "So the first time after I received that letter, the Raptors were in front by like 10 with about a minute and 20 to go, I thought that was safe, so I said, 'Get out the salami and cheese, mama, this ballgame is over!' It just caught on."

For many Raptors supporters, hearing Swirsky's voice triggers warm memories of the franchise's most exciting years. Chuck also fondly remembers those early days. "I joined the ballclub in year three—in 1998—and I think the honeymoon period was still going on, although fans were starting to get a little bit impatient as far as putting a winning club together," Swirsky told Sportsnet. ca. "It was a perfect storm because the club drafted Vince Carter, Glen Grunwald acquired Kevin Willis and Charles Oakley, Tracy McGrady was entering his second year, and the Raptors franchise was about to take off. I think the opening of the Air Canada Centre in 1999 really set the foundation for a world-class building with players that were not only in their primes, in terms of Oakley and Willis, but McGrady was just an up-and-coming star—everyone could see that—and then Vince arrived and made a huge splash."

After a great 10-year run in Toronto, Swirsky, who became a Canadian citizen in 2008, decided to accept a Chicago Bulls radio play-by-play position and leave a loyal Toronto fan base which, for the most part, would miss him. "There's lots of good play-by-play guys out there, but only one Chuck Swirsky," Tom Anselmi, then-executive vice president and chief operating officer of Maple Leaf Sports & Entertainment (MLSE), which owned the Raptors, said in a statement. "He is a big loss to our organization. His passion for basketball and passion for our fans makes him one of the game's great ambassadors."

54 Vince, Time to Be Clutch

Vince Carter never hit a playoff game-winner for the Raptors. Of course, Toronto's fans begrudgingly know that and don't appreciate you opening the old wound regarding his last-second Game 7 miss against the Philadelphia 76ers in 2001.

It still stings.

Regardless, Vince did delight his fans with many game-winning plays in the regular season. But they seemingly came in bunches during one month—March of 2000. During that time the Raptors were in the midst of a stretch where they'd win 11 of 12 games, and the streak was ignited by Carter's 51-point explosion against the Phoenix Suns on February 27. Vinsanity would rule the month of March with his last-second heroics, and here are the examples to prove it.

March 1, 2000

In Boston the Raptors trailed 94–93 with 3.2 seconds left, and Tracy McGrady inbounded a pass to Carter. With a Celtics defender draped all over him, VC drained a fadeaway three-pointer at the buzzer to win the contest 96–94. Carter finished with a game-high 28 points and stunned the Beantown crowd. "Well, there's a lot of startled Celtic players right now, but superboy did it. Wow," said Celtics television colour analyst and Hall of Famer Tommy Heinsohn.

March 8, 2000

At the Staples Center in Los Angeles, Carter put on a show. With Toronto down 90–82 and under 3:35 to go in the fourth quarter, Dee Brown sent an alley-oop lob pass, which Carter reached back for with one hand and then hammered a highlight reel jam that got the L.A. fans buzzing.

Even the Clippers television colour analyst was surprised. "How does he do this?" said a laughing Bill Walton.

Carter wasn't done.

The Raptors were behind 94–92 with 1.5 seconds remaining, and VC received a McGrady inbounds pass and then drilled a wide-open three at the buzzer to lock up the 95–94 victory. "He is invincible," said Clippers television play-by-play announcer Ralph Lawler.

Carter had a game-high 23 points in the win. "An incredible performance by Vince Carter," Walton said.

March 19, 2000

Hitting last-second game-winning three-pointers is nice, but Carter wanted to show you another way to get the job done. At the Air Canada Centre against the Houston Rockets, the game was tied at 98 with 11 seconds left. Houston made the mistake of having Shandon Anderson guard VC one-on-one. Carter blew past the forward for a clutch two-handed baseline slam that gave Toronto a 100–98 lead, which would be the final score.

Rockets television colour analyst Calvin Murphy loved Air Canada's aerial attack.

"Let me tell you what he just did," he said, "he made me a believer."

Carter, who scored a game-high 37 points, brought the ACC crowd to its feet, making March 2000 a month to remember.

55 Who Needs You?

Over the years Raptors supporters have had lots of practice booing players who wronged them in some way. Guys like T-Mac, VC, Antonio Davis, CB4, and Bargnani, have all felt the wrath of Toronto's passionate fan base. In 2010, while with the Detroit Pistons, McGrady called out Raptors fans suggesting they didn't even know why they were still booing him after all these years. "I'm telling you, they really don't," he said. "It's not like I was like Chris Bosh in selling out the city—like the city was horrible or something...making crazy comments about the city. [In 2000] it was Toronto or going back home to Orlando. That's pretty much it. I love the city. Every time I come back, I really enjoy my time here."

In 2011 lovable ex-Raptor Charles Oakley also couldn't understand the club's followers.

"They are into the numbers and the hype, but then when the hype leaves, they get mad at the person," Oakley told the *Toronto Sun*. "Like Bosh, they boo him. Why boo him? Why boo Vince, Tracy? I mean, why boo any of us? We didn't do nothing wrong. We didn't trade ourselves. Management did that."

Regardless of Oakley's logic, Toronto fans are always willing to vocalize their feelings even without knowing the full story. Here are a few other examples of players who will not be receiving a Christmas fruitcake from Raptors followers any time soon.

B.J. Armstrong
A three-time NBA champion on Michael Jordan's Chicago Bulls clubs of the early 1990s, he was a three-point specialist who would be Toronto's first pick in the 1995 Expansion Draft. But the

baby-faced shooter wanted nothing to do with the Raptors, so he was traded to the Golden State Warriors in a multi-player swap.

Kenny Anderson

The point guard, who was moved to Toronto in the 1998 Damon Stoudamire trade, refused to join the Raptors and forced them to deal him to Boston. In a 2010 interview with BackSportsPage. com, Anderson explained his decision. "No, I didn't want to play in Canada due to the tax issues. It was money at the time," he said. "People thought I didn't want to play with the team. It wasn't that. Back then it was like double the taxes, half your money. Nobody knew that. Now they set it up where if you're one of their players, you can get more money and bonuses to back it up. But back then I thought I couldn't do that. And I had my money saved and all that. So, I gave up my million dollars to not play because I had money at the time to deal with that."

Alonzo Mourning

The 2014 Naismith Memorial Basketball Hall of Fame inductee was a part of the 2004 blockbuster Vince Carter multi-player deal. At that time Mourning was hungering for a chance at an NBA championship and knew his title window was closing, considering his age and past health issues (2003 kidney transplant). As a result, he never reported to the Raptors plus the team had to eat the remaining $9 million on his contract.

Hedo Turkoglu

Acquired by Toronto via a sign-and-trade in a July 2009 four-team deal, the 6'10" forward was fresh off helping the Orlando Magic reach the NBA Finals. The Raptors thought he could assist their return to the postseason, but it didn't turn out that way. In March of 2010, with the club in a hunt for a playoff spot, Turkoglu, who signed a five-year, $53 million free-agent contract, was benched once it was revealed he was reportedly out in Toronto's trendy Yorkville district after a Raptors defeat against the Denver Nuggets, a game he didn't play in because of a stomach virus.

Busted!

Of course, Raptors fans and the club were angry. Not only was Turkoglu partying the night away when he was supposed to be sick, but he also was having a disaster of a season on the court, averaging 11.3 points in 74 games. With the rough way Turkoglu's year finished, he wanted out of Toronto.

In a Turkish television interview published on TheScore.com, he explained his side of things. "After a sleepless Thursday night and not having eaten much, [the Raptors] asked me how I felt. I explained the situation and said, 'I didn't sleep. I'm not feeling good.' Their answer was, 'We shouldn't put you on the court without practicing,'" Turkoglu said. "Our Italian physiologists said, 'You are not starting today. After training on Sunday, you'll give it a go against Miami and Charlotte.' I nodded and did some weight work on gameday. Although they allowed me to go home, I wanted to watch the [Denver] game with my teammates. After the game I went back home. Some European teammates called me and said, 'Hedo, are you sleeping?' Then they told me where they were hanging out, which is actually 100 metres away from my home. I said okay, and when I arrived, all the guys were here. And if you check the camera records, you will see that I left there in 15–20 minutes with Andrea Bargnani. I guarantee it. And if they prove me wrong, I will give back my contract!

"The day after, the whole controversy erupted. They claimed that I intentionally skipped the game. And the worst thing is that the people making the claims were from Raptors management and they wanted to suspend me for two games. My attorney settled the dispute, and Mr. Colangelo promised me that things would stay between us. The following day, I was fined and did not play against Miami. After the statements of the front office, everybody in Toronto heard the news. Think about the situation I am in...I have played for four different teams in 10 years in the NBA and I have never experienced anything like this. I bet nobody can prove these 'party machine' rumours."

Turkoglu's wild time in Toronto ended when he was traded to the Phoenix Suns in July 2010.

56 MLSE Buys the Raptors

If you were a Raptors fan in the early years, the thought of Toronto's hockey team, the Maple Leafs, owning your club sounded odd. But things started to change in November 1996, when John Bitove Jr., the man who built the Raptors organization from scratch, failed to gather an estimated $65 million for a shotgun clause exercised by fellow team part-owner Allan Slaight in time to buy out his 39.5 percent ownership of the club. As a result Bitove moved on, and Slaight, the owner of media giant Standard Broadcasting, was now the Raptors' new majority owner.

At the time Isiah Thomas had a minority stake in the team but would later suffer a similar fate as Bitove. One of Slaight's changes was to work with the Maple Leafs on a new building since he wanted to share a facility. In 1997 the Raptors officially broke ground on the Air Canada Centre (ACC) project, but in 1998 during the construction process, Maple Leaf Gardens Limited (MLGL), which owned the Maple Leafs and the aging arena, Maple Leaf Gardens, purchased the young NBA franchise and the ACC from Slaight and minority owner Bank of Nova Scotia for $467 million.

That same year MLGL changed its name to Maple Leaf Sports & Entertainment (MLSE).

Yes, the Maple Leafs and Raptors were now owned by the same company and would share a new home. It would begin a competitive relationship that still goes on to this day. Over the years MLSE would become larger and more profitable, owning not just the Leafs, Raptors, and ACC, but also the Major League Soccer team, Toronto FC; American Hockey League club, the Toronto Marlies; various digital television channels; and a stake in Maple Leaf Square, a multi-use development next to the arena.

In 2011 Canada's largest telecommunications giants and intense rivals, Bell and Rogers Communications, would officially pay $1.32 billion to the Ontario Teachers' Pension Plan for shared majority ownership of MLSE. Regardless of that landmark deal, it didn't change the fact the Leafs and Raptors were still part of the same family, which would always cause some tension at the dinner table.

57 1–15

Was November 2005 a good month for you? It certainly wasn't for the Raptors.

In their first full campaign without Vince Carter since his dramatic exit in late 2004, Toronto would get off to a horrific start. It didn't help that in the first month of the 2005–06 season, Loren Woods, Rafael Araujo, and Aaron Williams all received starting minutes at the centre spot. Plus, having an underachieving rookie forward, Joey Graham, in your first unit wasn't a positive either.

It all added up to a nasty 1–15 month, including a franchise worst nine straight losses to start a season.

Here's what happened:

November 2, 2005
Washington Wizards win 99–96, Raptors fall to 0–1

In Toronto's regular season opener, the home team was down by three with 12.7 seconds left, but rookie Charlie Villanueva air balled a three-pointer, and Jalen Rose also missed a three as the Raptors shot 24 percent in the fourth quarter in the defeat. "We had a chance to win the game. We missed shots down the stretch." Rose explained. "This team needs me to step up in crucial situations. I did not do that. I had a couple of turnovers down the stretch, missed a couple of shots and I can't do that. I take this loss upon myself."

November 4, 2005
New Jersey Nets win 102–92, Raptors fall to 0–2

Vince Carter scored 20, but it was Richard Jefferson, who had a game-high 35 points and 11 rebounds, that hurt Toronto the most in the New Jersey victory. During the loss Raptors fans showed no mercy for Rafael Araujo, who badly missed two shots and then had two quick fouls in just five minutes.

November 5, 2005
Detroit Pistons win 117–84, Raptors fall to 0–3

Joey Graham and second-year player Matt Bonner couldn't contain Pistons forward Tayshaun Prince, who scored 15 of his 27 points in the first half as Detroit blew out the Raptors. The Pistons dominated on the boards, outrebounding Toronto 57–35, including 16–3 on the offensive glass. "We didn't play with much energy," said Chris Bosh who scored 12 points. "It's the same story again."

Head coach Sam Mitchell added, "I think our guys are just overwhelmed. This is a brutal way to be introduced to the NBA. But no one feels sorry for us, and we can't feel sorry for ourselves. We just have to remember these beatings and give them back someday."

November 7, 2005

Cleveland Cavaliers win 105–93, Raptors fall to 0–4

LeBron James did his thing, scoring a game-high 27 points, but Toronto's centres, Loren Woods and Rafael Araujo, were invisible with zero and two points, respectively, in the loss. Mitchell was trying to find a solution to motivate his struggling players. "John Wooden said the best teacher is the bench," Mitchell said. "If I go that route, and I haven't decided, it won't be because I'm angry. It will be that we have to grab some people's attention. The only way to get people's attention is with playing time."

November 11, 2005

Utah Jazz win 99–84, Raptors fall to 0–5

Jazz big man Mehmet Okur had a 29-point, 12-rebound night as the Raptors delivered another uninspired performance, which resulted in Toronto fans booing them off the court after the game. Coach Sam Mitchell benched Loren Woods and Rafael Araujo, but Aaron Williams wasn't much of an upgrade, finishing with two points and three rebounds. "Teams are wanting the ball more than us right now," Chris Bosh said.

With the piling defeats, Raptors general manager Rob Babcock wanted the club's followers to be patient. "We just hope that the fans understand our plan, which is building for the future." At the game one Toronto supporter had a sign, which read "For Rent, Raptor fan."

November 13, 2005

Seattle SuperSonics win 126–121 in overtime, Raptors fall to 0–6
Toronto roared back after being down 18 in the fourth quarter to force overtime, but Rashard Lewis' 41 points and the fact Seattle outscored the Raptors 9–4 in the extra quarter would be too much to handle.

Lewis wasn't impressed with the victory. "This win doesn't mean anything. We've got to go out there and beat a legit team, a real good team. This team hasn't won a game." Added Raptors rookie Charlie Villanueva: "Nobody wants to be 0–6. We tried to get our first win and we came really close."

November 15, 2005

Philadelphia 76ers win 104–92, Raptors fall to 0–7
Philadelphia's duo of Allen Iverson (34 points and 12 assists) and Chris Webber (28 points and 16 rebounds) were a handful for Toronto to deal with in its seventh consecutive defeat. Chris Bosh, who had 19 points and 17 rebounds, is still puzzled about the Raptors' losing ways. "I don't understand it, I don't," he said. "I guess it comes with experience."

Carlos Villanueva had a suggestion: "We need to throw the first punch instead of letting teams throw the first punch."

November 16, 2005

76ers win 121–115, Raptors fall to 0–8
Allen Iverson would sting Toronto again—this time with 42 points while Andre Iguodala, who was selected behind Rafael Araujo in the 2004 NBA Draft, scored 26 in the victory. Araujo had another forgettable game with zero points. "The cameras were actually put on me when Toronto's pick came up, so I thought I was going here, but they passed," said Iguodala of his draft night experience. "I think I'm in a good situation right now."

During the second half, Mitchell smashed his clipboard into the scorer's table, throwing it in frustration. "People need to understand these guys want to win," Mitchell said. "They understand that we're 0–8 and they want to win. But the last two games and basically the whole year we've just gotten off to horrendous starts."

At one point a fan was escorted from the Air Canada Centre after holding up a sign which read "Raptor Killer" with a picture of Rob Babcock on it.

November 18, 2005
Boston Celtics win 100–93, Raptors fall to 0–9
Toronto was in this game when it cut the lead to one at 90–89 on a Chris Bosh slam with 1:59 left, but Boston answered with a 10–4 run, including some points from Paul Pierce and Ricky Davis, who both scored 26, to secure the Celtics victory. "We just have to learn how to win," said Carlos Villanueva who scored 18 points off the bench. "We played a decent half but didn't get it done when it counted the most. We dug ourselves this hole and now we have to dig out.

November 20, 2005
Miami Heat lose 107–94, Raptors improve to 1–9
It's a miracle!

Toronto would go on an 18–2 run in the fourth quarter to beat the eventual 2006 NBA champions and snap its longest season-opening losing streak in franchise history.

Afterward, the Raptors were all smiles. "Everyone likes each other again," said Mike James who had 25 points and six assists. "The mood always lightens after a win," said Chris Bosh, who put up 27 points and 12 rebounds in the victory. "People are nicer, the food tastes better, practice is a lot more fun,"

"I'm happy for those guys," Mitchell admitted. "Being the coach is one thing, but when you have to go out there in front of

19,000 people and prove yourself every night, the way the season started, that's where the focal point is. I get mine after the game, but during the game, those guys have to go out there and be the focal point and hear the cheers and boos."

November 22, 2005
Phoenix Suns win 90–82, Raptors fall to 1–10
Shawn Marion (28 points and 18 rebounds) and Steve Nash (23 points and nine assists) would put Toronto back in the loss column. Despite having a team-high 23 points, Chris Bosh didn't score in the fourth quarter and took responsibility for the defeat. "It's my fault. I just didn't make smart decisions," he said. "I had a turnover and three missed shots down the stretch. I just have to make sure I calm my nerves."

Sam Mitchell mentioned, "We're young and inexperienced and we just don't know how to win basketball games right now."

November 23, 2005
Los Angeles Clippers win 103–100, Raptors fall to 1–11
Los Angeles wouldn't take the lead in this game until less than two-and-half minutes to go in the fourth quarter. Sam Cassell had 10 of his 26 points in the final period while Corey Maggette had a game-high 30 points to help the Clippers earn the victory.

Jalen Rose, who missed his first eight shots and was 1-for-12 with six points, was irritated after another defeat. "It's frustrating to lose the ballgame, especially when we're giving a valiant effort. It's doubly frustrating because of the way I've been playing," Rose said. "The guys are doing what they can to help us win ballgames and they need me to step up and play the way I'm capable of playing."

November 25, 2005
Sacramento Kings win 106–104, Raptors fall to 1–12
After Morris Peterson tied the game at 104 with 21.2 seconds to go, Bonzi Wells, with the shot clock winding down, would score two of his 18 points with two seconds remaining. The Raptors had one last chance, but Rose missed a potential game-winning three-pointer at the buzzer. "We wanted to get Chris [Bosh] ducking in or Mike James going to the corner," Rose said. "But they did a good job of taking that away. Unfortunately, the shot didn't go down."

November 26, 2005
Golden State Warriors win 117–91, Raptors fall to 1–13
Jason Richardson was 10-of-18 from the floor with a game-high 25 points while Chris Bosh only scored two points in the second half, and the Raptors shot an ice cold 1-for-13 from three-point land in the lopsided loss. "It's disappointing," Sam Mitchell said. "I don't know if our guys were tired, but we just didn't do anything right."

November 28, 2005
Dallas Mavericks win 93–91, Raptors fall to 1–14
With just over two minutes to go, the Raptors were up 89–83 until Dirk Nowitzki scored eight straight points to give Dallas a temporary lead then with the game tied at 91, and then Jason Terry hit a running layup at the buzzer to close out Toronto. "No matter how bad this hurts," said Mike James, who scored 22 points, "you have to keep your head up."

November 30, 2005
Memphis Grizzlies win 92–66, Raptors fall to 1–15
Ex-Raptor Damon Stoudamire scored a game-high 19 points as Memphis pounded Toronto at home. The Raptors received an earful from the fans again. They booed their club off the court

at halftime, at the end of the third quarter, and once the game finished.

Mighty Mouse could empathize. "This is the same thing that went on eight years ago," said Stoudamire, referring to his time on the 1997–98 Raptors squad that lost 17 straight. "I remember them days like it was yesterday. I feel for them. I know what it's like to lose that many. What are they, 1–15? I've been there before. I know all about that."

The Raptors would start December with a showdown against the almost as bad 2–12 Hawks in Atlanta. Heading into this game, both teams collectively had a 3–27 record and the worst winning percentage in NBA history for opponents that have suited up for at least 30 games combined. Toronto would come out on top, thanks to a Carlos Villanueva go-ahead basket with 2.5 seconds left in the 102–101 victory. "This was a game we had to win," Villanueva admitted. "They were struggling. We were struggling. We hadn't won on the road yet, and this was our best chance."

The Raptors' full post-Vince Carter season was unforgiving and filled with many lows, including Kobe Bryant lighting up Toronto for 81 points, which led to a 27–55 record. Although that year was painful, hope would soon come in the form of the 2006–07 campaign where things would start to brighten up.

58 Richard Peddie

The former president and CEO of Maple Leaf Sports & Entertainment (MLSE), who was also the Raptors president and CEO, Richard Peddie was the man responsible for some perplexing moves, including hiring the inexperienced Rob Babcock, who'd pull off the worst trade in franchise history, as general manager. Back then, though, Peddie was confident in his hiring of Babcock. "Rob was on our list from Day One, and then we brought him in and he quickly went to the top of that list," Peddie explained. "I went back to Rob and said, 'Rob, this is such a critical hire for us. I want to make sure you are the right guy. I'm going to do that by doing more homework on you, but I'm also going to look at what else is out there.'"

He gave Babcock the job, but once the rookie NBA GM would later present the Vince Carter trade proposal to the MLSE board of directors, Peddie was concerned. "I had a new general manager that I had started to become really worried about," Peddie told TSN 1050. "I'm thinking if I pull the plug on this then I've meddled, then I've basically fired the general manager. In hindsight, I wish I had. It set back the franchise—years."

Peddie was skewered for his Babcock hire early on. "I had let Glen Grunwald go in 2004, and it was being played out in the media," Peddie told *The Globe and Mail*. "There was a firepeddie. com website. I got obscene phone calls and had the police come in. One fellow rented a plane with a banner. I remember one night I couldn't sleep and I walked into a Starbucks as soon as it opened in the morning, and the person behind the counter said, 'Who are you going to hire for GM?' I'm not a celebrity, but I'd bet I'm recognized much more often than any of the bank CEOs, and they run much bigger companies."

Peddie wasn't just unpopular with fans, but also with Vince Carter. During the GM search, VC endorsed Julius Erving for the role, but Peddie didn't have a formal meeting with Dr. J, instead opting for a quick chat at the airport that went nowhere. Carter felt disrespected especially since he wasn't kept in the loop.

In his book *Dream Job*, Peddie wasn't afraid to share his true opinion of Toronto's former superstar, stating, "Vince was a mama's boy, and his mother was a force." He also mentioned,

"Vince had amazing athletic talent, but didn't work hard—at all. [He] had little heart and no ability to rise to the occasion." Peddie then suggested Carter and his cousin, Tracy McGrady, weren't as close as Raptors fans thought. "There were jealousies between them," Peddie said. "Everyone played up that they were cousins. There was not a lot of closeness. Again, maybe it was the egos. They both wanted to be the man. And not everyone can be the man."

Once T-Mac left for Orlando, Peddie admitted the club did various things to keep VC happy. "We tried the appeasement, sucking-up mode with him with cars and his own security guard," Peddie said. "He was Vince. That didn't work out so well."

The ex-Raptors president and CEO certainly didn't get along with everyone and made his share of missteps, but he did hire GM Bryan Colangelo, who would construct two playoff teams, including a division title winner, but they would never get past the first round, and then Colangelo's lustre would soon wear off. "I might have stayed longer at MLSE," he said in *Dream Job*. "But, I just got tired of losing."

59 Oh Canada!

Canadians Jay Triano and Jamaal Magloire were basketball trendsetters.

A former star player at Simon Fraser University and 1981 eighth-round Los Angeles Lakers draft pick, Triano was mostly known as the head coach of the Canadian men's national team before Lenny Wilkens hired him as a Raptors assistant coach in 2002, making him the first Canadian-born coach in the NBA. Over the years Triano would serve under Wilkens, Kevin O'Neill, and Sam Mitchell until February 13, 2008. With Mitchell not available that night due to his father-in-law's death, Triano made league history by filling in as head coach, becoming the first Canadian to do so in a NBA regular season game. "Initially, it was where people just looked at, 'You're a Canadian and you're the fourth assistant, and that's good,'" said Triano, who was in his sixth year as a Raptors assistant. "Over time you work hard and you get yourself into position where something like this is a possibility."

Toronto would beat the New Jersey Nets 109–91 to give Triano his first NBA head coaching regular season victory. In December of 2008, Triano was named interim head coach for the rest of the season after the firing of Mitchell. Now, Triano was the first full-time Canadian NBA head coach in league history. He'd guide the club to a 9–4 record to finish the 2008–09 campaign. After waiting his turn, following three Raptors head coach dismissals, Triano finally got his chance. In May of 2009, the Raptors officially named him the team's full-time head coach and then signed him to a three-year contract. For Triano, being a Canadian NBA head coach was important. "It means a lot," Triano admitted. "When I took over halfway through the year, I didn't really have much of a chance to think about it, but now that the season's been over and I have a chance to go back to Vancouver and be in different places in North America, you see the joy that a lot of the other Canadian coaches have. I've always had a real affection for the Canadian coaches and wanting to help them and help them get better."

Triano would lead the Raptors to a 40–42 record in 2009–2010, but in the summer of 2010, his All-Star, Chris Bosh, would bolt to Miami to team up with LeBron James and Dwyane Wade, leaving the Raptors in bad shape. In the 2010–11 campaign, they'd finish last in the Atlantic Division with a 22–60 mark. Unfortunately for Triano, general manager Bryan Colangelo had seen enough. In June of 2011, he would not pick up Triano's contract option, ending the Canadian's run as Raptors head coach. "I am grateful

Magloire Shines at the 2004 NBA All-Star Game

When the full 2004 NBA All-Star rosters were announced, some questioned Jamaal Magloire's Eastern Conference selection. Since the East lacked premier big men, critics felt that was why the first Canadian born NBA All-Star (Steve Nash was born in South Africa) made the cut.

In his first All-Star classic, Magloire could have easily been in awe facing the West's incredibly talented frontcourt, which included Shaquille O'Neal, Tim Duncan, Kevin Garnett, Dirk Nowitzki, and Yao Ming, but instead the New Orleans Hornets centre went to work. On February 15, 2004, in Los Angeles, with the All-Star lights shining brightly and the NBA universe watching, Magloire scored an East-leading 19 points and grabbed eight rebounds in the 136–132 loss. "I felt in my heart that I am an All-Star," Magloire said. "This won't be the last time I will be an All-Star."

Well, actually, it was his lone All-Star appearance, but Magloire created a memory he and Canadian basketball fans won't soon forget.

to the organization for the opportunity to be a head coach in the NBA," Triano said. "I am proud of the work that I and the coaching staff have done with our young players and feel confident we have laid the foundation for a team that will continue to improve."

Despite his 87–142 record, Canada's first NBA head coach became an inspiration to those in the Great White North who wanted to follow his path for years to come. Jamaal Magloire was another Canadian inspiration. The Toronto native was a 6'11" centre who played his college ball at the University of Kentucky. After his time there, including a 1998 NCAA title in his sophomore season, "The Big Cat" would head to the 2000 NBA Draft, where he was picked 19th overall by the Charlotte Hornets.

In 2002–03 the Hornets moved to New Orleans, and Magloire began to shine. He started all 82 games, averaging 10.3 points, 8.8 rebounds, and 1.4 blocks per contest. In 2003–04 Magloire would have his best season with 13.6 points and 10.3 rebounds a night, earning him a spot in the NBA All-Star Game. He became only the second Canadian citizen—after Steve Nash—named to an All-Star squad.

Magloire, however, would never reach that level again. Injuries would take their toll, reducing him to mainly a bench player the rest of his career. The opportunity to play at home, though, was always attractive, so when the Raptors signed him in December 2011, making him the first Canadian-born player in franchise history, it was special. "It's an honour," said Magloire, who starred at Eastern Commerce High in Toronto. "I'm very privileged to have this opportunity. This doesn't happen very often. There's only 450 guys in this league and not only am I a part of it, I get an opportunity to come home. I'm so happy. I'm a Toronto Raptor. It's always been a dream of mine, and I'm looking forward to having a great year."

Magloire would only suit up for 34 games, averaging 1.2 points and 3.3 rebounds a night during that final season, but he helped pave the way for the next generation of Canadian NBA players like Andrew Wiggins, Tristan Thompson, and 2014 NBA Finals champion Cory Joseph, who signed with Toronto in the 2015 offseason.

60 The Red Rocket

The red-headed, wholesome-looking sharpshooter, who liked to eat Subway sandwiches, didn't have an entourage, nor did he drive up to the Air Canada Centre parking lot in a fancy car.

In fact, back in his Raptors days, Matt Bonner didn't even own wheels.

To get around town, he would either use the Toronto transit system, including the subway (otherwise known as The Red Rocket) or walk around. Thus, then-Raptors broadcaster Chuck Swirsky bestowed the nickname "The Red Rocket" upon Bonner.

Originally, he was acquired in a 2003 draft day trade from the Chicago Bulls. After playing his first pro season in the Italian league, his chances of making the Raptors in 2004 were slim. The franchise was in a bad place with new general manager Rob Babcock, who had no connection to Bonner and whose hands were tied due to various guaranteed contracts on the roster. And then two days before the start of training camp, Bonner would have his knee accidentally kicked by Morris Peterson on a drive to the basket. The 6'10" NBA hopeful was told he'd require four weeks to completely recover from a bone bruise and sprained ligament. He was devastated. Back in his downtown Toronto hotel room, Bonner, still feeling down, was taking a nap when a phone call woke him up. He answered and found out his high school best friend was killed in a car crash. "Here I was, injured...it felt like somebody shot me in the knee," he told the *Toronto Star*. "And then that phone call put things in perspective to where I thought, 'I can't give up at this point. I just can't give up.' It's one of those classic adversity stories, I guess, without being too cliché."

Knee injury or not, Bonner was determined to play in the pre-season. Toronto's new head coach at the time, Sam Mitchell, who liked the kid's "bring your lunch pail to work" mind-set, would give him an opportunity against the Philadelphia 76ers. Bonner was slated to play centre against Philly big man Samuel Dalembert, whose first choice wasn't leaving his comfort zone in the paint to guard the fresh-faced redhead beyond the arc.

Mitchell assured the young forward: "I told Matt, 'You're going to get wide-open shots. If you can make wide-open shots, you will make this basketball team. That's my promise to you.'" Bonner had nine points and nine rebounds in 23 minutes. "He

Matt Bonner, "The Red Rocket," was a very popular Raptors player—in part because he rode the subway to the Air Canada Centre.

189

made the shots and Rob [Babcock] couldn't cut him," Mitchell said. "And he became kind of a Toronto hero."

On December 15, 2004, Bonner's legacy as one of the Raptors all-time fan favourites was cemented. Toronto was hosting Kevin Garnett's Minnesota Timberwolves. After KG grabbed an offensive rebound in the fourth quarter, Bonner knocked the 2004 NBA MVP to the floor and then Garnett charged him. A referee, Anthony Jordan, and Mitchell held KG back. Garnett's teammate, Latrell Sprewell, also went after the rookie. "It was a hard foul. That really didn't even spark me until I saw him pointing into the crowd like he's some enforcer," said Garnett who had 23 points and 15 rebounds in the loss.

Though he would be ejected for his flagrant foul, fans chanted "Bonner, Bonner" in adulation. "I felt a lot of pride for myself, the team, the whole city of Toronto that they support me so much," Bonner said. "I feel honoured."

Raptors fans loved Bonner's edge, hustle, three-point touch, red hair, everyman mentality, and his embracing of the city. Heck, he even married a Canadian girl he met in Toronto, and in his post-Raptors days, he attempted (but failed) to get Canadian citizenship in time to play for Canada's national basketball team.

Unfortunately, the Bonner era would end with a multi-player trade sending him to the San Antonio Spurs, where the good guy would enjoy multiple NBA championships in his career. "When I see what Matt Bonner's doing, I'm more proud of that than I am of anything else I ever did as a coach," Mitchell said. "I get tired of the NBA because too often we'd rather take the bad guy who says he's sorry and give him all the chances. And we take the good guy and say, 'Hey, you're a great guy, but I'm sorry. I'm going to take a chance on the bad guy.' And my thing was, it's not that I'm not going to give bad guys a second chance, but let's give some of these good guys a chance and see what kind of player they turn out to be."

61 Why Raptors Fans Are More Fun Than Leafs Fans

The Toronto Maple Leafs and Raptors have the same owners, share the same arena but have starkly different fan bases. If you know a supporter of the Blue and White, he's probably been through a lot of losing, mediocrity, and empty promises.

He's likely jaded and whenever he attends a Leafs game he wants to get behind the bench because he thinks he can do a better job. Not winning a Stanley Cup since 1967 will do that to him. With all the negativity surrounding the club, especially in the 2014–15 campaign, it isn't surprising Leafs fans aren't enthusiastic about their team. "I know a lot of people say Toronto is the best place to play, but that's only if it's going miraculously well," Leafs head coach Ron Wilson said in 2014. "And the only way you're going to be cheered in Toronto is if you happen to be leading with five minutes to go. And if you've got a significant lead then, they might happen to get off their hands and give you a cheer. I was watching last night, and at the start of the second period, all the platinums are totally empty. It looked on TV like nobody was in the building. Everybody in Toronto talks about how bad it is in Florida, but in Toronto everyone sitting in the platinums are down in the suite drinking, and they're not even paying attention to the team. Hockey seems to be secondary, which is a shame. It's a morgue at the start of the game. You score a couple of goals early on the Leafs, and then the crowd wakes up and starts to give it to the Leafs instead of encouraging them."

To be fair, when the Buds made it into the 2013 playoffs, fans filled Maple Leaf Square and passionately cheered on the Blue and White, so they have it in them, but they just don't do it consistently throughout the year. Even attending a Leafs regular season game in which they're winning doesn't have nearly the electric atmosphere as a Raptors home affair. Raptors fans are more fun because…

- They're typically younger and more energetic. They'll cheer and boo with all their heart and do it for longer periods.
- Many of them just go for the experience and don't take the game too seriously, which allows them to enjoy the game more.
- They're positive. The Raptors have had some terrible losing seasons too, but their fans haven't been as jaded as Leafs supporters, so they can still have hope without being overly cynical.
- They go with the flow. If the Raptors mascot decides to throw a pie in their face, they'll most likely laugh along with everyone else.

During the Raptors' success over the last few years, the whole NBA and North American sports world have witnessed how passionate the team's fans are. "Throughout my years in the NBA, this is something I've never seen before," said Raptors big man Amir Johnson. "Just to see the whole country and the city come together like that is very inspirational. It just makes you hungrier to get there again, to do it for them. I felt like we have the best fans in the world, to see everybody come out. It's an unbelievable feeling to have that support behind you."

62 Moving Out of the SkyDome

The SkyDome was the Raptors' first home from 1995 to 1999. The massive multi-purpose retractable roofed stadium, which seated less than 30,000 for basketball, was never intimate enough, but it did serve its purpose. Soon though, hoops fans, who complained they could barely see game action from the Dome's 500 level, which was closest to the roof, would be in for a treat. The Air Canada Centre, which received its name in a 1995 partnership deal between the Canadian airline and the Raptors, was coming.

But before the ACC was completed, there was some drama surrounding it. During the 1990s the Toronto Maple Leafs ownership group shopped for a new home arena to replace Maple Leaf Gardens, which was considered too small and needed revenue-generating luxury boxes. In 1996 the Raptors agreed to build the $200 million-plus ACC at the former site of Canada Post's downtown Toronto postal delivery building and asked the Leafs to be a joint tenant. But they wanted nothing to do with it, feeling the building wouldn't be large enough.

In April of 1997, the Leafs ownership group surprised many by announcing its plans to create an arena very close to the ACC above Union Station, the Toronto transportation hub. In the proposal the Leafs wanted to turn the postal station into a bus terminal, and the Raptors would move in with them despite the new NBA franchise already sinking $80 million into the ACC's construction. Then-Raptors majority owner Allan Slaight wasn't interested, and in June of 1997, the Leafs' Union Station plans would be dashed by Toronto city council members, who rejected the proposal after both sides couldn't agree on annual rent costs.

In February of 1998, the Leafs ownership group caught everyone off-guard again by purchasing the Raptors and the ACC and then revamping the arena's original basketball-centric design to make it more hockey-friendly. After years of commotion, the ACC would finally open its doors as the Maple Leafs hosted the Montreal Canadiens in their first home game on February 20, 1999. As for the Raptors, following a win in their last home contest at SkyDome against the Milwaukee Bucks on February 19, they'd pack their bags and head east a few minutes where they'd make their ACC home debut on February 21 in a 102–87 victory against fellow expansion club, the Vancouver Grizzlies.

Today, the Air Canada Centre, located at 40 Bay Street, is a 665,000-square-foot sports and entertainment venue and has the following features:

- 19,800 seating capacity for basketball
- 18,800 seating capacity for hockey
- 19,800 seating capacity for concerts
- 5,200 seating capacity for theatre
- 1,020 club seats
- 40 platinum lounges
- 65 executive suites
- 32 theatre suites
- 16 loge suites (second and third-level loges)
- three group sales areas, including a 200-seat gondola
- Rickard's Brewhouse, an-in house brewery

63 Chant "Let's Go Raptors!" at a Leafs Game

Toronto Maple Leafs fans know what's been happening. With their team underperforming, the chant "Let's Go Raptors!" has been heard at home games at the Air Canada Centre. Obviously, it's a swift kick to the grapefruits for a club, which is considered the crown jewel of the Toronto sports scene. But it also shows the respect the Dinos are receiving from a fan base, which used to ignore them.

The "Let's Go Raptors!" chant epidemic isn't only reserved for home games, but it chases the Leafs on the road as well. During an embarrassing 6–2 Leafs loss on November 15, 2014, in Buffalo, some of the thousands of Leafs fans in attendance chanted "Let's Go Raptors!" in response to Toronto's uninspired performance. It seems like every time a Leafs fan is ticked off, he has his Raps chant armed and ready.

Raptors fans don't wish the Leafs any harm. In fact, many of them want the Blue and White to win the Stanley Cup again one day. It would be great for the city. But if the team continues to feed its long-suffering fan base more years of mediocrity, then the franchise deserves to hear about a winning club.

If you're a Raptors fan who is somehow invited to a Leafs game, here are some suggested moments when it's appropriate to deliver your chant.

If a Leafs player takes a dumb penalty then the other team scores…
"Let's Go Raptors!"

If a Leafs player gives up a terrible turnover, which leads to an opponent's goal…
"Let's Go Raptors!"

If a Leafs player goes on a breakaway but either falls and/ or misses the net entirely…
"Let's Go Raptors!"

If a Leafs player doesn't have his head up and accidentally but hilariously collides with his own player, and no one is hurt…
"Let's Go Raptors!"

If the Leafs are down four goals before you even had your first overpriced Air Canada Centre beer of the night…
"Let's Go Raptors!"

If the opposing goalie sends the puck down the ice, and it slips by the Leafs goalie for a score…
"Let's Go Raptors!"

If a Leafs fan proposes to his girlfriend at the game, and she turns him down…
"Let's Go Raptors!"

If a Leafs fan eats a hot dog, and the mustard squirts all over his new designer white shirt…
"Let's Go Raptors!"

64 Do You *Really* Know Your Raptors?

Here's where we find out if you're a true Raptors fan or just a pretender.

These 30 trivia questions will test your knowledge.

1. Which of these former Raptors became an NBA referee?
   (a) Haywoode Workman, (b) Michael Bradley, (c) Zan Tabak, (d) Earl Cureton

2. Who won NBA Coach of the Year in Toronto?
   (a) Butch Carter, (b) Sam Mitchell, (c) Lenny Wilkens, (d) Jay Triano

3. What two Raptors players on the 2000–01 roster would be NBA head coaches one day?
   (a) Antonio Davis and Dell Curry, (b) Chris Childs and Eric Montross, (c) Alvin Williams and Charles Oakley, (d) Mark Jackson and Tyrone Corbin

4. What ex-Raptor once acted in the movies *Bad Boys 2* and *Mr. 3000*?
   (a) Walt Williams, (b) Acie Earl, (c) Alvin Williams, (d) John Salley

5. True or False—former Raptors forward Amir Johnson attended Michigan State University.

6. What uniform number did the 1996 No. 2 overall pick Marcus Camby wear in Toronto?
(a) 21, (b) 25, (c) 8, (d) 13

7. Where was 2004 Raptors first-round draft pick Rafael Araujo born?
(a) Argentina, (b) Costa Rica, (c) Spain, (d) Brazil

8. Who was the Raptors' first selection in the 1995 expansion draft?
(a) Greg Anthony, (b) B.J. Armstrong, (c) Reggie Slater, (d) Tony Massenburg

9. Who hit the most three-pointers in a single game in Raptors history?
(a) Donyell Marshall, (b) Dell Curry, (c) Jason Kapono, (d) Terrence Ross

10. True or False—Jose Calderon won an Olympic gold medal playing for the Spanish national team.

11. In Kobe Bryant's 81-point game against the Raptors, who led Toronto in scoring and what was the amount?
(a) Jalen Rose—20 points, (b) Mike James—26 points, (c) Chris Bosh—33 points, (d) Morris Peterson—22 points

12. Name the 1999 NBA Draft pick that was traded to Indiana for forward Antonio Davis?
(a) Jonathan Bender, (b) Aleksandar Radojevic, (c) Lamar Odom, (d) Corey Maggette

13. Name the two players Toronto drafted in 1998?
(a) Vince Carter and Rafer Alston, (b) Antawn Jamison and Tyson Wheeler, (c) Keon Clark and Maceo Baston, (d) Robert Traylor and Sean Marks

14. What Toronto Raptor has hit the most three-pointers in franchise history?
(a) Morris Peterson, (b) Jason Kapono, (c) Andrea Bargnani, (d) Dell Curry

15. On March 24, 1996, in Toronto's upset win against the Chicago Bulls, what former NBA champion scored 12 points off the Raptors bench?
(a) Tracy Murray, (b) Doug Christie, (c) Carlos Rogers, (d) Zan Tabak

16. Who finished second to Terrence Ross in the 2013 NBA Slam Dunk Contest?
(a) Gerald Green, (b) Jeremy Evans, (c) Eric Bledsoe, (d) Kenneth Faried

17. What player holds the Raptors single-game rookie scoring record?
(a) Damon Stoudamire, (b) Acie Earl, (c) Vince Carter, (d) Charlie Villanueva

18. Who is the only Raptors player to win the NBA's Three-Point Shootout?
(a) Jason Kapono, (b) Terrence Ross, (c) Steve Novak, (d) Marco Belinelli

19. Andrea Bargnani is one of three Italian born players to ever suit up for the Raptors. Name the other two.

20. What former Raptor played the most consecutive games in team history?
(a) Morris Peterson, (b) Antonio Davis, (c) Chris Bosh, (d) Jose Calderon

21. Which of the following Raptors players was not drafted by general manager Bryan Colangelo?
(a) Andrea Bargnani, (b) Charlie Villanueva, (c) Roy Hibbert, (d) Ed Davis

22. Name the only Chinese-born player in Raptors history.
(a) Wang Zhizhi, (b) Mengke Bateer, (c) Yao Ming, (d) Yi Jianlian

23. During Vince Carter's rookie season, who was the first team he scored over 30 points against?
(a) Cleveland Cavaliers, (b) Houston Rockets, (c) New York Knicks, (d) Los Angeles Clippers

24. How many points did DeMar DeRozan score in his regular season rookie debut?
(a) 20 points, (b) 12 points, (c) eight points, (d) 24 points

25. True or False. Tracy McGrady was chosen ahead of Chauncey Billups at the 1997 NBA Draft.

26. During the 2009–10 season, besides Chris Bosh, name the other former Georgia Tech player on the team.
(a) Sonny Weems, (b) Jarrett Jack, (c) Reggie Evans, (d) Marcus Banks

27. On February 21, 1999, in the Raptors first ever regular season game at the Air Canada Centre, who did they beat and who was Toronto's leading scorer?
(a) Detroit Pistons and Kevin Willis, (b) Boston Celtics and Vince Carter, (c) New York Knicks and Doug Christie, (d) Vancouver Grizzlies and Vince Carter

28. Name the two members of the 2009 NCAA champion University of North Carolina team who played for the Raptors.
(a) Justin Watts and Wayne Ellington, (b) Ty Lawson and Danny Green, (c) Deon Thompson and Marc Campbell, (d) Ed Davis and Tyler Hansbrough

29. How many points did Chris Bosh score in his final Raptors regular season game?
(a) 15 points, (b) 29 points, (c) 2 points, (d) 21 points

30. Which future NBA head coach was a teammate of Isiah Thomas on the 1981 NCAA champion Indiana University squad?
(a) Randy Wittman, (b) Steve Kerr, (c) Keith Smart, (d) Doc Rivers

Trivia Answers

1. (a) Haywoode Workman
2. (b) Sam Mitchell
3. (d) Mark Jackson and Tyrone Corbin
4. (d) John Salley
5. False. Amir Johnson never went to college. He went straight from high school to the 2005 NBA Draft.
6. (a) Marcus Camby wore No. 21.
7. (d) Brazil
8. (b) B.J. Armstrong. He was a guard with the Chicago Bulls.
9. (a) Donyell Marshall. On March 13, 2005, he hit 12 three-pointers against the Philadelphia 76ers.
10. False. Jose Calderon won two Olympic silver medals in 2008 and 2012.
11. (b) Mike James had 26 points.
12. (a) Jonathan Bender
13. (b) Antawn Jamison and Tyson Wheeler
14. (a) Morris Peterson hit 801 three-pointers with the Raptors.
15. (d) Zan Tabak. During the 1994–95 season, he won an NBA title with the Houston Rockets.
16. (b) Jeremy Evans
17. (d) Charlie Villanueva scored 48 points vs. the Milwaukee Bucks on March 26, 2006.
18. (a) Jason Kapono. After winning the Three-Point Shootout with the Miami Heat in 2007, he did it again as a Raptor in 2008.
19. Marco Belinelli (2009–10) and Vincenzo Esposito (1995–96)
20. (a) Morris Peterson played 371 straight games from 2002 to 2006.
21. (b) Charlie Villanueva. Rob Babcock selected him seventh overall in the 2005 Draft.
22. (b) Mengke Bateer. During the 2003–04 season, the centre played seven games in Toronto.
23. (b) Houston Rockets. Vince Carter scored 32 points in Houston on March 25, 1999.
24. (c) DeMar DeRozan scored eight points against the Cleveland Cavaliers on October 28, 2009.
25. False. Chauncey Billups was selected third overall by the Boston Celtics while Toronto picked Tracy McGrady in the ninth spot.
26. (b) Jarrett Jack
27. (d) The Raptors beat the Grizzlies 102–87 while Vince Carter scored 27 points.
28. (d) Ed Davis and Tyler Hansbrough
29. (c) Chris Bosh scored two points against the Cleveland Cavaliers on April 6, 2010.
30. (a) Randy Wittman. He scored 16 points while Isiah Thomas had 23 to help Indiana beat North Carolina 63–50 to capture the NCAA championship.

65 Yes, He Was a Raptor

Here are some former NBA and college stars who you may have forgotten played for Toronto.

Chauncey Billups
Before being a 2004 NBA Finals MVP with the Detroit Pistons, "Mr. Big Shot" was Boston's third overall pick in the 1997 NBA Draft. In February of 1998, the Celtics shipped him along with Dee Brown, Roy Rogers, and John Thomas to Toronto for Kenny Anderson, Popeye Jones, and Zan Tabak. The guard wasn't a Raptor for long. In 29 career games, Billups averaged 11.3 points before being dealt again. In January of 1999, he was sent to Denver in a three-team, multi-player trade.

Peja Stojakovic
The three-time All-Star was one of the game's elite three-point specialists. In fact, from 2002–2003, the forward won back-to-back NBA Three-Point Shootout titles. In November of 2010, the 14th overall pick in the 1996 NBA Draft was traded along with Jerryd Bayless from the New Orleans Hornets to the Raptors for Jarrett Jack, David Andersen, and Marcus Banks. Stojakovic would only play two games before being sidelined for 26 contests with a sore left knee. In January of 2011, Toronto released him, but days later the Dallas Mavericks picked him up. The move worked out well. The Mavericks beat the Miami Heat for the NBA title that year, allowing Stojakovic to retire as a champion.

Shawn Marion

At his peak "The Matrix" was an athletic freak who attacked the rack many times during his years with two-time NBA MVP point guard Steve Nash and the up-tempo Phoenix Suns.

In February of 2009, Marion was dealt in a multi-player trade from Miami to the Raptors, which also involved six-time All-Star Jermaine O'Neal heading to the Heat.

During his 27 games in Toronto, the 1999 first-round selection showed off his scoring and rebounding abilities, recording 10 double-doubles, including 34 points and 11 rebounds against the Chicago Bulls in the last game of the season. In his brief Raptors stay, the four-time All-Star averaged 14.3 points and 8.3 rebounds per contest.

In July 2009, Marion was part of a four-team deal that sent him to Dallas where, in 2011, he'd win an NBA title with the Mavericks.

John Salley

In the 1995 NBA Expansion Draft, the Raptors selected this former Detroit Pistons Bad Boy. The 6'11" baller and actor played 25 games in Toronto's first season before being waived.

That move, though, worked out well for Salley. Just over a month later, the future four-time NBA champion signed with the Chicago Bulls who'd win a record 72 regular season games and an NBA title.

Jimmy King

The guard was a member of the University of Michigan's "Fab 5" team with Chris Webber, Juwan Howard, Jalen Rose, and Ray Jackson that went to back-to-back NCAA title games but came up empty both times. In the 1995 NBA Draft, the Raptors selected him in the second round with the 35th overall pick. He'd play 62 games in his rookie year, only scoring 4.5 points per contest.

In the offseason King was traded to the Dallas Mavericks in a multi-player move but was eventually waived. In April of 1997, he signed with the Denver Nuggets and played two games, but that would be it for his NBA career.

John Wallace

The Syracuse University star took his team to the 1996 NCAA title game before losing to Kentucky. Wallace, a 1996 New York Knicks first-round draft pick, was traded to Toronto in a three-team deal. During the Raptors' 16–66 season, the forward displayed some scoring touch by having two 30-point games and pouring in 20 or more 16 times. In 82 games that year, he averaged a career-high 14 points but would eventually leave Toronto in 1999, signing a free-agent deal to return to the Knicks.

Kris Humphries

You may have intentionally forgotten Humphries because of his heavily publicized association with Kim Kardashian, his former wife of 72 days, and her family's reality television show. Years before he got tangled up in that crazy situation, Humphries was a young forward from Minneapolis, Minnesota, who played three seasons with the Raptors. In those 159 games, he had 4.6 points and just more than three rebounds per contest while playing on two Raptors postseason teams.

66 Terrible Trades

Unfortunately, there have been many head-scratching moves in the franchise's history, which set the Raptors back in some way. Here's a list of some of the worst.

Trading Away Vince Carter

VC was traded for Alonzo Mourning, Aaron Williams, Eric Williams, a 2005 first-round draft pick (Joey Graham) and a 2006 first-round draft pick (Renaldo Balkman). At the time Raptors general manager Rob Babcock said it was the best deal he could make for the unhappy Carter. The trade, though, stunned Carter's teammates. "I'm still just shocked," Morris Peterson admitted. "Even with all the trade talks, it's hard to believe"

Besides losing Carter, one of the biggest kicks in the teeth about this trade was not the fact Mourning, who wanted to play for a winner, never reported, but he apparently told Babcock and other Raptors officials he wasn't coming up north before the deal was even struck.

"I made it clear to [the Raptors], and they were made aware by [Nets general manager] Rod Thorn who said, 'If you guys make this trade, there's a strong, strong possibility Alonzo Mourning won't even report,'" Mourning said. "It wasn't foreign to them, and they told me that. They knew what they were getting into. They adopted a problem. I didn't cause it at all."

Babcock pulled the trigger anyway, and the Raptors had to pay the remaining $9 million left on Mourning's contract.

Trading for Jermaine O'Neal

Bryan Colangelo took a chance on an injury-prone and expensive former All-Star to give Chris Bosh some frontcourt help. In the summer of 2008, Jermaine O'Neal and the draft rights to Nathan Jawai were dealt to the Raptors for T.J. Ford, the draft rights to Roy Hibbert, Rasho Nesterovic, and Maceo Baston.

The move failed miserably. O'Neal only played 41 games due to injuries and was soon traded to the Miami Heat in February 2009. As a result the Raptors missed out on seeing the 7'2" All-Star Hibbert play in a Toronto uniform.

Trading for Hedo Turkoglu

In July of 2009, Bryan Colangelo pulled off a four-team sign-and-trade to acquire Turkoglu, Devean George, and Antoine Wright while giving up Shawn Marion, Kris Humphries, Nathan Jawai, a second-round pick, and cash. Unfortunately, the 6'10" Turkish forward would disappoint. In a season where he allegedly partied after a game he missed because he was "sick" and on another occasion inexplicably answered a postgame Raptors television interview question with only the word "Ball," you knew things wouldn't work out.

He also didn't provide offence, so Colangelo would say goodbye to him via a trade to the Phoenix Suns in July 2010. "After much fanfare and high expectations, things just didn't seem to work out here for Turk," Colangelo said. "I'm certain he will move on and contribute great things to Phoenix. We wish him well."

Trading for Rudy Gay

In January of 2013, Bryan Colangelo put the finishing touches on a three-team trade, which brought Rudy Gay and Hamed Haddadi to Toronto while Jose Calderon, Ed Davis, and a second-round pick were sent out of town. Right away, Gay didn't seem like a fit for a roster, which already featured a high scoring wing talent in

DeMar DeRozan. At times, Gay would be criticized for his inefficient volume shooting but would still average 19.5 points in 51 games as a Raptor.

General manager Masai Ujiri, who took over for Colangelo, noticed how Gay and DeRozan weren't in sync on the court, so in December of 2013, he dealt Gay to the Sacramento Kings in a seven-player trade, which eventually turned the Raptors into a playoff team.

Trading for Hakeem Olajuwon
In the summer of 2001, general manager Glen Grunwald put together this highly anticipated trade, which brought the future Hall of Famer to the Raptors for two draft picks.

At the time this move created a lot of excitement for the fan base, and some thought it could make Toronto a possible title contender.

In 2001–02, however, the aging star was slowed by injuries, which allowed him to only play 61 regular season games. He did see some playing time in the Raptors' 2002 first-round postseason series against the Detroit Pistons, but at that point, he was a bench player with little impact.

Trading Away Chris Bosh
Bryan Colangelo offered Bosh an extension before he became an unrestricted free agent year in 2010, but CB4 refused. Bosh, who played seven years in Toronto, was ready for a change. The Raptors sent him to the Miami Heat, where he'd team up with his old friends, LeBron James and Dwyane Wade, in a sign-and-trade for two first-round draft picks and a trade exemption. Some fans criticized Colangelo for not dealing Bosh earlier, so Toronto could receive more for him, but one of those picks did turn out to be Jonas Valanciunas, so it wasn't completely terrible.

Other Notable Questionable Moves:

General manager Rob Babcock drafted Rafael Araujo eighth overall in the 2004 NBA Draft.

General manager Glen Grunwald re-signed Michael "Yogi" Stewart to a six-year, $24 million contract.

Isiah Thomas selected Marcus Camby second overall in the 1996 NBA Draft, passing over Kobe Bryant, Steve Nash, Ray Allen, and others.

Grunwald sent Tracy McGrady in a sign-and-trade to the Orlando Magic for a first-round pick.

67 Mother Nature Can't Stop Junkyard Dog

Few players in Raptors history could match the high energy effort on the court of "Junkyard Dog" and his fierce commitment to the team. Jerome Williams, the always smiling forward, showed his dedication early on.

On February 22, 2001, the Detroit Pistons traded him and Eric Montross to Toronto for Tyrone Corbin, Kornel David, Corliss Williamson, and a 2005 first-round draft pick (Fran Vazquez).

Williams was bound and determined to join his team as soon as possible—no matter the weather or the mode of transportation. "When they told me that I couldn't make it there for practice because the private jet that they were sending wouldn't be there until the morning, I said, 'Boy, that's unacceptable,'" Williams said. "I said, 'I don't need a jet. I got a car. Chevy Blazer with four-wheel drive that can make the trek.' I hop into the car. Kiss the wife bye and tell her, 'Okay, pack up the things. We're going up north.' It was funny because radio stations and a lot of fans actually knew

Known for his energy and enthusiasm, Jerome "Junkyard Dog" Williams was not even slowed by inclement weather.

about it because they were calling me while I was in the blizzard on my way. It did reach the airwaves. By the time I got there, a lot of the fans knew about it and were very happy and excited that they had a player that was willing to drive through the snow to get to Toronto."

68 Shake the Hand of the Raptors' Super Fan

Nav Bhatia is arguably the most passionate Raptors fan ever and possibly the most charming. "Everybody loves Nav," Raptors star DeMar DeRozan told *The New York Times.*

Bhatia's enthusiasm is undeniable, and it shines whenever you see him cheering courtside, wearing his signature turban, in the background of televised Raptors home games.

A season-ticketholder since 1995, he's witnessed some terrible basketball over the years, yet he's still having fun, especially when trash talking opponents with his G-rated (as in no swearing) material. "It's funny because I watch old games from the late 1990s," DeRozan said. "And you see Nav sitting in the exact same seat, doing the exact same things."

Bhatia, who owns 10 season tickets (for now), is a regular at the Air Canada Centre. Even opposing players ask where he is when he's not within their sight. He's the ultimate team ambassador not named Drake. "I don't drink, I don't smoke, I don't womanize, I Raptorize," Bhatia told CBC News. "That's all I do."

Before being a successful owner of multiple car dealerships, Bhatia, who trained as a mechanical engineer, and his wife moved to Toronto in 1984 during anti-Sikh riots in India. He struggled to adjust at first, working odd jobs and dealing with those who weren't used to his turban. But he persisted, eventually scoring a car salesman position at a Hyundai dealership.

Thanks to his lovable personality, natural sales talent, and strong work ethic, he soared up the company food chain until he became an owner and the successful man he is today.

Bhatia is an inspiring figure who's also deeply involved with charities and is quite generous—even with Raptors players. When DeRozan was a 2009 rookie, Bhatia educated him on everything Toronto, including the neighbourhoods, restaurants, and Raptors history. DeRozan once disclosed he was shopping for a car. After waking up the next morning, the rookie saw a Range Rover parked outside his place. Bhatia loaned it to the youngster until he could find his own wheels.

Over the years Bhatia has befriended many players, including Vince Carter, and has helped many in the South Asian community. "During Vaisakhi and Diwali, I buy 3,000 tickets for NBA games for over $300,000 and give them to Sikhs and non-Sikh children so that they can enjoy matches," said Bhatia, who has watched over 500 games. "The idea is make the mainstream in North America aware about turbans and my Indian identity. The idea is to integrate my Indian community with the mainstream."

Want to shake this do-gooder's hand? Even if you don't want to bother him at his seat or miss him in the Air Canada Centre concourse, you can always visit him at work. His car dealerships—Nav Bhatia's Mississauga Hyundai Superstore and Nav Bhatia's Mississauga Elite Cars—are located in a western Toronto suburb called Mississauga, Ontario.

69 Skip to My Lou

"He's smart. He's passionate. He's enthusiastic. He's got every attribute you'd want in a player."

—Jeff Van Gundy

Rafer Alston was the recipient of that praise. When former New York Knicks/Houston Rockets head coach Jeff Van Gundy, who doesn't give compliments often, says that about you, you're doing something well.

The former Raptors guard had come a long way since his days as a legendary streetball player from Queens, New York. Back then, "Skip to My Lou," who earned the nickname for his habit of skipping down the court while dribbling, embarrassed many playground opponents with his dazzling ballhandling skills which many felt inspired the AND1 Mixtape Tour. "What made me good was that any place, any borough, I didn't mind going in there and doing what I had to do to win a game and also put on a show," he explained. "Then I developed a following. I guess everyone who was a Rafer Alston fan, I never let them down out there. When you play in the New York City playgrounds, you hear so much [about] this guy or that guy being so good. At a young age, I was that guy."

The playgrounds definitely toughened him up, especially since he was a hotshot talent with a target on his head. "When you're a streetball player, it makes you more confident," he said. "It gives you a swagger, that you can go anywhere, any place and you can compete with the best out there. That's one thing growing up in New York City, playing on the playground circuit. People don't understand the things that are said to you, the threats that we have to endure when you go from Queens to Brooklyn, Brooklyn to Bronx, Bronx to Harlem. I'm from Queens, and they don't like it if a Queens guy comes and destroys them in Brooklyn."

Even though Alston tore it up on the New York City playgrounds, he still had big basketball dreams. "My eye was always on the prize, the NBA, and I was a student of the game," he said. "I played all day in the park and went home and watched basketball on TV. My mom would tape games for me. It was always in my heart to play at this level."

Fast forward a few years, he played some community college ball and then spent a year at Fresno State where his temper got him into trouble with his coaches and the law on occasion. After receiving anger management counseling, his shot at the NBA arrived. In 1998 the Milwaukee Bucks drafted him. His longtime dream finally came true. Following three years with the Bucks, Alston suited up for Toronto in January 2003. That 2002–03 squad was ravaged by injuries and severely underperformed, but it was a chance for Alston to impress. And in his final four games that season, he averaged 20.3 points and 7.8 assists. After playing the 2003–04 campaign with the Miami Heat, Alston returned to the Raptors in 2004, signing a six-year, $30 million contract.

It was a turbulent time in franchise history with the Vince Carter saga reaching its ugly end. To add to the drama, then-head coach Sam Mitchell and Alston were butting heads as well.

In a December road game at Boston, after teammate Loren Woods received two quick fouls with less than two minutes left in the third quarter, Alston wasn't happy with the officiating, so he threw a basketball down the court, resulting in his technical foul. Woods also pleaded his case, which led to a technical, too. Mitchell benched Alston and Woods. "We are supposed to be professionals. Nobody has the right to do that in a close game," Mitchell said. "They embarrassed themselves and the Toronto Raptors."

After the loss Alston shared his frustration. "It's tough right now for me," he said. "I'm going to talk to Sam [and general manager Rob Babcock]. I think it's time. I'm tired of getting into it with my teammates and my coaches. I don't know if I'm a good fit for this team and I don't know if I'm a good fit for this league. I'm going to take some time off. I might not even play the rest of the season."

Mitchell considered not playing Alston the next game in Cleveland, but the guard did suit up, scoring 20 points and dishing out 10 assists off the bench in the loss to the Cavaliers. Their rocky relationship continued. In late January of 2005, Mitchell gave Alston a two-game suspension for storming out of a practice. Then, during a February 8 road game against the Cavaliers, Mitchell benched Alston with 3:46 left in the first quarter after he had three turnovers in eight minutes, marking the end of his night. According to *The Globe and Mail*, Mitchell and Alston had a physical showdown at halftime. "[Alston's] in trouble," a security guard, reportedly standing outside the Raptors locker room, told *The Globe*. "He got in a fist fight [with Mitchell]."

Alston would leave Gund Arena during the fourth quarter while Mitchell addressed the speculation after the game. "No, there wasn't anything physical," Mitchell said. "It's a basketball thing that Rafer and I have to sort out. Rafer is determined in his way, and I'm determined in my way. He is struggling with some basketball things, and I wasn't planning on playing him in the second half." For Alston's teammates, this was a distraction. "It's like one big soap opera," Raptors sharpshooter Morris Peterson said.

Besides Mitchell, Alston reportedly also didn't get along with forward Jalen Rose. During a tough loss in Orlando one night, Rose criticized his teammates for their selfish play at times and not being fully committed to playing winning basketball. Alston was offended. "That night he said that coach had opened the floor for anybody to say anything, and 'this man' chose not to say anything to the players. But...then he talked to the media and he bashes us as players and myself? That's not right," Alston said. "A lot of us are like, 'What do you mean?' So, you're the only one playing hard? We all know that's not the case."

As for his drama-filled stay in Toronto, it would only last until October 2005 when he was dealt to Houston for guard Mike James. Despite the circus, Skip to My Lou enjoyed arguably his best season during his last one in Toronto with a career-high 14.2 points per game, including scoring 20 or more 13 times that year. He also had 10 double-doubles and drilled 139 three-pointers. The ex-flashy streetball star didn't have to be a showman anymore. He had proven to be a legit NBA player.

70 The First Raptors Squad

Back in 1995 it was an exciting time for Toronto basketball fans. Their team was finally taking shape via the NBA expansion and lottery drafts, trades, and other transactions.

On June 24 the Raptors and Vancouver Grizzlies took part in their expansion draft featuring 27 players. Toronto would choose first and here were their selections:

No. 1 overall—Guard, B.J. Armstrong (from the Chicago Bulls)
No. 3 overall—Forward, Tony Massenburg (Los Angeles Clippers)
No. 5 overall—Forward/Centre, Andres Guibert (Minnesota Timberwolves)
No. 7 overall—Guard, Keith Jennings (Golden State Warriors)

No. 9 overall—Forward, Dontonio Wingfield (Seattle SuperSonics)

No. 11 overall—Forward, Doug Smith (Dallas Mavericks)

No. 13 overall—Forward, Jerome Kersey (Portland Trail Blazers)

No. 15 overall—Centre, Zan Tabak (Houston Rockets)

No. 17 overall—Guard/Forward, Willie Anderson (San Antonio Spurs)

No. 19 overall—Forward, Ed Pinckney (Milwaukee Bucks)

No. 21 overall—Forward/Centre, Acie Earl (Boston Celtics)

No. 23 overall—Guard, B.J. Tyler (Philadelphia 76ers)

No. 25 overall—Forward/Centre, John Salley (Miami Heat)

No. 27 overall—Centre/Forward, Oliver Miller (Detroit Pistons)

Of course, not all of the above would stick around. Armstrong wasn't happy about leaving the Bulls to head to Toronto, so he was dealt to Golden State for five players, including Carlos Rogers, Victor Alexander (who never officially played with the Raptors), Martin Lewis, and Dwayne Whitfield. Other players such as Kersey, Guibert, Jennings, Wingfield, Smith, and Tyler were either released, waived, or retired.

Throughout the inaugural season, players would come and go, but here were the ones who saw action in a Raptors uniform:

Willie Anderson

The 6'7" swingman averaged 12.4 points in 49 games before being traded with Victor Alexander to the New York Knicks for Doug Christie, Herb Williams, and cash in February of 1996.

Doug Christie

The young guard/forward was traded three times, including by the Los Angeles Lakers and Knicks, before playing his first game with the Raptors. During 1995–96 Christie average 10.1 points, 3.8 rebounds, 2.9 assists, and 1.8 steals in 32 games.

Acie Earl

The Boston Celtics first-round pick in 1993 mainly came off the bench in Toronto's first season, averaging 7.5 points and 3.1 rebounds in 42 games.

Vincenzo Esposito

The Italian was the Raptors' first ever European free-agent signing. In 1995–96 the guard was a part of Toronto's second unit where he scored 3.9 points per contest in 30 games.

Acie Earl—the Funniest Raptor Alive

There are some candidates for the most amusing Raptors teammate ever, but one guy is at the top of the mountain. "It's got to be Acie Earl," ex-forward Popeye Jones said during *The Breakdown with Dave & Audley* podcast. "He was just such a comedian. He was really quick-witted. He always had something to say that was really funny. He was the guy also who could come up with funny nicknames for guys. It has to be Acie. He always kept us laughing."

Sharone Wright and former Raptors forward Tracy Murray also enjoyed being around No. 55, though sometimes you wanted to be far, far away from the 6'10" big man. They recall a funny incident involving the tall jokester. "He had gas like every five minutes," Sharone Wright said.

"We had to literally stop the bus, pull over, and get the hell out," Murray said. "Ace is my boy. We joked a lot. Ace is a good dude. I don't know what he ate, but he let one go that just cleared out the *whole* bus. Ace kind of sat in the front of the bus, but when it reached us in the back and wasn't going anywhere and we had no windows on the bus, it was time to get off."

Jimmy King

During the Raptors' first campaign, the 1995 second-round selection only scored 279 points in his 62 appearances and would then be traded in July 1996.

Martin Lewis

The 20-year-old forward arrived in the B.J. Armstrong multi-player deal and would suit up in 16 games with Toronto, averaging 4.7 points in 1995–96.

Tony Massenburg

The veteran big man played for five NBA clubs before his pit stop in the T-Dot, but after 24 games he'd be on the move again in a multi-player trade to the Philadelphia 76ers for Sharone Wright.

Oliver Miller

A talented player with weight issues, he capped off his 1995–96 campaign with 35 points, 12 rebounds, nine assists, four steals, and three blocks against the 76ers on April 21, 1996.

Tracy Murray

A skilled marksman from beyond the arc, Murray would score 30 or more points five times in Toronto's opening season, including a 40-point game, which featured six three-pointers against the Denver Nuggets on March 18, 1996.

Dan O'Sullivan

The 6'10" big man only played five games in 1995–96 but had a season-high 15 points on April 17, 1996.

Ed Pinckney

In the Raptors' first season, the former NCAA champion averaged seven points and six rebounds in 47 games before being packaged with Tony Massenburg and draft picks in a trade to the 76ers for Sharone Wright.

Alvin Robertson

Prior to joining the club, the University of Arkansas product had already been a four-time NBA All-Star, Defensive Player of the Year, Most Improved Player, and an owner of a quadruple-double in a game. In 1995–96 the veteran was still active defensively with three or more steals in 27 games, including seven against the New Jersey Nets on January 23, 1996.

Carlos Rogers

A 6'11" Seattle SuperSonics first-round pick, Rogers averaged 7.7 points in Toronto's opening campaign, including a season-high 28 points against Magic Johnson's Los Angeles Lakers on March 31, 1996.

John Salley

Years before joining the Raptors, the Georgia Tech alum played alongside Raptors general manager Isiah Thomas on Detroit's Bad Boys teams, which won back-to-back NBA titles. As for Salley's Toronto stay, it didn't last long. The Raptors bid farewell to him in February 1996.

Damon Stoudamire

The 1995 Pac-10 Player of the Year received a tough home reaction on NBA draft night, but the kid turned those fans into believers in Toronto's first campaign. The 5'10" guard scored 20 or more points 37 times in what would be a Rookie of the Year award-winning season.

Zan Tabak

As a rookie in 1994–95, the young Croatian centre was part of a NBA champion Houston Rockets club led by Hakeem Olajuwon. After moving to Toronto in 1995–96, Tabak would produce six double-doubles, including a 26-point, 11-rebound, and two-steal effort against the 76ers on March 27, 1996.

Dwayne Whitfield

After arriving in the B.J. Armstrong trade, the Raptors waived him in November 1995 but then signed the 6'9" forward as a free agent in February 1996. In eight games he would average five points that season.

Herb Williams

Traded along with Doug Christie from New York to Toronto, Williams would only play one game before being waived five days after the deal.

Sharone Wright

The Clemson University star fit in right away after being traded to Toronto from Philadelphia on February 22, 1996. The 6'11" 23-year-old scored in double figures in 10 of his 11 games, including 25 points on March 5 against the Detroit Pistons.

71 The Naismith Cup

In honour of the Canadian inventor of basketball, Dr. James Naismith, the Toronto Raptors and Vancouver Grizzlies faced each other in an annual neutral site exhibition game called The

I'm Half-Grizzlie, Half-Raptor

Before the Grizzlies moved to Memphis in 2001, only six men played for both Vancouver and Toronto, here they are:

Forward/Centre, Tony Massenburg

Toronto's 1995 Expansion Draft pick was a member of the franchise's first ever team, averaging 10.1 points and 6.9 rebounds in 24 games. Massenburg also played for Vancouver on two separate occasions and in 156 games he had 7.1 points and 4.5 rebounds per contest.

Centre, Benoit Benjamin

Vancouver's expansion draft selection played in the Grizzlies' inaugural season, averaging 13.9 points and 7.9 rebounds in 13 games before being traded to the Milwaukee Bucks. The very next season, Benjamin signed with the Raptors as a free agent but only lasted four games, averaging 3.3 points before being waived.

Forward/Centre, Aaron Williams

Mainly known as one of the pieces in the 2004 Vince Carter trade to New Jersey, Williams played in 37 games as a Raptor. In 32 games with Vancouver, he averaged 6.2 points and 4.3 rebounds.

The other members of this exclusive group are former guards **Milt Palacio**, **Darrick Martin**, and forward **Roy Rogers**.

Naismith Cup. The preseason showdown didn't mean much except for bragging rights, but it did allow the nation's basketball fans from various Canadian cities to see their teams up-close.

For some the Naismith Cup conjures up bittersweet memories of a Vancouver franchise that moved to Memphis in 2001. Names such as Mike Bibby, Bryant "Big Country" Reeves, Shareef Abdur-Rahim, Blue Edwards, Greg Anthony, Doug West, Antonio Daniels, Michael Dickerson, Cherokee Parks, and Stromile Swift have long since faded from our minds. What if the Grizzlies chose Vince Carter or Dirk Nowitzki or Paul Pierce instead of selecting Bibby second overall in the 1998 NBA Draft? Would that have saved the franchise? What if Steve Francis didn't pout and want out of Vancouver when the Grizzlies selected him in the 1999 NBA Draft?

We'll never know.

As for The Naismith Cup results, the Raptors dominated the series 4–1.

- In 1995 Toronto beat Vancouver 98–77 in Winnipeg, Manitoba.
- In 1996 the Grizzlies defeated the Raptors 80–77 in Calgary, Alberta.
- In 1997 the Raptors won 107–98 in Halifax, Nova Scotia.
- In 1998 the game was cancelled due to the NBA lockout.
- In 1999 the Raptors blew out the Grizzlies 110–84 in Edmonton, Alberta.
- In 2000 Toronto was victorious 97–92 in Ottawa, Ontario.

72 The Other Head Coaches

Brendan Malone, Darrell Walker, and Kevin O'Neill are the forgotten head coaches in Raptors history. They didn't take the club to the playoffs like Lenny Wilkens, Butch Carter, Dwane Casey, and Sam Mitchell did. Nor were they like Jay Triano who was remembered for being the NBA's first Canadian-born head coach. Malone, Walker, and O'Neill were the other guys who saw some dark days in franchise history.

Here's a look back at their time in Toronto:

Brendan Malone

From the 1988–89 to the 1989–90 seasons, Detroit Pistons "Bad Boys" basketball ruled the NBA, winning back-to-back titles. Malone was an assistant on those teams and he met his future

Raptors boss—Isiah Thomas. Years later, once the Pistons star became Toronto's general manager and part owner, he hired Malone to steer the expansion franchise's maiden voyage in 1995.

This was Malone's first full-time NBA head coaching position. With the help of Rookie of the Year Damon Stoudamire and others, Malone would guide the club to a 21–61 record, including surprising victories against Michael Jordan's 72-win Chicago Bulls, Shaquille O'Neal's Orlando Magic, and Shawn Kemp and Gary Payton's Seattle SuperSonics.

But Malone and Thomas had a different philosophy. Malone wanted to win playing his best lineup every night, and Thomas pushed for the youngsters to suit up more. Once the season was over, Malone was fired. "I enjoyed my opportunity being the head coach of the Toronto Raptors very much. I also thanked the team for working very hard. I would say to everybody in Toronto that supported us, thank you. You were fantastic, great crowds even until the end."

Darrell Walker

A guard in the NBA for 10 years, he played for five teams, including the Detroit Pistons and the Chicago Bulls, where he was part of the 1993 NBA championship team. Walker, who was a teammate of Isiah Thomas in Detroit, was one of Brendan Malone's assistants in Toronto's first season. After Malone was let go, Walker would get his first crack at a full-time NBA head coaching job.

In the 1996–97 season, the Raptors finished with a 30–52 record under his guidance, a nine-win improvement compared to Year One. It appeared Toronto was on the way up until the 1997–98 campaign—and then everything crumbled. A multitude of injuries occurred. There was a 17-game losing streak. Isiah Thomas wasn't able to buy out the team's majority owner, Allan Slaight, so he resigned. Damon Stoudamire was unimpressed with how the Raptors handled the Thomas situation, so he wanted out of Toronto and was dealt on February 13, 1998, in a multi-player trade to the Portland Trail Blazers.

In an added twist that same day, Walker resigned. "I just thought that if they were going to trade Damon, they were going in a different direction than I wanted to," Walker said. "I don't mind coaching an expansion team, but I wanted to see some light at the end of the tunnel. I don't see any light."

Butch Carter would replace Walker as the Raptors finished their chaotic season with a 16–66 record.

Kevin O'Neill

The hard-nosed O'Neill was yet another one of the Raptors' first-time NBA head coaches they seemed to enjoy hiring. After working as an assistant under Rick Carlisle with the Detroit Pistons and before that under Jeff Van Gundy with the New York Knicks, O'Neill signed a two-year deal with Toronto to replace Hall of Fame coach Lenny Wilkens.

During the 2003–04 season there was a rift between O'Neill and Raptors general manager Glen Grunwald after a local newspaper reported current players were tired of the coach's abrasive style. The team would finish 33–49 and out of the playoffs for the second straight year leading to Grunwald's dismissal. O'Neill was by no means safe, but he still felt brave enough to criticize the franchise. "I can just tell you right now, the focus is not on winning here all the way through the organization all the time. There needs to be drastic measures taken."

A day later, he was fired. In June of 2004, he would be replaced by another first-time NBA head coach, Sam Mitchell.

73 He Did What?

One of the fun things about being a Raptors fan is when an unlikely player does something cool you would have never expected. There have been several of those moments throughout franchise history.

April 12, 1996—Acie Earl had 40 points and 12 rebounds against the Boston Celtics.
The 6'10" big man was an ex-Celtics first-round draft pick who didn't perform well in his Beantown days, but in this game, he would stick it to his old team by making 13-of-23 field goal attempts and 14-of-19 free throw attempts.

December 11, 1996—Popeye Jones had 22 points and 21 rebounds against the Celtics.
For the 6'8" forward, this would be his only 20–20 game in a Raptors uniform, which came during 56 minutes of work in a 115–113 triple overtime loss in Boston.

November 4, 2002—Mamadou N'Diaye had eight blocks against the Chicago Bulls.
The seven-foot centre from Senegal, who only played a combined eight games and had two total blocks in his first two Raptors seasons, recorded a season high in blocked shots and he added 12 points in a 109–105 overtime win. "I'm thankful I got some minutes," N'Diaye said.

February 17, 2004—Donyell Marshall grabbed 24 rebounds against the Bulls.
He set a Raptors single-game rebounding record with his effort versus the team that traded him to Toronto in December 2003.

March 13, 2005—Donyell Marshall hit 12 three-pointers against the Philadelphia 76ers.
The forward tied an NBA single-game record and set a Raptors franchise mark with his three-point shooting spectacle. He scored 38 points in the 128–110 win. "The basket just looked humongous out there today," Marshall said. "My teammates kept telling me to shoot it. They kept saying no matter what play we run we're going to look for you in the corner."

March 26, 2006—Charlie Villanueva scored 48 points against the Milwaukee Bucks.
With Chris Bosh leaving the game with an early injury, Villanueva took over by scoring a Raptors single-game rookie record in points, including 29 of them in the second half in a 125–116 overtime defeat. "When Chris went out, someone had to step up, and I stepped up to the challenge," Villanueva said. "It feels good. It feels real good. It feels like you can't be stopped. The basket feels bigger than it already is."

April 11, 2011—Joey Dorsey had 20 rebounds against the Bucks.
The University of Memphis product ripped down his Raptors single-game career-high boards in what would be his lone season in Toronto.

April 26, 2012—Ben Uzoh had a triple-double against the New Jersey Nets.
After signing a couple of 10-day contracts and then staying with the Raptors for the remainder of the season, Uzoh surprised everyone

by having 12 points, a career-high 12 assists, and 11 rebounds for his first career triple-double in a 98–67 victory. "It's pretty cool," he said. "My teammates were rooting me on and pushed me to try and get there. That's a big thing in this league. I'm definitely happy that it happened."

January 25, 2014—Terrence Ross scored 51 points against the Los Angeles Clippers.

For a man who had a disappointing rookie season, the high-flyer amazed the Air Canada Centre crowd with his 10 three-pointers and single-game, club-record-tying point total in a 126–118 loss. Afterward, Ross talked about being in his zone: "You don't really realize what you're doing until it's all over."

74 Great Guards

Some of the Raptors' biggest games and moments featured a terrific effort from a guard.

Just pick any awesome Vince Carter achievement. Or how about Alvin Williams' first-round series-clinching shot against the New York Knicks in 2001? Who could forget Damon Stoudamire pouring in 30 points against Michael Jordan and the 72-win Chicago Bulls in 1996?

The franchise has seen its share of solid point and shooting guards. Here's a list of some of the finest to ever wear a Toronto jersey.

Damon Stoudamire, the franchise's first draft pick, developed into one of the best guards in Raptors history.

Vince Carter
The legendary dunker was the most exciting player in Raptors history. At his peak Mr. Half-Man, Half-Amazing was one of the NBA's top five elite talents.

Kyle Lowry
Credited with being one of the main reasons why the Raptors returned to the playoffs in 2014–15, Toronto's fearless little floor general is a good offensive player but also endears himself to fans with his all-out hustle, tenacity, willingness to take charges, and his ability to sometimes snatch rebounds against bigger and stronger men.

Damon Stoudamire
In 1995–96 the 5'11" point guard adapted quickly to the NBA, ranking second in rookie scoring and leading all first year players in assists. His deadly left-handed three-point shooting touch, ability to penetrate for a layup, or pass to a teammate made him a challenging weapon to contain.

DeMar DeRozan
After Chris Bosh's exodus in 2010, the Raptors' 2009 first-round pick was counted on to elevate his game—which he did. In 2014 the shooting guard played in his first NBA All-Star game and was a key contributor in Toronto's postseason run.

Jose Calderon
A gifted passer, who had his share of bumps during his long Raptors tenure, and efficient shooter, the Spaniard will go down as one of the best point guards in Raptors history.

Doug Christie
A lockdown defender and respectable scorer, who played in Toronto's inaugural season, Christie averaged 14.2 points and 2.1 steals in 314 career Raptors games.

Anthony Parker

A reliable 2-guard with overseas playing experience, he shot 46 percent in 235 Raptors regular season games and averaged a career postseason-high 15.2 points per contest against the New Jersey Nets in the 2007 playoffs.

T.J. Ford

Possessing terrific speed and athleticism for a six-foot point guard, the injury-prone 2003 first-round pick shared the starting point guard duties with Jose Calderon at times but still averaged 13.2 points and 7.2 assists during his 126 regular season games in a Toronto uniform.

Alvin Williams

A longtime Raptor and effective playoff performer, Williams scored a career postseason high 23 points in Game 2 against the New York Knicks in a 2001 first-round match-up.

Mike James

The well-traveled former NBA champion only spent one season in Toronto, but it was the best year of his career. In 2005–06 James scored 30 or more points 14 times while averaging 20.3 points in 79 games.

Rafer Alston

The streetball star was criticized for his attitude while in Toronto, but it didn't distract him from having a career-best 14.2 points and dishing out 6.4 assists per game in the 2004–05 campaign.

Jarrett Jack

Like Ford, Jack also battled Calderon for Toronto's starting point guard role. During the 2009–10 season, the Georgia Tech product was a durable and productive option, scoring in double figures 45 times and shooting 48.1 percent from the floor.

75 Dunk You Very Much

When it came to the fine art of greeting the rack with power and creativity, Vince Carter was a master. In the 2000 Slam Dunk Contest, VC was a jaw-dropping and unstoppable force.

But he wasn't the only Raptor to have "NBA Slam Dunk champion" on his resume.

There was one high-flyer who accomplished the feat in a Toronto uniform while two former Raptors captured the crown with other teams. Here are those three men who showed off their aerial talents in the NBA's popular All-Star Weekend event.

Dee Brown
At the 1991 Slam Dunk Contest in Charlotte, North Carolina, the 22-year-old Boston Celtics rookie guard would face the following contestants: Rex Chapman (Charlotte Hornets), Blue Edwards (Utah Jazz), Shawn Kemp (Seattle SuperSonics), Kenny Williams (Indiana Pacers), Otis Smith (Orlando Magic), Kenny Smith (Houston Rockets), and Kendall Gill (Hornets). During the competition Brown delighted the crowd when he pumped up his Reebok Pump shoes, which had an internal inflation mechanism, before delivering a slam. "People think Reebok told me to do that with the shoes," Brown told *The Breakdown with Dave & Audley* podcast. "That was unrehearsed and thought about on the spur of the moment."

The 6'1" Brown would match up against the super athletic 6'10" Shawn "Reign Man" Kemp in the final. The guard would finish off Goliath as a result of his famous no-look left-handed jam, which featured Brown covering his eyes with his right arm, to win the dunk title. "Never practiced it," the 1990 first-round pick said, "just made it up on the spot. Just wanted to do something that was different, like a signature dunk. People remember Michael Jordan taking off from the foul line and Dominique doing the windmill dunk, so I wanted to do something that was, obviously, totally different."

Prior to the dunk contest that evening, Brown and Kemp actually had a funny run-in with a fan, involving a case of mistaken identity. "All the contestants were sitting all together in a little area before the contest watching the other NBA All-Star activities that night," Brown said. "Everyone is asking Shawn Kemp for his autograph and Rex Chapman and all the guys who were sitting there. I was sitting next to Shawn Kemp. One kid goes, 'Hey Shawn, you gonna win the contest?' Shawn [says], 'Yeah, I'm gonna win it.' [The kid] goes, 'Hey, what does your little brother think?' At that time, me and him [Kemp] had the same haircut. So they thought I was his little brother. That pissed me off so badly, *Oh okay, you ain't going to win nothing.* So when I got to the finals, I remembered that. It kinda motivated me a little bit more. I thought it was a funny story."

Since winning the dunk championship, Brown still reminded Kemp what happened that night. "I played with him (Kemp) a few years right before I retired," Brown mentioned. "I say, 'Hey Shawn, I got a trophy at my house. You wanna come look at it, man? Because you don't have one.'"

In the mind of 1992 Slam Dunk champion Cedric Ceballos, Brown's victory was a hollow one. The ex-NBA forward said the Celtics guard used his ideas after losing to him in a college dunk contest. "Fortunately for Dee Brown, everything that I beat him in college, he used on the NBA stage," Ceballos told *The Breakdown with Dave & Audley* podcast, "the pumping up of the shoes, the covering of his face. All those dunks that I beat him with in college, he used in the NBA, so I was really hot then. Him winning that dunk contest gave me determination to go next summer, work hard to get playing time where I can go and be in a dunk contest, and beat him with more creative ways that I *showed* him before he used that to get his shoe endorsements and put his name on the map and all that."

It's safe to say Ceballos and Brown won't be exchanging Valentine's Day cards anytime soon.

Fred Jones

In 2004 at the Staples Center in Los Angeles, the 6'4" Indiana Pacers bench player would have to deal with these competitors: 2002 and 2003 NBA Slam Dunk champion Jason Richardson (Golden State Warriors), Chris Andersen (Denver Nuggets), and Ricky Davis (Boston Celtics). During the contest Jones excited the crowd with an impressive one-handed reverse jam after lobbing a bounce pass to himself from the three-point line.

He and the reigning champion, Richardson, met in the final. After Jones missed his last slam attempt twice, on a pass from a friend in the stands, J-Rich had a chance to win his third consecutive dunk title, but he missed his final jam as well, giving the championship to Jones.

It wasn't pretty, but Frederick Terrell Jones was your 2004 Slam Dunk champion. "It was an honour to be out there because Jason Richardson is one of the greatest dunkers ever," Jones told the media. "I was just trying to be creative and do something different."

Terrence Ross

The 2013 Slam Dunk Contest in Houston featured a solid group of gravity-defying men, so the Raptors rookie would be facing the likes of 2012 Slam Dunk champion Jeremy Evans (Utah Jazz), Kenneth Faried (Denver Nuggets), Eric Bledsoe (Los Angeles Clippers), 2007 Slam Dunk champion Gerald Green (Indiana Pacers), and James White (New York Knicks). Ross would advance into an entertaining final against the defending champion.

Evans' first dunk involved leaping over a black cloth covered easel and then revealing it was a painting of himself performing the exact same slam. He'd autograph it on the spot.

Ross' opening dunk in the final—while wearing a Vince Carter No. 15 purple Raptors jersey—was a twisting and thunderous baseline one-hander off a pass from the side of the backboard. "It was weird, but I was honoured," Carter said. "It was great to see that jersey on the floor in that atmosphere of the dunk contest."

The kid with prime-time hops, Ross, then sported his own No. 31 Raptors top and would seal the dunk title by soaring over a ball boy while taking the ball between the legs then unleashing another one-handed jam. "I told [the ball boy] the day before that I was going to jump over him, but I never told him I was going to go through the legs," Ross admitted. "He was kind of nervous. When I first grabbed him, he said, 'You're not going to hit me, right?' I said, 'No, I'm not going to hit you.' So I had to calm his nerves."

It was a fun night as Ross joined Carter as the only Raptors Slam Dunk champions in franchise history. "I feel blessed, but it's still overwhelming," Ross said, "just trying to soak it all in."

76 Herbie Kuhn

Employed since the franchise's 1995 inception, Herbie Kuhn, the Raptors' public address announcer, has one of the sweetest jobs in sports, and the Toronto native knows it. "First and foremost, sitting in the seat that I have and watching the growth and evolution of professional basketball here in my home city has been an unparalleled privilege," said Kuhn, who has announced over 800 NBA games. "It has been at times incredibly frustrating, it has been at other times incredibly exhilarating, and on occasion it has been depressing. You know we have done so well at points looking at those Vince Carter, Charles Oakley, and Antonio Davis years, and then there have been times where it has been a lot of 'Oh my goodness, I can't believe they just did that again.' I guess if you were to put it into one term, I'd say it has been a roller coaster, but it has been a fun one."

Kuhn definitely keeps a busy schedule and has a consistent gameday routine. "I usually arrive at the arena for a 7:00 PM game at 3:30 PM and the first thing I do is go to the media room and get the notes and the rosters," Kuhn told CP24.com. "I am an old school guy that likes handwriting everything so I have a book where I will then write all my introductions as well as the rosters and the statistics that I will want to know. By the time I have done all that, it is 4:45 PM or so and I try to get some dinner and have some quiet time. Then at 6:00 PM every game myself and another gentlemen named Steve Kearns are co-chaplains for the team, so we have a pregame chapel service that is open to both home players and visiting players as well. That wraps up by 6:15 PM, and my first read is usually around 6:20 PM or so. When I say, 'Ladies and gentlemen, welcome to whatever sponsor night at the Air Canada

Centre, tonight's game is between the Dallas Mavericks and your Toronto Raptors,' and that's it, we are off to the races."

If you're hosting a community outreach, sports fund-raiser, school fund-raiser, charitable cause, or business initiative and want Kuhn to appear at your event, contact the Raptors by filling out an online form at http://www.nba.com/raptors/community/playerappearances.

77 Fantastic Forwards

The Raptors have been blessed. Since 1995 the club has had some talented forwards wear its uniform, including Chris Bosh and Tracy McGrady. Here's a list of some of Toronto's top all-time small and power forwards:

Chris Bosh
A franchise leader in numerous all-time categories, the Raptors' skilled and agile former first-round pick was a 20 and 10 talent who could score inside and out, which made him a frustrating mismatch for many opposing big men.

Charles Oakley
"Oak" was a burly and tough player who wasn't afraid of confrontation and working hard on the court. He was an integral leader and motivator for the young Raptors playoff teams of the early 2000s.

Donyell Marshall
Whether it's hitting 12 three-pointers or grabbing 24 rebounds in a single game, the 6'9" Pennsylvania native could hurt you in multiple ways.

Tracy McGrady

Young, long, and supremely athletic, T-Mac was a good shot blocker, especially in 1999–00, and on the verge of great things offensively in Toronto before he left the Raptors in 2000.

Andrea Bargnani

When healthy and motivated, the seven-foot Italian could light up opposing teams with his shooting ability as evidenced by his 41-point performance against the New York Knicks in 2010.

Morris Peterson

The durable, good shooter hustled on the court and, of course, always looked cool with the headband. What's not to like about one of Toronto's most popular players?

Amir Johnson

He was a blue-collar worker. It didn't matter if he was hurt and/ or tired, the former Detroit Pistons draft pick applied maximum effort on the court and was always looking to improve his game, including the addition of shooting three-pointers to his offensive arsenal a few seasons ago.

Rudy Gay

Despite his short 51-game Raptors sample size and fondness for excessive shooting at times, the 6'8" scorer did produce by putting up 19.5 points and 6.8 rebounds per contest.

Jalen Rose

In 177 games as a Raptor, the versatile former University of Michigan Fab 5 member hit 185 three-pointers and averaged 16.2 points per night.

78 Raptors Kids Have Become Pro Stars

As Raptors players Ronald "Popeye" Jones and Dell Curry weren't All-Stars or Hall of Famers, but they executed their roles. Jones did the dirty work, providing rebounding help in the paint while Curry was mainly a sharpshooter off the bench. But who knew that years later, it would be their offspring grabbing the headlines?

Popeye was a 6'8" forward, who mainly played in cities with National Hockey League clubs such as Dallas, Denver, Boston, Washington, and Toronto. In fact, during his Raptors days, he remembers having puck fever. "I loved going to Gretzky's [restaurant] and hanging out there," said Jones in a podcast interview on *The Breakdown with Dave & Audley.* "I actually started watching ice hockey when I was in Toronto. My kids didn't play when I was there, but I started watching the sport, *Hockey Night in Canada* and Don Cherry. I'm a huge hockey fan now."

Soon enough, Jones wouldn't be the only one. His sons, including Seth, expressed a desire to play the game. Popeye, who was a rookie hockey dad, knew he needed some advice, so he reached out to a Colorado Avalanche star. "I was playing for the Nuggets and I was working out at the Pepsi Center and I saw Joe Sakic. I said, 'Hey Joe,' and he had no idea who I was," Jones said in an NHL.com article. "I just said, 'My kids want to play hockey.' He turned and looked at me and said, 'From the look of you, your kids are going to be huge. They need skating lessons.'"

After those wise words, Popeye's kids dove right into hockey, especially Seth, who attended Colorado's Game 7 Stanley Cup win against the New Jersey Devils in 2001. "It just kind of took off from there," Seth Jones said.

Sweet-shooting Dell Curry played 16 seasons in the NBA—including three for the Raptors—but the accomplishments of his son, Steph, would dwarf his own.

If you ask Popeye, Seth's hockey passion began when he tried to copy his brother, Justin, who is three years older. "When we moved to Denver, Justin asked to play, and like any other little brother, you want to do what you're big brother is doing," Jones explained. "Seth is a little guy tagging along. He wanted hockey stuff. He wanted skates. He wanted to skate with the rest of the kids. It just took off. It seemed like he never wanted to play any other sports."

Years later, Seth would emerge as a highly touted 6'4" defenceman who'd be drafted fourth overall by the Nashville Predators in 2013 after some speculation he could have been the first ever African American hockey player chosen in the top spot. For a kid who was born in Texas and whose dad played in the NBA, Seth Jones was carving out his own unique path.

"I'm proud he's my son," Popeye said. "I know how much work he's put into it."

As for Dell Curry's boy, Stephen, he showed his promise early on. During his father's career in Toronto, the young Curry would take pregame practice shots at the Air Canada Centre, which caught the eye of Dell's teammates. "It's just amazing. Steph Curry, I remember I used to watch him play," ex-Raptors player Morris Peterson said. "He used to have a crowd before the game. He'd be out there shooting, shooting from halfcourt, shooting NBA threes, and here he is, 12, 13 years older, and look at him now."

For Stephen, a kid who'd follow in his dad's path, those Toronto years proved to be a great learning ground. Not only did he develop his quick-fire shooting touch, but his underrated passing game was coming of age. "Stephen learned everything from his daddy," said Muggsy Bogues, who played with Dell on the Charlotte Hornets and Raptors. "Stephen [was] always coming to our practices, was always shooting around with the guys. He really got to watch how the game is supposed to be played, and as he grew up, information stayed in his head. He's always known how to make his teammates better. It's why he has those pure point guard skills today."

In a March 2010 *Toronto Star* article, Curry mentioned how much he valued his time in Toronto. "It helps to have that kind of experience," said Curry who'd average 17.5 points per game in his first NBA season. "It's a lot different when you're going through the grind of an NBA season yourself. That goes without saying, but I think it's definitely a benefit to be around players like Alvin Williams, like Vince Carter, when he was there and see how they handled themselves on a day-to-day basis. I can just have a little leg up in my first year and feel comfortable here."

Dell's boy would turn out just fine. Steph received the NBA's 2014–15 MVP award, won the title that season, and has become one of the league's deadliest shooters and overall most outstanding talents.

Just ask the New York Knicks.

Curry lit them up for 54 points in the Mecca of Basketball—Madison Square Garden—on February 27, 2013. Even his father couldn't explain it. "There's zones and there's zones in New York City," Dell Curry told SBNation.com. "I was never in a zone like he was. To be in New York, in Madison Square Garden, and put on that type of show—I've been in zones where obviously you feel like you can't miss, you just want the ball, you're going to shoot it from wherever you're at. He's in that kind of zone, but to do it on that type of stage, national audience, honestly, I can't say I've ever felt that way."

79 Three-Point Streakin'

On February 26, 1999, Vince Carter hit a first quarter three-pointer against the Minnesota Timberwolves. No big deal, right? Well, game after game, year after year, the Raptors kept sinking at least one three-ball per contest until January 24, 2011, when they were 0-for-13 from beyond the arc against the Memphis Grizzlies in a 100–98 loss.

After nearly 12 years, Toronto's streak of 986 consecutive games with a made three-pointer was over, a feat the head coach found out about after he was walking off the floor. "Somebody yelled at me that I should be fired because we didn't make a three," Jay Triano said. "The organization should be very proud of the streak that it had, but for us to go into a game thinking that we should try to make a three and for us to have a depleted lineup with guys like [Leandro] Barbosa and [Linas] Kleiza and [Jose] Calderon not in uniform, I mean those are guys that are going to sometimes step up and make them for us. You know what, it's a record, and that record did not help us climb one spot in our race to try to get better as a team. It's one less thing we can put in our media notes. Alright? So that's about the extent of that streak being broken."

Message received, Jay.

The Dallas Mavericks, though, started a streak that would eclipse Toronto's NBA record that same season with 1,108 straight games with a made three-ball. But knocking down threes, you could say, has been a regular Raptors habit over the years. Here are some of the Raptors' better long-range shooters:

Morris Peterson

Mo Pete has a team-record 801 made three-point field goals and hit more than 100 three-balls in six straight seasons.

Andrea Bargnani
Whether you liked the seven-foot Italian or not, he was a tough cover when he had his long-distance game working. The 2006 No. 1 overall pick is second behind Peterson with 579 career three-pointers.

Vince Carter
VC was more than just a dunker. In the 2000–01 campaign, Mr. Half-Man, Half-Amazing hit 162 regular season three-balls and in the playoffs against the Philadelphia 76ers that year he drained nine threes in Game 3 of their second-round series. Carter is third in the team's all-time history with 554 made three-pointers.

Jose Calderon
This longtime Toronto point guard was more of a skilled play-maker than a long-range marksman, but Calderon still made three-pointers—456 to be exact.

Doug Christie
A member of Toronto's original 1995–96 squad, Christie wasn't afraid to hurt teams from beyond the arc. In the 1996–97 season, he drilled 147 threes and would finish his Raptors career with 431.

Kyle Lowry
In 2013–14 the Raptors' tough-minded guard was lethal from three-point land, sinking a franchise single-season record 190 threes.

Damon Stoudamire
The 1995–96 Rookie of the Year did not suffer a sophomore jinx. In his second season, Mighty Mouse would knock down 176 three-pointers on the way to scoring 20.2 points per game. Stoudamire would end up with 374 threes in a Raptors uniform.

Anthony Parker
Never flashy, but always steady, Parker drained 342 three-pointers in his three seasons in Toronto.

Donyell Marshall
The forward had 271 career threes with the Raptors, and an NBA record-tying 12 of them came in one game against the Philadelphia 76ers in 2005.

Terrence Ross
In his second season, T-Ross made 161 threes, but on one magical night in January 2014, the kid would sink 10 from downtown on the way to his franchise record-tying 51 points against the Los Angeles Clippers.

Dee Brown
Yes, the 1991 NBA Slam Dunk champion was a sharpshooter. In fact, during the league's lockout-shortened year, Brown led the NBA with 135 made threes and would eventually end up with 267 in his Toronto career.

Walt Williams
In 1996–97 the Wizard was solid from three-point land, drilling 175 three-pointers. The forward knocked down 224 from beyond the arc as a Raptor.

Lou Williams
In his lone Raptors season, Williams drilled a career-high 152 three-pointers on the way to winning the NBA's Sixth Man of the Year award.

Tracy Murray

Another member of Toronto's debut 1995–96 club, the UCLA product was a three-point artist who sunk 151 in the Raptors' opening season. Overall, Murray would finish with 220 in the T-Dot.

Jason Kapono

A winner of back-to-back NBA Three-Point Shootouts, Kapono earned the latter as a Raptors player in 2008. A 2006 NBA champion while playing with the Miami Heat, he hit 155 threes in his time with Toronto.

Dell Curry

With 1,245 made career regular season three-balls on his resume, Stephen Curry's dad sank 202 of them as a Raptor in his final three NBA years.

80 Beasts of the Boards

The real rebounding beasts are the guys who bring their lunch box to work every night and clean the glass consistently. They do the dirty job most NBA stars don't have the desire, will, or strength to do. Fortunately, Raptors history is filled with those working-class guys.

Here are some of the best:

Chris Bosh

The five-time Toronto All-Star crashed the boards better than anyone in team history, becoming Toronto's all-time rebounding leader (4,776). He was more highly skilled than just an average blue-collar player, but when it came to rebounds, his effort was all in. The Georgia Tech product averaged more than 10 boards per game in three different seasons. On March 25, 2005, the future multiple NBA champion had a 24-point and 22-rebound (his Raptors career-high) performance against the Philadelphia 76ers while on November 14, 2006, Bosh had 23 points and 22 rebounds versus the Golden State Warriors.

Antonio Davis

An undersized centre for much of his time in Toronto, Davis had to really earn his rebounds. The 6'9" veteran averaged more than 10 per game in 2000–01 (including an all-time franchise best 787 total boards that year), which would be his lone All-Star season. In 310 games in Toronto, the Oakland, California, native had 9.2 rebounds per contest.

Charles Oakley

Over the years, the tough, surly, and intimidating forward would outmuscle many guys for rebounds. Even in his late 30s, Oakley was still a formidable force in the paint. In 2000–01 the ex-New York Knicks enforcer ripped down more than 10 boards in six straight games, including an 18-rebound effort against Kobe Bryant, Shaquille O'Neal, and the Los Angeles Lakers, a day before his birthday, on December 17, 2000. That season Oakley averaged 9.6 points and 9.5 rebounds per game.

Donyell Marshall

Mostly known for his three-point touch, the 6'9" forward had a nose for rebounds, too.

After being traded to Toronto from Chicago in December 2003, Marshall would average 10.7 boards in 66 games as a Raptor. During that season he had back-to-back 19-rebound outings against the New York Knicks and Orlando Magic, respectively, and a Raptors career-best 24 against his former team, the Bulls, on

February 17, 2004. During his 131 games in Toronto, the UConn star finished with 8.7 rebounds per contest.

Amir Johnson

This Los Angeles native always delivered a first-class effort on the court. The forward proved it on March 15, 2013, when he had a career-high 21 rebounds in a 92–78 win against the Charlotte Bobcats. Raptors head coach Dwane Casey said: "That was a heck of an effort by Amir Johnson. I can't sing his praises enough." Johnson was more humble. "Career highs are one thing, but getting wins is what I really want," he said. "We're just going to keep playing hard and get as many games as we can."

Jerome Williams

The Junkyard Dog was all about high energy and working hard on the court. He did whatever he could to grab a rebound and/or contribute any other meaningful plays to help Toronto win. During the 2002–03 campaign, JYD had 10 consecutive games with 10 or more rebounds, including his Raptors career-high 20 boards against the Washington Wizards on January 14, 2003.

Reggie Evans

Despite only a 58-game sample size in Toronto, Evans, when healthy, was a relentless and passionate rebounder who wasn't afraid to go all out. The 6'8" forward was the epitome of a blue-collar guy, which Raptors fans and his teammates loved. On November 24, 2010, Evans had his Raptors career-high 22 rebounds in a 106–90 win against his former team, the Philadelphia 76ers. "He's just a big, crazy dude who gets rebounds," DeMar DeRozan said, "a tough guy out there on the floor."

Evans' old 76ers teammate, Andre Iguodala, praised him. "It's just about hard work. There is no equation behind that," he said. "He just goes out there and works hard, and you can only respect that. If anything, our guys should learn from the way he plays the game." In his final Raptors season, Evans averaged 11.5 rebounds in 30 games.

One to watch: Jonas Valanciunas

The young Lithuanian centre is gradually becoming a better rebounder and showed some of his brilliance on April 11, 2014, when he set a career-high with 21 boards against the New York Knicks. Later that season he made an impressive playoff debut against the Brooklyn Nets. He averaged double-doubles in the first three games of the series, including a 17-point and 18-rebound Game 1 performance.

81 Take a Raptors Road Trip

Cheering your face off at the Air Canada Centre and Jurassic Park is cool. The Raptors enjoy the love at home. But bringing your enthusiasm on the road is a whole new level of die-hard fandom. Well, passionate Raptors followers have been travelling in bigger numbers to see their team.

On November 22, 2014, an energetic group from Toronto were rooting loudly in Cleveland as the Raptors beat up LeBron James and the Cavs 110–93. The team noticed the support. "It's dope, man," said Lou Williams, who scored 36 points in the win. "This has been an incredible experience as far as the fans go. We have a very, very excited fan base." DeMar DeRozan agreed. "It felt like a playoff game, honestly, with our fans being in there, cheering and singing the national anthem," he said. "It was just an amazing thing." Head coach Dwane Casey called it "unbelievable." "It was like old-school soccer, travelling with the flag and all that," Casey said. "That was big."

But not just fans were making the trips. In December of 2014, general manager Masai Ujiri also hit the road. He joined a bus full of Pistons supporters as they rode to Detroit, where Toronto would defeat the Pistons 110–100. During the ride Ujiri sang a song with the die-hards called "We Love You Raptors." There's no doubt that kind of thing didn't happen in the Rob Babcock days.

So, if you're thinking of taking a Raptors single or multi-city road trip, there are some things you'll need to know. Who better to ask than Peter Robert Casey, a man who attended "30 games in 30 days" at every NBA arena from November 7–December 6, 2013? He's the founder and chief community officer of Sports Passport (http://sportspassport.co/), a tool that lets fans easily track every sporting event they attend.

Casey had some helpful tips, regarding tickets, apps to use, and other valuable information: "We recommend using SeatGeek. com—a ticket app and aggregator—that compares ticket prices across many sellers and ranks each deal based on biggest bargain or worst rip-off. StubHub.com and its app are another great resource for spotting deals on the secondary market. Generally speaking, it's cheaper to buy tickets in advance.

"Hotels.com is our preferred resource for finding the widest range of accommodations to fit your budget. If you're being spontaneous by extending your trip at the last minute or have pro-crastinated (we don't recommend the latter), the Hotel Tonight app offers seamless discovery and booking of hotel rooms at the 11th hour, all from the convenience of your smartphone. You'll obviously need additional tickets for a multi-city NBA trip, and we encourage you to book those well in advance. But if you find yourself in an NBA city on gameday and are looking to go, check out the Gametime.co app or the aforementioned SeatGeek and StubHub sites to see if there's any inventory.

"Since Canada only has one NBA team, a multi-city trip means you'll be crossing the border. So not only will you need your passport, but the currency changes, too. Check U.S. exchange rates periodically to stay abreast of any major changes. You will usually get the best exchange rates at banks and post offices. Avoid the change bureaus you encounter in touristy areas."

Other essential apps include:

- **Waze.** It's an effective crowdsourced traffic-avoidance app. Download it. You'll thank us later.
- **Sporcle app.** It has Raptors trivia for a Raptors road trip. 'Nuff said. It also helps avoid long bouts of silence on long driving intervals.
- **Pogoseat app.** Use this to upgrade your seats.

82 Hello, Mr. Williams

If you thought Smith was a popular last name, go back and look at the Raptors' all-time player roster. You'll notice there were eight men who had "Williams" stitched to the back of their jerseys.

Sorry Corliss Williamson, you just missed the cut.

This exclusive group may not have been All-Stars, but they all contributed in their own way. Here's a brief look at who they are:

Aaron Williams
A journeyman frontcourt player, he saw action in two NBA Finals with the New Jersey Nets; was involved in the Vince Carter trade; and suited up for 10 NBA teams (the Utah Jazz, Milwaukee Bucks, Denver Nuggets, Vancouver Grizzlies, Seattle SuperSonics,

Washington Wizards, Nets, Raptors, New Orleans Hornets, and Los Angeles Clippers).

Alvin Williams
Known for hitting the shot, which sealed Toronto's first ever playoff series win in 2001, the fan favourite guard averaged 9.3 points, 4.3 assists, and 1.2 steals in 417 games as a Raptor.

Eric Williams
Another piece from the Vince Carter deal, he averaged four points in 62 games with Toronto. Williams played for seven NBA clubs (the Boston Celtics, Denver Nuggets, Cleveland Cavaliers, New Jersey Nets, Raptors, San Antonio Spurs, and Charlotte Bobcats).

Herb Williams
The centre/forward was part of the February 1996 trade with the New York Knicks, which brought him and Doug Christie to Toronto. Williams would only play one game in a Raptors uniform before being waived.

Jerome "Junkyard Dog" Williams
One of the most popular players in team history, JYD won over the hearts of the Toronto fans with his unlimited energy and effort on the court. The forward was also a helpful piece off the bench during the Raptors' 2001 postseason run.

Lou Williams
Instant offence had been the sharpshooter's role ever since joining the Raptors via a steal of a trade with the Atlanta Hawks in June 2014. He developed a knack for hitting last-second shots, giving Toronto's offence a lethal scoring option behind DeMar DeRozan and Kyle Lowry.

Micheal Williams

A guard, who won an NBA title as a Detroit Pistons rookie, played only two games with the Raptors in 1999.

Walt Williams

"The Wizard" was a three-point specialist who loved wearing high socks. The forward averaged 16.4 points per game and shot 40 percent from beyond the arc in his first Raptors season (1996–97). But the good times didn't last. He was shipped out to the Portland Trail Blazers in the February 1998 Damon Stoudamire multi-player deal.

83 Former Raptors Gone Bad

If you're an NBA player about to retire, it's probably a challenging period in your life. That's especially the case for the following ex-Raptors, who have been on the wrong side of the law.

Alvin Robertson

One of the original Raptors is used to having a mug shot.

Here were some of his infractions:

- On October 28, 1995, days before Toronto's first regular-season game in franchise history, Robertson was arrested on an assault charge for a reported "incident" with an unidentified Toronto woman. In a 2010 Deadspin article, ex-Raptor John Salley, known for his storytelling abilities, alleged "the incident" involved Robertson "kicking a naked prostitute out of his hotel room after deciding he didn't want to pay."

- In August 1997 Robertson pled no contest to four misdemeanor charges of abusing an ex-girlfriend and was sentenced to one year in prison.
- In 2002 Robertson was sentenced to three years in jail for a probation violation involving a rape accusation, even though his longtime girlfriend recanted the account she mentioned to police.
- In January 2007 he was arrested in San Antonio on various charges, including several relating to domestic violence.
- In February 2010 Robertson was arrested for the alleged sexual assault of a 14-year-old girl, trafficking an underage child for purposes of sex, and forcing a sexual performance by a child. Authorities believe in 2009 he was one of seven people who kidnapped and coerced her into prostitution and made her dance at a Corpus Christi strip club.
- In January 2015 Robertson was arrested after being on the run since cutting off a GPS monitor while out on bond in the 2009 case involving the sex trafficking of a minor. He'd been released from jail on December 12, 2014, and was required to wear the monitor.

Keon Clark

In December of 2013, Clark was sentenced to an eight-year prison term after pleading guilty to weapons and driving under the influence charges in two separate cases. He was given four years for each count. A Raptors shot-blocking master back in the day, the 1998 first-round pick had a long battle with alcohol even during his NBA career. At one point he admitted he wasn't mentally prepared to deal with the life of a professional athlete. "The money, the fame, the fact that I was on TV, people think money will make your life better," said Clark who played for the Raptors, Denver Nuggets, Sacramento Kings, and Utah Jazz. "Money didn't dissolve my problems. It increased them."

Rafer Alston

The streetball legend's temper had been an issue, off and on, for years, which resulted in various run-ins with the law. One incident, in particular, in July 2010 involved Alston, who reportedly beat a 31-year-old man over the head with a beer bottle during a wild melee, which began inside a New York strip club and then spilled into the streets. In August of 2011, Erick Franceschini sued Alston and the Perfection Gentleman's Club in Queens for an unspecified amount of damages. "My client had 12 staples in his head," Franceschini's attorney, John Rapawy, explained. "He suffered a concussion."

According to Rapawy, Alston assaulted his client in the street. He also mentioned Franceschini filed a police report, but the ex-Raptors point guard wasn't arrested. This lawsuit arrived in May after Alston was hired as the new head coach and athletic director at a Houston-area school called Christian Life Center Academy. It was not exactly a great impression to leave with the new boss at a religious school.

Benoit Benjamin

The former Raptors centre made millions in his NBA career, so you'd think if he had kids, they'd be well taken care of. But in 2010 the former 1985 third overall pick was ordered by a court in Monroe, Louisiana, to pay a whopping $517,200 in back child support payments.

Oliver Miller

Another original Raptor, the overweight talent had problems in April 2011 when he allegedly pistol-whipped a man during a fight at a family cookout in Maryland.

He was arrested and given the following charges: first and second-degree assault, reckless endangerment, possessing a handgun, using a handgun in a violent crime, possessing a handgun in a vehicle, and disorderly conduct plus other charges.

He pleaded guilty in the fall of 2011. He was originally sentenced to five years in prison, but Miller would only serve one year in jail. After his release he was placed on probation for five years.

84 NCAA Champion Raptors

March Madness is that time of year where millions of delirious sports fans get all giddy with the hope their bracket will win their Tournament pool. It's also when Cinderella teams rise, college Goliaths fall during thrilling upsets, and unknown players make a name for themselves in this frenzied "win-or-go-home" battle of basketball survival.

When looking back at the Toronto Raptors' all-time roster, quite a few players have travelled that chaotic path and have come out on top. They've experienced the ultimate joy of cutting down those nets and calling themselves NCAA national champions. Four of them were even awarded Most Outstanding Player of the Final Four.

Here are the NCAA title winners:

Lonny Baxter—Maryland (2002)
Ed Davis—North Carolina (2009)
Juan Dixon—Maryland (2002)/Final Four Most
   Outstanding Player
Tyler Hansbrough—North Carolina (2009)
Antonio Lang—Duke (1991 and 1992)

Before playing seven seasons with the Raptors, Morris Peterson earned a championship ring at Michigan State in 2000.

Jamaal Magloire—Kentucky (1998)
Eric Montross— North Carolina (1993)
Morris Peterson—Michigan State (2000)
Ed Pinckney—Villanova (1985)/Final Four Most
   Outstanding Player
Charlie Villanueva—UConn (2004)
Jake Voskuhl—UConn (1999)
Corliss Williamson—Arkansas (1994)/Final Four Most
   Outstanding Player

Note: **Hakeem Olajuwon** won the 1983 Final Four Most
Outstanding Player, but his University of Houston Cougars were
upset by the North Carolina State Wolfpack in the title game.

85 Best Off the Bench

Throughout Raptors history, there have been a few men who
excelled exclusively on the second unit. Here is a list of some of the
best bench players who ever played for the Dinos:

Dell Curry

During the Raptors playoff runs of the early 2000s, the veteran
three-point specialist could always be counted on to deliver from
long distance. In 19 career postseason games with Toronto, Curry
shot 44.4 percent from beyond the arc, sinking 20-of-45 attempts.

Lou Williams

Williams was a lethal perimeter threat who scored in bunches
and didn't fear any opponent. For example in a November 2014

road game in Cleveland, facing LeBron James and his new-look Cavaliers, Williams exploded for a game-high 36 points in the Raptors win.

Leandro Barbosa

The Brazilian speedster could burn you with his feet or his three-point touch. He was the ultimate bench player, never starting in any of his 100 career Raptors games, while hitting 112 three-pointers during his Toronto stay.

Greivis Vasquez

The former New Orleans Hornets and Sacramento Kings starting point guard accepted and excelled in his backup role upon arriving in Toronto, via the Rudy Gay trade. A skilled passer and shooter, Vasquez, who hit a career-high 133 three-pointers in 2014–15, was one of the key reasons Toronto made a surprising trip to the 2014 playoffs and another postseason appearance in 2015. In fact, in his Raptors playoff debut against the Brooklyn Nets, he didn't crumble under the pressure, scoring 18 points and dishing out eight assists in Game 1.

Dee Brown

More than just a former Slam Dunk champion, he could frustrate teams with his three-point shooting skills. Two games in particular stand out. In April 1999 against the Milwaukee Bucks, Brown made nine three-pointers and then he sank eight against the Cleveland Cavaliers in March 1999.

Patrick Patterson

Another valuable piece in the Rudy Gay deal, the versatile 6'9" forward could hurt you from the beyond the arc and use his size to crash the glass. During his first ever NBA playoff series in 2014, Patterson was effective, averaging 10.4 points and 6.7 rebounds, including a 17-point effort in Game 3 and a 16-point, eight-rebound performance in Game 7 against the Brooklyn Nets.

86 Rooming with Montell

During his three years at Pepperdine University in beautiful Malibu, California, ex-Raptors guard Doug Christie once shared his space with a 6'8" sweet-singing kid, Montell Jordan.

He is the musician who sang the catchy 1995 hit single, "This Is How We Do It." "Montell was a funny guy. A great guy," said Christie who attended Pepperdine from 1989–1992. "As tall as he was, he never played basketball. He liked the game but didn't never really play it a whole lot. He would come watch. It was just fun being around him. I never thought that he would take off the way he did, but man, could he sing. I got those concerts that no one got to hear."

Christie knew Jordan's calling was pretty clear, and basketball wasn't it. Jordan, who played high school but not college basketball, realized it as well especially during his early prep years in Los Angeles. "What's really hilarious to me, is that a 6'2" guy shows up at your school named Jordan and just never played basketball before," Jordan admitted. "So I walked in to a place where expectation was very high and productivity was extremely low. I walked in there. I couldn't dunk. I couldn't drive. I couldn't do anything. I had a Jheri curl and I walked into that school, and they just knew that I was going to be the school saviour, and I really, really sucked."

Jordan ended up pursuing a career path better suited for him while Christie would carve out a solid NBA living. Not bad for a couple of roommates pursuing their dreams. Not bad at all.

87 Meet a Raptors Player

Here are the best ways to meet one of your favourites on the Raptors roster:

Greet Players Before Tip-Off

The Air Canada Centre gates typically open one hour before the game starts, and during this time, fans can spot many of their beloved players participating in an optional on-court shootaround. Some players can often be seen working on specific aspects of their game, warming up, or just stretching. It's a less hectic time, and if you arrive at the ACC early enough, you just might catch them.

Once you get into the arena, head toward the lower-bowl entrance where you'll meet an event staff member that will greet you when come in. The person you'll likely meet will be either a security guard or usher. Since the security guard wants to keep the environment safe, he/she is more prone to turning down requests from eager and excited fans. This is why you'll want to speak with an usher. His/her role is to help the fans. "The job of the usher is to create a championship experience for guests," said Audley Stephenson, a former ACC usher for close to 15 years and a basketball personality.

So when approaching an usher, be honest and say, as an example, "Hi, this is my first Raptors game. My kids and I are really excited to be here. Is there any way we can sit and watch practice near the players exit tunnel and then say hi or ask for an autograph afterward?" It doesn't matter if you have a lower-bowl seat or not, you can still make this request. Ushers are willing to work with you if you're upfront and not trying to sneak in. So if you politely ask, and the seating area isn't busy, the usher might let you sit there. But they can't guarantee you'll receive an autograph. That's obviously up to the player.

Once you're in your prime location, Stephenson offers some tips to positively attract a player's attention:

Know the Personality of the Player You're Targeting

By focusing on one player, you'll waste less time. As for a player's personality, you can typically tell by his on-court body language and/or his behaviour in public appearances how receptive he might be. For example, Amir Johnson did a lot of charity work and was very fan friendly when he was with the team, so was likely to be more open to signing autographs.

Stand Out

Stephenson suggests bringing big, colourful signs expressing appreciation for the player or any of his old school and unique team jerseys, which could spark a conversation. The key is to be different but in a fun, bright, and endearing way.

Bring Kids

Stephenson says it doesn't hurt to bring along cute little children wearing Raptors jerseys to appeal to a player's softer side. It's tough to resist hanging out with an adorable little Raptors fan.

Take the Toronto Subway

As crazy as it sounds, sometimes you bump into a Raptors employee on public transportation. For example, in May 2014 head coach Dwane Casey took the subway on the way to the ACC before Game 7 of Toronto's first-round playoff series against the Brooklyn Nets.

Also before winning NBA titles with the San Antonio Spurs ex-Raptor Matt Bonner used to regularly ride the subway to work.

Host a Community Event

The Raptors are very involved with the community, so if you're working with a community outreach initiative, a charity, business initiative, or school fund-raiser, you can potentially meet a player by having him at your event. To start the process, just fill out the player request form at http://www.nba.com/raptors/community/playerappearances.

88 Do You Have a 50?

Hall of Fame big man Wilt Chamberlain had 50 or more points 118 times in his career including 45 in one season (1961–1962). But he was an exception. The fact is, for mere mortals, scoring 50 or more just once is tough enough—unless you're facing the Raptors. The Dinos have been on the wrong end of several big performances.

Kobe. Enough said. Yet, Toronto has had 50-point guys of its own. Vince and T-Ross please stand up.

Whoever scores 50 in a game, it's still always a sight to behold. Here are some players who dropped a cool 50 and some change against or with the Raptors.

Opponents

Kobe Bryant—81 points—January 22, 2006—Staples Center
On a regular Sunday night in Southern California, Kobe was extraordinary. The 27-year-old had the game of his life by carving up the Raptors for a Lakers-record 81 points on 61 percent shooting in the 122–104 win.

The line—81 points, 28–46 field goals, 7–13 three-point field goals, 18–20 free throws, six rebounds, three steals, two assists, and one block

LeBron James—56 points—March 20, 2005—Air Canada Centre

Do you remember what you were doing at 20 years old? Maybe you were partying at college?

At 20 years old LeBron James was busy unleashing thunderous dunks and carrying the Cleveland Cavaliers on his back in his second year in the league.

On a Sunday afternoon at the ACC, the young King decided to drop 56 points on his future Miami Heat teammate, Chris Bosh, and the Raptors. Despite Cleveland's 105–98 loss, the NBA world got a taste of LeBron's future greatness.

The line—56 points, 18–36 field goals, 6–12 three-point field goals, 14–15 free throws, 10 rebounds, five assists, and two steals

Allen Iverson—51 points in January 2001, 54 points in Game 2, and 52 points in Game 5 in 2001 second-round playoff series—First Union Center

In 2001 The Answer was the NBA's Most Valuable Player. The Raptors found out why.

On January 21 that year, Allen Iverson dropped 51 on Toronto, but in a 110–106 overtime loss. Later, his Hall of Fame resume would grow in the 2001 playoffs. The future four-time scoring champion was unstoppable in his superstar postseason battle with Vince Carter.

A.I. barbecued Toronto with more than 50 points twice in the series on the way to helping the Philadelphia 76ers win the seven-game showdown.

Iverson would score a league playoff-best 723 points in 22 games that year. All you can do is tip your cap to the MVP.

The lines—January 21—51 points, 20–40 field goals, 4–8 three-point field goals, 7–8 free throws, four assists, three rebounds, and one steal

Game 2—54 points, 21–39 field goals, 3–5 three-point field goals, 9–9 free throws, five rebounds, four assists, and one steal

Game 5—52 points, 21–32 field goals, 8–14 three-point field goals, 2–2 free throws, seven assists, four steals, and two rebounds

Kevin Durant—51 points—March 21, 2014—Air Canada Centre

It's late in the second overtime. Your team is down by two. The game is on the line.

Who gets the ball? You better believe Kevin Durant does. With under 10 seconds left, the 2013–14 NBA MVP hit a clutch go-ahead three-pointer to seal a 119–118 double overtime thriller. "That was the craziest game I've ever been a part of," said Durant who erupted for 51 points including seven three-pointers.

The line—51 points, 15–32 field goals, 7–12 three-point field goals, 14–19 free throws, 12 rebounds, seven assists, one block, and one steal

Jamal Crawford—50 points—April 11, 2004—Air Canada Centre

Entering the fourth quarter, the 24-year-old sharpshooter heated up. Crawford scorched the Raptors with 28 of his 50 points in the final period and overtime to give the Chicago Bulls a 114–108 win. "I just tried to put two halves together," Crawford said. "I had it going, and my teammates did a great job of finding me. But more importantly we won. You don't want to take bad shots and alienate your teammates."

The line—50 points, 18–34 field goals, 6–11 three-point field goals, 8–11 free throws, seven rebounds, two assists, two steals, and one block

Raptors

Vince Carter—51 points vs. Phoenix Suns in 2000 and 50 points vs. Philadelphia 76ers in 2001 playoffs—Air Canada Centre

VC always knew how to excite a crowd. On February 27, 2000, in front of a national television audience, Vinsanity took flight. The 23-year-old dazzled Toronto fans with a franchise regular season record 51-point performance, which helped the Raptors edge the Phoenix Suns, 103–102.

Then in Game 3 against the Philadelphia 76ers in a 2001 second-round playoff series, Carter answered Allen Iverson's 54-point effort in Game 2 with a Raptors playoff-record 50 points and nine three-pointers in Toronto's 102–78 win.

The lines—vs. Suns—51 points, 17–32 field goals, 4–8 three-point field goals, 13–13 free throws, nine rebounds, three steals, and one assist

Game 3—50 points, 19–29 field goals, 9–13 three-point field goals, 3–3 free throws, seven assists, six rebounds, four blocks, and one steal

Terrence Ross—51 points—January 25, 2014—Air Canada Centre

After an underwhelming 2012–13 rookie campaign, the athletic Ross was still raw and developing until January 2014 when a flash of brilliance occurred. Facing the Los Angeles Clippers on Saturday night, Ross put on a three-point shooting clinic, draining 10 from beyond the arc.

He would surprisingly tie Vince Carter's regular season single-game team-record with 51 points in a 126–118 loss. Has Ross ever scored 50 in a game before?

"Never," Ross said. "That's my first time."

Raptors head coach Dwane Casey was impressed. "For the fans it was a great exhibition of basketball," Casey said. "The young man, Terrence, picked it up. We lose DeMar [DeRozan] and put on a heck of a display. Not only did he have 51 points, he had nine rebounds, which was huge too."

At the time Ross became the first player in NBA history to score 50 while averaging less than 10 points per game.

The line—51 points, 16–29 field goals, 10–17 three-point field goals, 9–10 free throws, nine rebounds, one assist, and one steal

89 Look at My NBA Title Ring!

For Toronto Raptors fans, who are still waiting for the franchise's first NBA title, it hurts to see their former star, Chris Bosh, have two NBA championship rings after leaving the club in bad shape in 2010.

But there are ex-Toronto players that Raptors followers don't mind rooting for such as multiple NBA champion Matt "The Red Rocket" Bonner who endeared himself to the city with his hustle, red hair, three-point stroke, and fondness for the local subway system.

Someday, though, Toronto will have an NBA title to call its own, but for now here's a list of former Raptors players who've already won on the league's biggest stage.

Leandro Barbosa—Golden State Warriors—2015
Mengke Bateer—San Antonio Spurs—2003
Marco Belinelli—San Antonio Spurs—2014
Chauncey Billups—Detroit Pistons—2004 (NBA Finals MVP)
Matt Bonner—San Antonio Spurs—2007 and 2014
Chris Bosh—Miami Heat—2012 and 2013

Earl Cureton—Philadelphia 76ers and Houston Rockets—1983 and 1994

Austin Daye—San Antonio Spurs—2014

Greg Foster—Los Angeles Lakers—2001

Lindsey Hunter—Los Angeles Lakers and Detroit Pistons—2002 and 2004

Mike James—Detroit Pistons—2004

Linton Johnson—San Antonio Spurs—2005

Cory Joseph—San Antonio Spurs—2014

Jason Kapono—Miami Heat—2006

John Long—Detroit Pistons—1989

Shawn Marion—Dallas Mavericks—2011

Sean Marks—San Antonio Spurs—2005 (as a player) and 2014 (as an assistant coach)

Tony Massenburg—San Antonio Spurs—2005

Jelani McCoy—Los Angeles Lakers—2002

Tracy Murray—Houston Rockets—1995

Radoslav "Rasho" Nesterovic—San Antonio Spurs—2005

Hakeem Olajuwon—Houston Rockets—1994 and 1995

John Salley—Detroit Pistons, Chicago Bulls, and Los Angeles Lakers—1989, 1990, 1996, and 2000

Peja Stojakovic—Dallas Mavericks—2011

Zan Tabak—Houston Rockets—1995

Corliss Williamson—Detroit Pistons—2004

Micheal Williams—Detroit Pistons—1989

Kevin Willis—San Antonio Spurs—2003

Note: Raptors head coach Dwane Casey was an NBA champion as a Dallas Mavericks assistant in 2011, and former Raptors general manager and part-owner Isiah Thomas won two NBA rings while playing for the Detroit Pistons.

90 Best of the Big Men

When you look at the centres that've played for the Raptors, you won't see any homegrown Hall of Fame talent. No offence Aleksandar Radojevic and Rafael Araujo, but Toronto has always struggled in drafting and/or developing elite big men.

The Raptors are hoping Jonas Valanciunas will end that drought. Years before JV, the club attempted to patch up the centre problem by acquiring two-time NBA champion Hakeem Olajuwon. Unfortunately, his advanced age and injuries restricted his effectiveness, which led to his retirement after one season in the Great White North.

Over the years, even though there hasn't been an Olajuwon (in his prime) or Shaquille O'Neal or Patrick Ewing patrolling the 5-spot for Toronto, there have been players who have definitely held their own amongst the land of trees in the paint. Here are some of those warriors:

Antonio Davis

Before being traded to the Raptors for Jonathan Bender in 1999, Davis was mainly a solid bench piece for many 1990s Indiana Pacers playoff clubs. During those years 7'4" Rik "The Dunking Dutchman" Smits was their centre, so once AD arrived in Toronto and took over the 5-spot, it would have rattled many who didn't think they could cut it in a new role. Not Davis. In his first Raptors season, the 6'9" centre had 23 double-doubles, played steady defence, and provided leadership to a young Toronto team on the cusp of big things. Those "things" would turn out to be the franchise's first three trips to the postseason.

Marcus Camby

The 1995–96 NCAA College Player of the Year didn't have your typical centre build. When he was drafted, the baby-faced kid was gangly and lean and would never be confused with chiseled San Antonio Spurs centre David Robinson. What Camby did have was the ability to be a disruptive force defensively with his shot-blocking talent. As a rookie he had seven games with five or more swats and in his second year he raised that number to 22 games. Unfortunately, he was traded away in 1998 before he could fulfill his potential in a Raptors uniform.

Oliver Miller

The heavy-set Forth Worth, Texas, native, who was a Toronto centre/forward, was a wide body but had a finesse to his game that smaller players would envy. Despite weighing over 280 pounds at times, he was a good passing big man blessed with terrific hands who could use his girth to score around the basket and rebound as evidenced by his 12.9 points (a career-high) and 7.4 boards per game in Toronto's opening season. In 1995–96 Miller was surprisingly effective on the defensive end, too. That season the Big O averaged 1.4 steals and 1.9 blocks per game, including nine swats in a near triple-double (18 points and 15 rebounds) against the Los Angeles Clippers on April 2, 1996.

Keon Clark

Looking at Clark, you would think he'd be frail because of his extremely thin legs and build. But once you drove the lane, he seemed like a big stone wall. With terrific athleticism packed into his wiry 6'11" frame, Clark would average 10.5 points, 6.7 rebounds, and 1.8 blocks per game in a Raptors uniform.

Jonas Valanciunas

JV is expected to be the main man in the middle when the Raptors become NBA title contenders. He is the future and a rare breed indeed. In an era filled with hybrid big men such as Dirk Nowitzki, Andrea Bargnani, and others, Valanciunas is a true centre who is focused more on converting high-percentage field goals and rebounding instead of hitting shots from beyond the arc. JV, though, is still a work in progress defensively and having issues with covering quicker big men due to his lack of Usain Bolt-like speed and conditioning at times.

There, though, is no questioning his offensive game. On January 12, 2015, he flashed some of his ability by having a 31-point and 12-rebound performance against a Detroit Pistons frontcourt starring young studs Andre Drummond and Greg Monroe.

Radoslav "Rasho" Nesterovic

The seven-footer from Slovenia wasn't a flashy player but just one who executed the little things properly. The 2005 NBA champion was a serviceable centre on the Raptors' first division title-winning team in 2006–07, in which he averaged 6.2 points, 4.5 rebounds, and 1.1 blocks per game and was also on their playoff roster in 2007–08.

91 Go to Real Sports Bar & Grill

Located on 15 York Street, seconds away from the Air Canada Centre and the rowdy Jurassic Park outside cheering section in downtown Toronto, Real Sports Bar & Grill has become a go-to destination before and/or after games for hungry and thirsty Raptors fans.

Once voted ESPN Mobile's Best Sports Bar in North America, this 25,000-square foot bar/restaurant has become a fan favourite. It doesn't hurt that it features a 39-foot HD big screen and 199 HD TVs. (A warning: once you see the Raptors on that monster HD big screen, you'll never want to use your old TV again.) And yes, they have 14 chicken wing flavours, 11 types of burgers, and 40 beer selections to choose from. Plus, the busy atmosphere feels like it's always a hip place to be. Granted, the prices are expensive, but for the occasional experience, it's worth it.

Even the Miami Heat like it. On February 3, 2013, after beating Toronto earlier on Super Bowl Sunday, head coach, Erik Spoelstra rewarded his team by allowing his players to watch the big game between the Baltimore Ravens and San Franchise 49ers from a Real Sports Bar & Grill private room. Two-time NBA champion Shane Battier said at the time, "I'd like to think it was a team-bonding activity that will propel us to bigger heights," he mentioned with a smile. "It was one of the best team days I've had in the NBA. It was one of the best days I've had as a pro socially with my teammates."

That would mark the start of Miami's 27-game winning streak, which would be the second longest in NBA history, and the Heat would go on to win the title. So perhaps Real Sports is truly the destination of champions.

92 Defensive Dinos

Defensive play isn't considered sexy. But throughout Raptors history, there have been more than a few players who embraced their defensive skills, which proved to be profitable for them and useful for the club. The moral of this story is dunking a ball can bring a crowd to its feet, but blocking that attempt can be just as sweet. Here are some of the best defenders in team history:

Doug Christie

Widely considered the best Raptors defender in team history, Christie is the club's all-time steals leader with 664. He also set franchise marks with most steals in a season (201) and most in a single game with nine against the Denver Nuggets on February 25, 1997. After his Raptors days, Christie would land on the 2003 NBA All-Defensive first team and become a three-time member of the NBA All-Defensive second team.

Marcus Camby

The future four-time NBA blocks leader was a pain for opposing offences early on. During the 1997–98 campaign, Camby set a Raptors single-season record with 230 blocks and he'd lead the league in swats per game at 3.65. Even more impressive was in two of his final four games of his Raptors career, he'd record triple-doubles with help from his shot-blocking skills.

Antonio Davis

You'd never see AD with any flashy chase-down blocks from behind or acrobatic steals, but he was solid. The undersized centre

While also known as a burly defender, Antonio Davis backs down New York Knicks forward Kurt Thomas in the post during the 2000 playoffs.

had 405 career blocks in a Raptors uniform with 151 coming in his All-Star 2000–01 campaign.

Keon Clark

A talented, 6'11", thin-legged, rim protector with a reported 7'5" wingspan and 40-inch vertical leap, Clark wreaked havoc on anyone looking for an easy trip to the hoop. On March 23, 2001, he set a Raptors single-game record with 12 blocks against the Atlanta Hawks.

Tracy McGrady

Before T-Mac became a two-time NBA scoring champion and seven-time All-Star, he was a shot blocking terror especially in the 1999–2000 season. That year, the 6'8" sleepy-eyed forward totaled 151 in 79 games.

Amir Johnson

In the 2012–13 season, the fan favourite forward had arguably his best year defensively. In 81 games he set career highs with 110 blocks and 81 steals while mostly coming off the bench.

Alvin Robertson

The 1986 NBA Defensive Player of the Year still had something left in his final NBA season. The 33-year-old guard, who led the league in steals three times, would have 2.2 per game in the Raptors' inaugural 1995–96 campaign.

Honourable mention: Chris Bosh, Charles Oakley, Anthony Parker, Jerome Williams, Morris Peterson, Alvin Williams, Kevin Willis, Kyle Lowry, Donyell Marshall, and James Johnson

93 Triple-Double Treats

If you're a fantasy basketball league junkie, you love it when your players fill up the stat sheet and rack up numbers in various categories. Over the years, there have been a few Raptors players who accomplished the feat. Here are members of that exclusive group:

Kyle Lowry

The All-Star has recorded multiple triple-doubles as a Raptor, but possibly the most special was on January 24, 2014, when he achieved the feat in his hometown of Philadelphia.

Lowry had 18 points, 13 assists, and 10 rebounds in front of family and friends in Toronto's 104–95 victory against the 76ers. "As long as it's with a win, I'm happy to have it," he said. "I'll take the thanks from the team and congratulations from all my teammates. But as long as it came with a win, that's all that really matters."

Damon Stoudamire

As a Raptor, Mighty Mouse put up three triple-doubles.

November 21, 1995—20 points, 12 rebounds, 11 assists against a 64-win Seattle SuperSonics team that would play in the 1996 NBA Finals.

November 8, 1996—21 points, 10 assists, 10 rebounds in a 93–92 home win against a Los Angeles Lakers squad featuring Shaquille O'Neal and a rookie Kobe Bryant.

March 18, 1997—30 points, 12 assists, 10 rebounds in a 117–105 win against another rookie Allen Iverson and his Philadelphia 76ers.

Alvin Williams

The longtime Raptor would record his only triple-double (11 points, 14 assists, and 10 rebounds) against the Atlanta Hawks in a 112–86 home win on March 23, 2001.

Marcus Camby

The second overall pick in 1996 racked up two triple-doubles with Toronto and used his shot-blocking talents to help make them happen. On April 14, 1998, against the New Jersey Nets, he put up 15 points, 12 rebounds, and 11 blocks in a 96–92 win. Then five days later on April 19 versus the Philadelphia 76ers, Camby did it again, this time with 13 points, 11 rebounds, and 10 blocks in a 107–78 loss.

Jose Calderon

During his Toronto stay, the Spaniard had two triple-doubles, including one on November 13, 2012, against the Indiana Pacers when he had 13 points, 10 assists, and 10 rebounds in a 74–72 Raptors victory. Over a month later on December 16, he'd hurt the Houston Rockets with a triple-double by recording 18 points, 14 assists, and 10 rebounds in a 103–96 Toronto win.

Vince Carter

With all his accolades as a Raptor, VC only had one triple-double, but it was a good one. On April 10, 2000, "Air Canada" had 31 points on 13-of-19 shooting to go along with 11 rebounds and 10 assists in a 112–103 Toronto triumph against the Cleveland Cavaliers.

Charles Oakley

In a Raptors uniform, the bruiser once put together a triple-double. Back on November 11, 2000, versus the Chicago Bulls, "Oak" had 12 assists, 11 rebounds, and 10 points in a 98–75 win.

Mark Jackson

Like Oakley, the talented playmaker also victimized the Chicago Bulls with his only Raptors triple-double. On November 26, 2000, Jackson totaled 11 points, 11 assists, and 11 rebounds in a 101–89 Toronto home victory.

Ben Uzoh

The most obscure name on the list had a triple-double in the last game of the Raptors 2011–12 regular season on April 26, 2012. The University of Tulsa guard had 12 points, a career-high 12 assists, and 11 rebounds in Toronto's 98–67 victory against the Nets.

94 Baby Dinos

For a first-year player to have any success in the NBA is quite remarkable. Fortunately, for the Raptors, they've had a few kids start their careers with a bang. Here are some of the best rookie seasons in team history.

Damon Stoudamire—1995–96

Mighty Mouse was a pint-sized point guard with big-time skills who set franchise rookie records with 1,331 points, 653 assists, and 133 made three-pointers. In 70 games Stoudamire averaged 19 points and 9.3 assists, which earned him the Rookie of the Year award.

He quickly knew he belonged in the league. "As crazy as it sounds, it was the second game of the season against the Indiana Pacers," he said. "They're a team that goes to the playoffs every year and they have great players. I had a good game against them, and that was when I knew that I could be something special."

Vince Carter—1998–99

During a lockout shortened 50-game season, Vinsanity put on a nightly aerial highlight show, which wowed fans, players, and even head coaches like Minnesota's Flip Saunders. "I want to see somebody better than Vince Carter," he said. "He single-handedly beat us." VC averaged 18.3 points per game and took home the franchise's second Rookie of the Year award.

Marcus Camby—1996–97

The 6'11" shot blocker had no trouble denying NBA players on a regular basis. Camby set a rookie team-record with 130 blocks, averaging 2.1 per contest. In 63 games the former University of Massachusetts star also had 14.8 points per night, including 36 points against the Philadelphia 76ers on March 18, 1997, and 37 points against the Atlanta Hawks on March 23. As well, the NBA All-Rookie first team member averaged 6.3 rebounds a game with a season-high 16 against the Charlotte Hornets on March 21.

Charlie Villanueva—2005–06

The 2004 NCAA champion with UConn began his career in good form. In 81 games the NBA All-Rookie first team selection had 13 points and 6.4 rebounds per game. But the highlight of his first year was scoring a Raptors rookie single-game record 48 points against the Milwaukee Bucks on March 26, 2006.

Andrea Bargnani—2006–07

The 2006 first overall pick played mainly off the bench, scoring 11.6 points per contest and sinking 100 three-pointers in 65 games. The seven-foot Italian had a decent playoff performance against the New Jersey Nets where he averaged 17 points in the final three games of that first-round series. For his efforts he landed on the NBA All-Rookie first team.

Chris Bosh—2003–04
Entering the NBA as a 19-year-old can be a daunting proposition—unless you're CB4. The 6'11" kid would put up 13 double-doubles while averaging 11.5 points and 7.4 rebounds, including a club rookie record 557 total boards, in 75 games and became a part of the NBA All-Rookie first team.

95 Remember 1995

It was the start of the Raptors' first NBA season, but 1995 was also an interesting year for the league and in media for the rest of North America. Here is a look back at the sports, movies, music, television shows and news that shaped our world back then.

In the NBA Detroit Pistons forward Grant Hill became the first rookie to lead in All-Star votes. "Leading the entire NBA in All-Star voting makes me feel awestruck," said Hill, who'd become the 1994–95 co-NBA Rookie of the Year award winner with Dallas Mavericks guard Jason Kidd.

On March 18 after Michael Jordan's attempt at professional baseball didn't work out, the retired Chicago Bulls superstar made a new announcement: "I'm back." Since the Bulls already retired his No. 23, Jordan returned wearing No. 45. On March 29, in his fifth game back, he torched the New York Knicks, scoring 55 points in a 113–111 win at Madison Square Garden.

Jordan would wear his old No. 23 in the playoffs, but the Bulls would eventually lose in six games to 23-year-old Shaquille O'Neal,

Penny Hardaway, and the Orlando Magic in their second-round match-up. Shaq's squad would make their first NBA Finals appearance, facing future Raptor Hakeem Olajuwon and the Houston Rockets. The reigning NBA champions would outclass the young Magic by sweeping them 4–0 to win their second straight league title. Olajuwon would be a back-to-back NBA Finals MVP.

San Antonio Spurs centre David Robinson won the NBA MVP, and Shaq captured the league scoring title with 29.3 points per game. Denver Nuggets centre Dikembe Mutombo won the Defensive Player of the Year award. Twelve-time NBA All-Star Moses Malone retired. University of Maryland forward Joe Smith was selected No. 1 overall by the Golden State Warriors in the 1995 NBA Draft. Other familiar names picked included Kevin Garnett, Rasheed Wallace, Jerry Stackhouse, Antonio McDyess, Michael Finley, and, of course, Damon Stoudamire. The NBA had its first ever lockout that lasted from July to September, but no regular season games were affected.

In the news O.J. Simpson, who was tried in the "Trial of the Century" for the murder of his wife, Nicole Brown Simpson, and her friend, Ronald Goldman, received a "not guilty" verdict, which outraged millions.

In the movie world, the top 10 grossing films were:

1. Toy Story—$191,796,233
2. Batman Forever—$184,031,112
3. Apollo 13—$172,071,312
4. Pocahontas—$141,579,773
5. Ace Ventura: When Nature Calls—$108,385,533
6. GoldenEye—$106,429,941
7. Jumanji—$100,475,249
8. Casper—$100,328,194
9. Seven—$100,125,643
10. Die Hard With A Vengeance—$100,012,499

As for popular songs, if iPods existed back then these tunes might have made your playlist:

"Gangsta's Paradise"—Coolio featuring L.V.

"Waterfalls"—TLC

"This Is How We Do It"—Montell Jordan

"One Sweet Day"— Mariah Carey and Boyz 2 Men

"You Oughta Know"—Alanis Morrissette

"You Are Not Alone"—Michael Jackson

"Fantasy"—Mariah Carey

"Exhale"—Whitney Houston

The top television shows were dominated by NBC stars like George Clooney, Jerry Seinfeld, and Jennifer Aniston.

E.R. (NBC)

Seinfeld (NBC)

Friends (NBC)

Frasier (NBC)

Home Improvement (ABC)

NYPD Blue (ABC)

96 Master P Tries Out for the Raptors

NBA players becoming rappers is a trend that happens all the time. Guys like Shaquille O'Neal, Allen Iverson, Tony Parker, and Ron Artest were all rocking the mic. Well, if the legendary Metta World Peace (aka Artest) can cross over into music, why can't entertainers make the move into the NBA?

Enter Master P (aka Percy Miller).

The rap star and multimillionaire entrepreneur had hoop dreams in his youth when he was on the verge of playing basketball

DeMar, Romeo, and the Suspicious Scholarship

Percy Miller's son Romeo (formerly rapper Lil' Romeo) played on the same club team as DeMar DeRozan as an eighth grader. According to *The Wall Street Journal*, DeRozan traveled with the Millers to cross-country tournaments, ate holiday meals with them, and often slept over at their Bel-Air home.

While DeRozan, a highly rated prospect, starred at Compton High School in California, Romeo battled injuries in his senior season at Beverly Hills High, scoring only 8.6 points per game. But both players received full University of Southern California scholarships from head coach Tim Floyd. In a phone call with Miller, Floyd remembered the music mogul asking, "DeMar and Romeo are ready to make their decision, and would you like to have them both on scholarship?"

The article questioned if the Millers took advantage of their resources and relationship with DeRozan to secure Romeo a free ride. USC did not break any rules, and Floyd admitted the publicity would help. "The more buzz you can create, the more news stories you can create," he said, "the better served you are as a program."

Ultimately, in two seasons at USC, Romeo would score five points in nine games before leaving the team.

at the University of Houston until a knee injury ruined his plans, forcing him to focus on music instead, which paid off big time. In 1998 he released *MP da Last Don*, which sold more than 4 million copies, becoming his best-selling album ever from the artist who spent much of his young life living in poverty in the New Orleans projects. "I never had nothing," Miller said. "I had to go out there and do something for my family, and the music stuff blew up for me. I come from a poor family. I had to do what I [needed] to take care of them. Now I got that straight, I want to do something I like while I can still do it."

That's where the roundball comes in. "Basketball is what kept me alive when I was growing up in the hood. My whole dream was to be a basketball player and play in the NBA, and this music thing blew up for me, and now I'm just chasing my other dream."

During the 1998 preseason, Miller began his NBA journey with the Charlotte Hornets. He was in their training camp but couldn't crack their regular season roster. Then, during the 1999 exhibition season, Miller attempted again, this time with the Raptors. In a preseason game against the Vancouver Grizzlies, the 6'4" guard scored eight points off the bench in a Toronto win.

Despite his slim odds of making the cut, Miller did receive some praise. "We've made investments in many young players here and we've got to decide if we're going to make an investment in someone like him," Raptors head coach Butch Carter said. "He's been nothing but positive here."

Unfortunately, Master P didn't make the team and would never be on an NBA regular season roster. He'd have to settle for moments like scoring 17 points in the 2008 NBA All-Star Celebrity Game to satisfy his NBA hunger. Fortunately, he has millions of dollars to fall back on. Yeah, he'll be just fine.

97 The All-Time Starting Five

If you're the general manager and can pick any Raptors players (past or present) in team history to assemble your ultimate starting five, who would you pick? This section will provide the answers (or at least my answers). The winning choices were based on the player's individual Toronto statistics, character, and meaningful contributions to the club's success.

Here's a breakdown of the winners and those left behind. Let the debate begin…

Point Guard
Damon Stoudamire
Mighty Mouse was the Raptors' first franchise star. His teammates and fans loved his style of play and why not? The 1995–96 NBA Rookie of the Year would dish out 19 assists one night and then later in the year he'd drop 30 points on Michael Jordan and the 72-win Chicago Bulls. Not bad for a guy who was booed by his future hometown fans on draft night.

Kyle Lowry
The Raptors' little bulldog had a breakthrough 2013–14 campaign, which saw him hit a single-season club record 190 three-pointers. His great leadership abilities and clutch performances helped Toronto make a surprising trip to the playoffs. In 2014–15 Lowry didn't slow down, becoming an All-Star starter for the first time.

Jose Calderon
Toronto's all-time assists leader was as classy as can be. The Spaniard at times had to deal with multiple starting point guard platoons, but he didn't let it affect his play. During his 525 regular season games with Toronto, Calderon dished out 3,770 assists and would be a part of two Raptors playoff teams, averaging 12.5 points and 6.1 assists per postseason contest.

Winner: Lowry
No other point guard in Raptors history has ever willed his team to victory more than this six-foot floor general. His intensity, grit, determination, and fearlessness to even grab rebounds in traffic with massive men around him have become his trademark. You add those traits to his knack for hitting big shots and making his teammates better, that's why he's the best point guard in franchise history.

Shooting guard

Vince Carter

You know the resume: 1998–99 NBA Rookie of the Year winner, 2000 Slam Dunk champion, multiple All-Star, 50 points in a playoff game, and the guy who put Toronto on the NBA map. Without a doubt VC is the best player in franchise history.

DeMar DeRozan

In 2013–14 the kid from USC had his best year yet, averaging a career-high 22.7 points while securing his first All-Star appearance and helping Toronto reach the playoffs for the first time since 2008. DeRozan wasn't flustered in his first taste of the postseason. He averaged 23.9 points against the Brooklyn Nets in the seven-game series.

Doug Christie

Christie, a terrific defender, is the Raptors' all-time steals leader, but he was also deadly from beyond the arc with 431 threes during his Toronto days.

Winner: Carter (in a landslide)

Small Forward

Tracy McGrady

Before becoming a two-time NBA scoring champion and seven-time All-Star, T-Mac was a raw talent the Raptors knew would be explosive one day. McGrady had all the tools—terrific scoring ability, great length, and outstanding athleticism. In the 1999–00 campaign, T-Mac started stuffing the stat sheet more consistently, averaging 15.4 points, 6.3 rebounds, 1.9 blocks, and 1.1 steals per game. Alas, it wasn't destined to be in Toronto.

Morris Peterson

One of the most beloved Raptors in franchise history, the all-time club leader in made three-pointers and regular season games played was a part of Toronto's playoff success in the early 2000s and the 2006–07 campaign. The left-handed sharpshooter was an ironman, too, playing every game between the 2002–03 and 2005–06 seasons.

Andrea Bargnani

The seven-footer was listed as a power forward/centre, but don't be fooled. The Italian's perimeter game and agility resembled more of an oversized small forward. As a result, when healthy and motivated, this hybrid talent was a handful for opposing big men. During his seven seasons in Toronto, Bargnani had 579 threes and scored 6,581 points.

Winner: **Peterson**

Even though McGrady was incredibly skilled, T-Mac didn't stick around long enough to realize his All-Star potential. As for Bargnani, he never lived up to his No. 1 overall pick status due to his injuries, which prevented him from being the elite scorer fans and the team expected, and lack of commitment in the defensive and rebounding departments. As a result Peterson gets the nod over them both for his consistent contributions toward the club's success and his durability.

Power Forward

Chris Bosh

The Raptors' all-time leading scorer and rebounder was a five-time Toronto All-Star who, at one point, averaged more than 22 points in five straight seasons. He took over the franchise after Vince left and didn't look back.

Charles Oakley

Whether it's slapping grown men in the face or trying to motivate Vince Carter during the playoffs, "Oak" was never afraid to share his opinion. His hard-nosed style and veteran leadership were perfect for the young Raptors playoff teams of the early 2000s. Oakley wasn't just roughing people up, though, he could still play ball. During the 2000–01 regular season, he averaged 9.6 points and 9.5 rebounds in 78 games.

Amir Johnson

The former Raptor was all effort on the court and was known for playing through pain without complaining. He was a respected teammate who rebounded, did the little things, and sank the"summertime three" from time to time. In a 2013–14 playoff series against the Brooklyn Nets, Johnson elevated his game with 11 points and six rebounds per contest.

Winner: Bosh (in a landslide)

No power forward in franchise history had his All-Star combination of inside and outside talent. CB4 is the Raptors' second best player ever and clearly deserves the all-time starting spot.

Centre
Antonio Davis

The 6'9" Davis was an undersized centre who held his own at the 5-spot. Physically sculpted and durable, the All-Star was a great frontcourt complement to Oakley as the young Raptors made their playoff runs in the early 2000s. During that time Davis stepped it up in the postseason, averaging 16.1 points and 10.6 rebounds in 20 games.

Marcus Camby

The future Defensive Player of the Year displayed his shot-blocking prowess early on as a Raptor. In fact the 1996 No. 2 overall pick had 360 swats in his only two Toronto seasons, including 230 in 1997–98. During his Raptors days, the University of Massachusetts star finished with 13.5 points, 6.8 rebounds, and 2.9 blocks in 126 games.

Keon Clark

The 6'11" UNLV product also majored in the fine art of shot-blocking. As a Raptor, he swatted 232 shots in 127 games.

Winner: Davis

AD had to battle bigger centres all the time, but he still found a way to become an All-Star and excel in the postseason. He was tough and provided consistent production and leadership to a young team that needed it. That's why he is Toronto's all-time best centre.

So, the Raptors' all-time starting five looks like this:

PG— Kyle Lowry
SG—Vince Carter
SF—Morris Peterson
PF—Chris Bosh
C—Antonio Davis

98 Stan Van Gundy Doesn't Like Free Pizza

Whenever Toronto would score 100 or more points, win or lose, the whole arena used to receive a redeemable ticket for a free pizza slice. Awesome, right? Well, it was great until then-Orlando Magic head coach Stan Van Gundy ruined the party. During Orlando's 117–101 blowout win on March 26, 2012, a late bucket by Raptors forward Ed Davis enabled Toronto to reach the century mark in scoring, provoking loud cheers from the crowd due to its impending free slice to come.

After the game Van Gundy took some jabs at Raptors fans and the pizza promotion. "I mean, everybody's on their feet, standing ovation, and the whole thing, and then a guy in the crowd next to me sitting baseline said everybody gets a free pizza, so I guess that was exciting," Van Gundy said. "That was the loudest the crowd was all night. They were into that. That was a big basket by Ed Davis. They're going to put that on the highlight film at the end of the year. I was like, 'Wow, what happened, I thought they had like an 18-point play and tied the game or something.'"

Then Van Gundy was told the fans received a slice—not an entire pizza. "Really? We got a standing ovation for a slice?" He said. "They told me they got a free pizza. A slice? A slice you have to sit in your seat and clap. You can't stand up on a slice; that's bad etiquette."

In late October of 2013, it was announced a free pizza slice would still be given out, but only if the Raptors scored 100 in a *winning* performance.

Damn you, Stan Van Gundy.

99 Vince, We Forgive You

On November 19, 2014, 37-year-old Vince Carter, whose high-flying superhero days disappeared long ago, was back at the Air Canada Centre (ACC), but this time as a Memphis Grizzlies bench player. It was unbelievable that nearly 10 years had passed since the most devastating divorce in Raptors history.

Both Vince and the team moved on, but as you know, Toronto fans had not.

Carter, now a seasoned veteran sporting a touch of gray in his beard, was entering the twilight of his NBA existence. Despite all the drama, he still fondly remembered his time in Toronto. Whenever he strolled into the ACC, he always looked for the banner that listed the arena's debut date. "They move this flag every time," Carter told reporters. "I struggle finding it. When I walk in here and see February 20, 1999, that's the first thing I think of—when this building opened. I just remember getting the opportunity to make history, making the first shot. That's one of the first things I think of. You can't take that away."

The eight-time All-Star learned the Raptors, celebrating their 20th anniversary, would honour him with an in-game video tribute later that night. "It's something that is memorable to me," Carter admitted. "To see the video right here in the building where it all happened, you can't beat that. It's one thing to sit at home and watch it with your friends, like, 'Oh yeah,' or watch it on your computer. But right here? It's special."

When asked how he thought the crowd would react, VC played it cool. "You never know. You just go through it and deal with it," he said. "It's still special coming here. It's still fun."

Heading into the game, no one really knew how the fans would respond. Would they finally forgive Vince or just throw knives his way as usual? During a first-quarter timeout, we'd get the answer. On the big video scoreboard hanging above the court, the tribute featuring Carter speaking about his time in Toronto and highlights of his greatest Raptors dunks filled the screen.

At first some fans began booing, then as the video progressed, many of the nearly 20,000 on hand started to rise and loudly cheer, which grew into a goose bump-inducing standing ovation for a player they loved many years ago. The emotional moment brought Vince to tears. Looking surprised, he even mouthed "Wow" during the crowd's reaction.

After the game Vince was still moved by the heartwarming response. "You can't prepare for that, whether it was a surprise or you knew it was coming. It's just an amazing feeling. Amazing just to be in the moment, to see it, and to kind of relive it. As it was happening, you see all the stuff and you see all the people that you've played with, and as each play was happening, I can remember all of that stuff like it was yesterday. It was awesome. It was an honest reaction. Like I said, just seeing the moment. Just a feel-good moment."

100 The 2016 NBA All-Star Game

What better way to spend Valentine's Day in 2016 than watching the NBA's most exciting and popular players run up and down the Air Canada Centre court in the league's first ever All-Star game outside of the United States.

The game means nothing to the standings, but for the city of Toronto and Canada, it's a great platform to showcase themselves as passionate basketball markets to the world.

The NBA officially awarded the event on September 30, 2013, the same day Toronto-born Grammy Award winner Drake was introduced as the Raptors' global ambassador. "The city of Toronto and the Raptors mean everything to me, and the chance to be able to play a role with this team is something I could have only dreamed of growing up," Drake said. "I'm really excited about the direction of the Raptors, and today's announcement about Toronto hosting the NBA All-Star Game in 2016 is another reason why Canadian basketball fans have a lot to look forward to."

Throughout All-Star weekend history, there have been some great Raptors moments, including Vince Carter's 2000 NBA Slam Dunk championship, Terrence Ross' 2013 dunk title, Kyle Lowry's surprising 2015 All-Star Game putback jam, and Jason Kapono's 2008 Three-Point Shootout victory. But only five Raptors players have ever made an All-Star team. Here's a look at how those gentlemen performed on the big stage:

Vince Carter

"Air Canada" was a five-time All-Star and four-time leading vote-getter with the Raptors. Here's the breakdown of his stats from those games.

2000—12 points (6–11 field goals), four rebounds, two assists, and two steals

2001—16 points (7–18 field goals), four assists, three rebounds, one block, and one steal

2002—Did not play due to injury

2003—Nine points (4–9 field goals), two assists, and one rebound

2004—11 points (5–7 field goals), two rebounds, and two steals

Chris Bosh

CB4 made five All-Star squads while with the Raptors, including starting in two of them.

2006—Eight points (3–7 field goals), eight rebounds, and two assists

2007—11 points (5–7 field goals), seven rebounds, and one assist

2008—14 points (7–15 field goals), seven rebounds, and one assist

2009—Did not play due to injury

2010—23 points (9–16 field goals), 10 rebounds, two steals, and one assist

Antonio Davis

In Washington, D.C., AD started for the Eastern Conference after making his only All-Star team as an injury replacement.

2001—Eight points (4–11 field goals), nine rebounds, one block, and one steal

DeMar DeRozan

DeRozan had a big year in 2014. Not only did he make his playoff debut, but he also landed on the NBA All-Star squad for the first time.

2014—Eight points (4–7 field goals), three rebounds, and two assists

Kyle Lowry

Lowry was the Raptors' first All-Star starter since Bosh. The point guard stunned the New York crowd on February 15, 2015, with a one-handed putback slam. "Best moment of the game by far," Lowry said.

2015—10 points (4–13 field goals), eight assists, four steals, and three rebounds.

After all the losing seasons and disappointing star player defections in club history, the 2016 All-Star Game is a symbol of how far the Raptors have come. This will be a great moment for the franchise and its fans to let the NBA universe know on a bigger scale that Toronto and Canada love more than just hockey pucks. "It's going to be a show," Lowry said. "The city is amazing. The fans are amazing. The culture is amazing. It will be an unbelievable time."

Sources

Researching and writing this book was a large and enjoyable task. There were many late nights when it was common for me and my bloodshot eyes to be working on this project hours before heading to my day job.

But I didn't mind.

Since I'm a basketball junkie, I was so immersed in the tales of turmoil and joy in Raptors history that I couldn't stay away. In my hours of digging, I came across the work of terrific storytellers who were on the frontlines of the club's news every day—the Toronto sports media. Being a member of that fraternity once upon a time, I have an in-depth understanding of what their jobs likely entailed and respect them for their consistent high caliber work. Without their great efforts over the years, I wouldn't have been able to craft *100 Things Raptors Fans Should Know & Do Before They Die.*

Right now, I'd like to personally credit the following current and past Toronto sports media talents for some of the information and quotes I used: Michael Grange, Doug Smith, Paul Jones, Dave Feschuk, Eric Koreen, Eric Smith, Steve Buffery, Mike Ganter, Ryan Wolstat, Jack Armstrong, Chuck Swirsky, Matt Devlin, Leo Rautins, Josh Lewenberg, Tim Micallef, Sid Seixeiro, Michael Landsberg, Audley Stephenson, Tas Melas, Phil Elder (J.E. Skeets), Trey Kerby, Leigh Ellis, Cathal Kelly, Morgan Campbell, Lori Ewing, Dave Zarum, Rob Sinclair, Sherman Hamilton, Sean Fitz-Gerald, Steve Simmons, Mike Ulmer, Kevin Nielsen, Bill Harris, Marty York, and Rachel Brady

I'd also like to give recognition to the following: Raptors.com, NBA TV Canada, NBA.com, Sportsnet.ca, TSN.ca, The Score. com, *The Globe and Mail, Toronto Sun, Toronto Star, National Post,*

BlogTalkRadio.com, Grantland.com, ESPN.com, USAToday.com, Yahoo! Sports, YouTube, Associated Press, Canadian Press, Basketball-Reference.com, ProBasketballTalk.NBCSports.com, RaptorsRepublic.com, RaptorsHQ.com, NBA on TNT, TSN's *Off The Record*, Sportsnet 590 The Fan, TSN 1050, FanSided.com, SBNation.com, Deadspin.com, VancouverSun.com, SI.com, BleacherReport.com, SlamOnline.com, DimeMag.com, NYDailyNews.com, NYTimes.com, YesNetwork.com, WSJ.com, WashingtonPost.com, FoxSports.com, FoxNews.com, Basketball.RealGM.com, ChicagoTribune.com, CP24.com, NHL.com, ProHockeyTalk.NBCSports.com, CBC.ca, CSNPhilly.com, MTV.com, HuffingtonPost.com, TampaBay.com, and LaTimes.com.

As well, these books were a good reference during the research process:

Dream Job: My Wild Ride on the Corporate Side with the Leafs, the Raptors and TFC
Authors: Richard Peddie and Lawrence Scanlan
Publisher: HarperCollins (October 2013)

Glory Days: Legends of Illinois High School Basketball
Author: Taylor Bell
Publisher: Sports Publishing (October 2006)

Basketball Talk The Way It Should Be!
A Baller & Celebrity Quote Book
Authors: Dave Mendonca and Audley Stephenson
Publisher: Lulu Press Inc. (July 2011)

For all those whose work I researched, thank you again for your contributions.

Acknowledgments

On December 10, 2014, Triumph Books editorial director Tom Bast sent me an email I would never forget, greenlighting this project. It was one of the best Christmas gifts I had ever received. Tom, thank you for giving me this amazing opportunity and for the patience you showed every time I pitched an idea. I hope I produced a book you and Triumph can be proud of.

Of course, Tom was one of many people who were a great help along this challenging and rewarding journey.

A tip of the cap goes to my talented Triumph editor, Jeff Fedotin, who was always supportive, provided terrific advice, and was open to new ideas.

As well, I'd like to thank Triumph's managing editor, Adam Motin, for his guidance as I tried to figure out how to tackle this fun project.

Definitely, a book of this detail demanded hours of research, focus, and sacrifice to complete.

As a result, I didn't see my newlywed wife, Linda, our families, and friends very often from December 2014 to March 2015.

I know it wasn't an ideal situation, but they, especially my lovely bride, were all tremendously patient, encouraging and understanding as I chased one of my dreams.

For that, I'm forever appreciative and thankful.

Another key figure who deserves much credit is a man I co-hosted a fun basketball podcast with—Audley Stephenson.

When we teamed up to broadcast *The Breakdown with Dave & Audley* in 2008, it began a memorable five-year ride, which featured interviews with some former Raptors whose quotes made their appearance in this book.

"The Audman," thank you for always providing great friendship, wisdom, and laughs along the way.

As for this next gentleman, without him, I would have never been allowed to enter the club's dressing room in the first place.

I'd like to say a big thank you to the Toronto Raptors director of media relations Jim LaBumbard for always being gracious in granting me media passes even during my podcasting years when Audley and I filmed wacky and funny pregame interviews with players.

Thank you for not calling security on us.

Also, I'd like to send much gratitude to the Toronto Raptors organization for giving Canadian hoops fans, like myself, an entertaining team to cheer for.

As well, I'd like to thank some of the club's ex-players for their contributions.

First, Jerome "JYD" Williams, thank you for taking the time out of your busy life to write a terrific foreword, which was filled with the same energy and enthusiasm you delivered on the court every night.

In addition, many thanks to Tracy Murray, Sharone Wright, Tracy McGrady, Damon Stoudamire, Morris Peterson, Sam Mitchell, Doug Christie, and others who Audley and I interviewed, whose engaging stories became a part of this Raptors celebration.

Finally, I'd like to praise my hard-working parents who battled a lot in their lives to make sure their children could have every opportunity to succeed.

Thank you always for your love, support, and sacrifice.

This book is for you.

About the Author

Dave Mendonca is a longtime NBA fan who covered Vince Carter's Raptors days as a Score Television (now Sportsnet 360) national sports reporter during the 2000s. The Toronto native later co-hosted a successful basketball podcast, *The Breakdown with Dave & Audley*, where he and Audley Stephenson had entertaining conversations with many current/past NBA stars, celebrities, and former Raptors, including Tracy McGrady, Damon Stoudamire, and Jerome "JYD" Williams. Using their fun and outrageous podcast chats, Mendonca and Stephenson co-authored *Basketball Talk, The Way It Should Be! A Baller & Celebrity Quote Book*. Nowadays, Dave is a sports and entertainment freelance writer and broadcaster who has interviewed the likes of Beyonce Knowles, Jamie Foxx, and Canadian astronaut Chris Hadfield, while his work has appeared in ESPN.com, SLAM Online, *The Dallas Morning News*, and *Star Wars Insider*.

You can visit his website at www.DaveMendonca.com and follow him on Twitter @DaveMendonca.